ALSO BY GREG GILMARTIN

Crew

Spy Island

Published by
Greg Gilmartin
PO Box 124, Mystic, CT 06355

ISBN: 978-0-578-25196-7 (sc)
ISBN: 978-0-578-25197-4 (e)

Library of Congress Control Number: 2021913858

Cover design by Courtney Moore of
CMB Creative Group of Mystic, CT
Courtney@cmbcreativegroup.com

Photo courtesy of Peter Barlow.
PeterBarlow@att.net

CAN'T
SAIL IN JAIL!

BY
GREG GILMARTIN

TABLE OF CONTENTS

Dedicated to all the

*POTRAFs, MFOs, PROs,
MRMSA Racers and
Racer Chasers.*

Prologue

My name is Morris, although they call me Big Mo. The story I'm going to tell you happened many years ago in a watery town called Mystic located on the sandy coastline of Southern New England. Long Island Sound, Fishers Island Sound and Block Island Sound all buffer the Atlantic Ocean as it splashes up and fills the glacial cuts in the earth that are all around here. The area is a natural haven for messing around in boats.

The young men and women who did the messing never saw it coming, but their mutual passion for sailboat racing, and partying, evolved into a community movement that continues to this day.

They raced hard and they partied harder. Sometimes they got into trouble. Sometimes, they made bad decisions. It's not like they did anything wrong, really, like murder or rape or obstruction of justice, but just the same, people shake their heads when talking about some of the trouble they got into, even though that trouble might better be called "mischief". You know, "frat-like". However, some of it was heroic. Epic even.

They weren't alone, of course, although they acted on their own, followed their own instincts, always focused on the prize, which was winning sailboat races and taking home trophies. The others involved traveled their own paths, pursued their own dreams, and ran into their own problems along the way. The "epic" part came when the many different paths crossed on one fateful weekend in the early summer.

I was there for some of it, and for the parts when I wasn't

there, well, I knew the people who were, or they knew people who knew those who were. I was certainly there enough to hear about the stories which led me to ask others about those who were involved or knew those involved. Someone once said all big legends start with a small lie. Or is it a small truth? Whichever, I can promise you a good tale.

1 – Saturday Jail Time

The way I heard it, Billy couldn't get the clanging of metal out of his head. It pressed against the inside of his skull and rattled through every corner of his messed-up mind. The noise was oppressive, as if someone was slamming a metal bible against prison bars and the souls in that tome of morality were collectively crying out for release from their own, very public hell.

The incessant clash of hard metals interrupted the pleasant revelry floating through Billy's semi-consciousness, fighting for his attention. The sleek moist form of his latest obsession slid easily through the seemingly endless wetness, her skin as smooth as a teenage model's, the friction lost in the technological brilliance.

"We put ourselves in jail with that move!" cried a voice within the metal madness. Billy immediately recognized his tactical advisor, Teddy Trumanlee, the thinker, the tactician, the guy who spoke only in declarative sentences that described the immediate situation, usually in terms so obvious it clarified what everyone was thinking; terms usually spoken on a sailboat during a race, but Billy did not feel like he was on a sailboat.

The noise suddenly stopped. Billy woke up, rolled onto his

back and off the narrow bench upon which he had been dreaming, falling two feet to the hard cement floor. His head hit with a sickening slap, but it didn't hurt. At least, he didn't feel it. It did, however, wake him up completely and he smartly pivoted on his elbow, sucked his feet under him and stood upright in a blink.

"Foking damn nasty bull crap momma!" Billy shouted, rubbing the back of his head. He felt it now! Then in an instant he realized the metal bar symphony was real. Billy "Gunny" Gunning was, in fact, in jail!

"Oh, crap!" he sighed. The clanging started up again and he turned around to see his bowman, Brian Bellows, running his steel-toed shoe across the bars of the prison cell. As a younger boy, Bellows suffered a terrible accident when the front of his right foot was ripped off by a chain saw, toes and all. It was a bloody scene that forever estranged him from his father who was manning the saw at the time. Drunk, apparently. To this day, Bellows had a psychotic reaction to saws of any type, power or not. He was, however, not afraid to live up to his family name, and coupled the shoe slapping clangs with his raised voice.

"Would someone please bring us something to drink!" he shouted.

"Would you please shut the fok up!" Billy shouted back.

Bellows stopped for an instant and looked at his skipper, leader, and mentor. The M.M.F.I.C. Main Mother Foker In Charge. He was surprised to see Billy standing upright because just moments ago he seemed lost to the world on the slab of bench that served as a bed in the corner of the cell.

"Oh, sorry, Gunny," Bellows said sheepishly, his shoe poised for another rattle across the bars.

Billy stared at his young friend and then the shoe. He had to smile because at one time he could not even imagine anyone would consider making a steel-toed, plate lined, boat shoe, much less see one right in front of his eyes. Then he felt other eyes and realized the rest of his crew were staring at him. Six of them spread about in various stages of repose in the 12-by-20-foot steel and cement box.

"Oh, crap!" he sighed again.

In the corner, another sound, this more a metallic echo from a hollow well.

"You can't sail if you're in jail!"

It was Teddy, again, but in real time. The hollow echo came from the metal toilet bolted to the jail cell wall. Trumanlee's head was deep into it, his neck resting on the seat, his shoulders apparently the only thing that kept him from falling in.

Billy marveled at the polished and shiny appliance bolted against the wall, and the pristine efficiency of the City of Westmont's civic mindedness. It was the cleanest damn toilet seat he had ever seen. Not that Billy Gunning ever spent a lot of time in jail.

Then there was the incident earlier that night.

It had started so innocently after the protest hearing brought by Commodore Montgomery Fillmore Prescott III of the prestigious Westmont Harbor Yacht and Tennis Club. The crew had been hanging in the shadows of the modern built-to-look-old building sitting on a small mound, once a landfill, now meticulously turned into the gracious grounds of Connecticut's most exclusive yacht club. Despite the magnificent view of Long Island Sound from its front porch, Billy often said the millions of dollars spent on landscaping and construction had failed to completely eliminate the odor of the past. He was usually just trying to get a rise from his guys.

"Smell something funny?" Billy would ask as their wind powered race craft glided across the finish line with Prescott's vessel, named LykytySplyt, still minutes behind. "Is it something or someone that still stinks?"

"Smells like money is what it smells like," was the frequent reply from Billy's spinnaker trimmer and best friend, Tank McHale. The crew would cackle as they cracked open a beer and toasted their humiliated opponent once again. "To M.F. Prescott. May we always whip his M.F. ass!"

"Lick this split!" was another refrain oft thrown toward their competitors, but loud enough only for Billy's crew to hear it. They would each slam back a beer and fire the empties into the cockpit where they formed the initial layer of aluminum debris that would reach several high by the time the boat was back at the dock.

Billy and his crew from the Mystic River had won two straight Eastern Seaboard Yacht Racing Union Championships and it looked like this year Prescott was destined to be an ESYRU bridesmaid again. It wasn't going to be easy. The scion to the Millard Fillmore fortune reached into the Rules of Sailing and, with a battery of lawyers at his side, filed a protest with the Organizing Authority alleging the racing machine Smoked, a Dave Vee designed speedster, built by Billy and his boys from Mystic, had an illegal keel and her handicap rating should be changed. Fillmore demanded the results from the previous two days of racing be tossed, which would in effect, put him in the lead.

"This crew, this boat, this bunch of 'Raceheadz'…these POTRAFs!" Prescott spat the last as a curse, expending his final gasp of air before he paused and then gulped another big breath to start again. "They are a disgrace to the sailing community!" Prescott continued in front of the International Jury convened for the annual regatta. "They cut corners, steal information and clearly are cheating…how else could they be so successful?

And their personal behavior pushes the limits of any civilized person, with public drunkenness, lewd carousing and a general ne'er-do-well attitude that makes them appear a gang of deckhands in for a weekend leave! Their very existence violates

Rule 2!!"

Prescott's tirade left him red-faced and puffy-cheeked. Billy watched from his chair in the corner of the protest room like a slow eyed cat with just the hint of a grin. He personally loved the phrase POTRAF. It was coined for the Parasites Of The Rich And Famous. His boys, his crew of sailboat racers who jumped on other people's boats and made them go fast. He knew when Prescott used that buzz word as a denigrating weapon, well, they had really gotten to him. And that made Billy happy.

The staid panel of esteemed judges, three of the top minds in the sport, sat stiff-lipped and wide-eyed at the outburst. They were familiar with Prescott's tactics and knew Billy's crew were good sailors. They, like many, were aware of their race hard, party harder reputation, earned through quality performances at regattas from Key West to Block Island over many years. The post-race carousing was as well tuned as their performances on the water, and would likely garner trophies, if they were awarded for that aspect of sailboat racing. Regardless, good racing always trumped good partying in the minds of event officials. No one bothered them, as long as no laws were broken.

Montgomery Fillmore Prescott III, likely sick of his runner up reputation, pressed the attack against Billy and his crew with a final swing of the powerful club he wielded as Commodore of the ESYRU.

"I'm recommending to the Board that these hooligans be kicked out of the Union and banished from sanctioned racing forever! They will not be taking any trophies home if I can help it! After all, I am the foking Commodore!"

With that final outburst, Prescott turned on his topsiders and stormed out of the jury room leaving his attorneys to deal with the official protest. It was dismissed in minutes; one of the judges had personally observed the measuring of the keel and found it to be well within the design rules. The suggestion of a conflict of interest on the part of the jury also fell on deaf ears and was dismissed by the judges with a wave and a laugh.

"We find nothing to indicate Smoked does not meet specifications, nor do they violate Rule 2. This protest is disallowed." Such was the official proclamation from the panel and the hearing was over.

Billy thanked the judges and left the room more angry than pleased. He expected the ruling, but not the amount of time it took for the entire process.

Outside in the glow of the magic hour just after sunset, Billy saw Monty waiting for him. He was stretched out on a paisley couch, easily six feet long, that graced the front porch of the structure that was the center of the Westmount Harbor youth sailing and tennis programs. Billy had to admit it was a nice couch. He wondered if the benefits of having money in a yacht club, outweighed the hassles of having money in a yacht club.

"Gunning. You think you're so smart, right! Well, you should follow the rules just like the rest of us!" he declared, poking the air with his finger.

Billy turned his hands upwards as if to say, "C'mon, Monty, get over it." But he didn't say a word, figuring it would be a waste of breath.

"You guys are a disgrace!" Monty added in response.

Billy smiled. "We'll be out there tomorrow!" he said.

"I'll be waiting!" was the response, but Billy just kept walking. He had already shifted his focus from the nice couch to the expanse of orange that splashed across the sky. The 'solset" he called it. A purity of color that reached into his very soul and made him appreciate what Mother Nature had to offer.

2 - PISSED OFF PISSED ON

Minutes later Billy carried word of the protest and the decision to his crew at the marina as they tidied up Smoked and enjoyed another round of post-race partying. The air was pungent with their favorite wacky weed and freshly spilt beer. The protest clearly pissed Gunning off.

"That M.F. blowhard! He goes ahead with the protest, forces a hearing, and cuts into my party time? Piss on him!"

"Now you're on the right tack," smiled tactician Trumanlee. He nodded toward the parking lot at the end of the dock where a shiny red Alfa Romeo Spider convertible sat in all its automotive glory.

"Is that what I think it is?" asked Gary "Darts" Goman, the navigator, who, on most occasions, was the most level-headed of the Smoked crew. He was certainly the oldest at the ripe age of 35.

"It is," said Johnny "The Kid" Flash, nodding a mop of long blonde hair that spilled in front of his eyes. He was the primary helmsman on the boat, the driver. Most who saw him drive marveled at his quiet demeanor and steady touch despite the apparent difficulty seeing through his blonde locks. The mere fact he spoke caused everyone to turn toward him in amazement and, for a moment, all seven of the crew waited to hear if there was more.

There wasn't, just a long pull on his ever-present cigarette, a

Winston this time.

"It is M.F. Prescott's land dinghy," Tank said finally, even as he started to move toward the shiny machine. Brian, the bowman, dropped the spinnaker sheet he was coiling and stepped over the lifeline onto the wharf. The click-click-click of his metal-toed boat shoe against the aluminum dock set a marching beat for the others.

In seconds the crew had left their boat, walked up the dock and encircled the sports car with a myriad of ideas stewing in their slightly off centered brains. Poised at the front bumper, Billy unzipped his fly.

"What do you think?" he laughed, looking around at his crew. "Like I said - piss on him!"

"Tack or gybe. Feels right to me," said Teddy, following suit. The sound of another half dozen zippers followed as the rest of the crew found a spot around the car. Billy, Tank, Teddy, Brian, Flash, Toby, Trip and Darts instinctually set up evenly spaced and let go, defiling the foreign road toy as if it were a fire hydrant and they a pack of drunken dogs.

As one, they washed the car as best they could without splashing each other. Tank moved to the open window and let go his beer filled bladder on the Corinthian leather seat. They were so intent on the total freedom and pleasure of release that they failed to notice the police car roll up and stop right next to them.

Inside was Westmont Harbor Police Chief Jason Pastor. He let loose a quick bleep of his high-pitched emergency horn and suddenly the entire crew, dicks in hand, turned with a start toward the sound, and realized they were busted. The entire crew, that is, save one. Gary Darts Goman, who did not do alcohol, was so focused on trying to piss that he did not see or hear anything. He was in his usual drug induced haze and was pissed that he couldn't go.

"Oh, crap!" sighed Billy, shaking the last few drops at the

Alpha Romeo badge on the hood. He zipped up and stood back as if he had innocently just arrived.

"Step away from the car and put your hands where I can see them!" came the voice of the law over the police car's speaker. Chief Pastor was surprised at how quickly the group of men around the car reacted. They all stepped back and put up their hands.

"Please! Keep your hands where they were!" came the correction from the loudspeaker. The crew lowered their hands, and all started to zip up. All except Darts, who was still slow on the uptake.

"Darts! Dickhead, wake the fok up!" hissed Billy.

Darts looked up this time and suddenly realized what was happening. He stepped back from the car and put up his hands. Everyone couldn't help but look at Darts' blessed endowment, the clear winner among the lot. Chief Pastor couldn't help but see as well.

"Hey, luckyhead! Zip up!" came the metallic voice from the loudspeaker. Darts realized he was the center of attention and somewhere in the dimmed recesses of his mind he thought he should milk the moment and he did, slowly packaging his piece into his sailing shorts.

"All of you, zip it up and stand against the fence!" said the chief. Then Pastor stepped out of the car with his gun drawn and motioned the crew from Smoked to move together by the parking lot fence.

"Hey, hey! No guns!" cried Billy as he shuffled with the others in a line.

"Shut up and move!" the chief barked, waving his gun.

The distant sound of police sirens drifted from the interstate across the open water of the marina cove as the crew slowly lined up, each keeping an eye on the gun.

"Hey, Sarge, ah, Chief, you don't need backup here," laughed

Billy. "We're cool with the law."

Chief Pastor looked over his shoulder briefly trying to identify the source of the sirens and then turned back to his pissing deviants. He waved the gun to herd them against the fence.

"That's not my chase," he said, slowly relaxing as the boys lined up. He holstered his weapon and pulled out a note pad.

"Must be Dr. Z!" exclaimed Tank, laughing at Billy and the rest of the crew. "He's late again!"

Dr. Z was the actual MFO of Smoked, the Mother Fokin' Owner, who had become increasingly unreliable through this particular summer. He was clearly involved with some other activity that the crew was not aware of, except for Toby, the pitman, who did have an inkling into what it was, but he wasn't telling.

"He's probably tied up with that other thing," was all Toby would offer, leaving the crew nodding their head as if they knew what Toby was talking about. They didn't, even Toby didn't know for sure, but all enjoyed acting like they did. Only Billy, however, really knew.

Dr. Z was thought to dabble in smuggling a variety of illegal drugs, but found sailing to be the strongest narcotic of all. He was constantly hiding from various factions of state and federal law enforcement agencies. Invariably, he found the desire to be on a fast sailboat so strong that he would venture out toward the marina anyway, hoping to hop on board for each race.

Sadly, for him, he was under near constant surveillance and every time he moved from his hiding spot, no matter what regatta Smoked had entered, the law would give chase. At least, it had seemed that way for much of this particular summer.

"He hasn't made a race all year, why should we expect anything different today." It was Brian, the steel-toed bowman, shaking his head sadly. He had heard the stories of Dr. Z, but Brian had met him only once in the winter. He was beginning to believe he was just an MFO myth conjured up by Billy and Tank at every sound of a cop's siren.

"Oh, he'll make it tomorrow," Billy said with a small smile. "He loves final days."

"I've got five that says he doesn't," shot back Tank.

Chief Pastor tapped his pencil against his notebook in annoyance. "Hey, Betheads! Pay attention here. I'm the law and you are all under arrest for public urination. Vandalism. And disorderly conduct. Let's start the list with that. Now, names and numbers, let's go, starting with you, big mouth in the blue hat! Gunny, right?"

Everyone looked at Billy and his trademark double billed cap, a bill in front and one in back. A logo on the front, stained by years of abuse, was hardly recognizable. Close examination would have shown a pair of yellow bars resembling the letter "L", but upside down, sticking up out of a black splash of color into a blue splash of color. The bill in back prevented his tender neck from feeling the damaging effects of the sun. As silly as it looked to those who did not know him, it was very practical.

After a moment, he identified himself to the Chief which started the process of street booking. Within a few minutes, everyone was in the record book and Chief Pastor began to herd them toward his car. It was immediately clear there were too many for the back seat of his cruiser.

"Hey, Chief, what do you say, I drive the van with the overflow," Billy said with a friendly smile. "You can trust me. I wanna be with my boys."

Chief Pastor sized up the situation quickly and realized he had no choice other than to agree with Billy's suggestion or let them all go. That wasn't going to happen. The fact that Pastor often sailed on Prescott's boat, LykytySplyt, and regularly felt the sting of losing to these knuckleheads insured that.

"Okay, Gunning," Chief Pastor nodded. 'Take these four and follow me in the van." He looked at him eye to eye. "You know I know where you live, so…." Billy laughed and nodded.

And so, another milestone in the young history of these racing, partying zealots from Mystic. Billy 'Gunny' Gunning drove his own crew to jail, meekly following the police chief while finishing half a joint left in the ash tray from their 90-minute ride down I-95 two days ago.

In the confusion, Gary 'Darts' Goman slipped away down the dock and hid in the cockpit of Smoked while the two-car caravan of 'pissoir' violators drove off. Billy's eyes silently sent the signal loud and clear to Darts as they drove off.

"Call Goldee for bail money!" Darts read Billy's lips through his mushroom induced haze.

He dialed her number from the dock office once the arrestees had left and silently hoped she was not with the guitar player. She was the only one who had access to enough money to get the crew out of jail. With the final race scheduled for tomorrow, she was their only chance to be on the starting line to battle for the championship.

3 - QuiKee Gs

About two hours east from the City of Westmont jailhouse, just south of the former mill town of Norwich, Connecticut, and two weeks prior to the rattling of the jail cage, the day had unfolded for Mike Kansas like most he had learned to enjoy since coming to America. The crinkle of the cellophane wrapped cakes, loaded with gooey centers, was music to his ears as he stacked them neatly on both sides of the main aisle leading to the cash registers. The chocolate covered discs and tubes sat tantalizingly on the shelf, glazed nibbles reflecting the morning sun through the large pane of glass across the storefront. He gently pushed and prodded the packages, taking special care to fill the gaps, yet not cram them so close they wouldn't each stand on their own.

He learned early in his days as co-owner of QuiKee Gs that American drivers could not resist the soft, hand sized snacks with names like Ring Dings, Yodels, Devil Dogs and Little Debbie Nutty Bars. What a country! Every time a package left the shelf, Mike Kansas pocketed $.66. And they flew off by the dozens! He could hear the cash register's digital ding in his sleep and smiled at his new appreciation for the American Dream.

"You got any Ding Dongs?" asked a young woman behind him with a small boy in tow. "You know, chocolate with cream inside."

"Like the Ring Ding?" he offered, pointing to the open boxes with the chocolate cakes on the wrapper that showed off the creamy inside.

"No, Ding Dongs…they're different," she said, her voice trailing off as she examined the shelves for other gooey wonders.

Mike sighed and shook his head.

"No, we have the Ring Dings, the Yodels…same chocolate covered chocolate cake with white, gooey, crème filling. No Ding Dongs."

The woman nodded, a slight frown on her face and moved off toward the bright red Twizzle Sticks one rack over. Her young son was already pawing at the packages of twelve.

Mike made a mental note to order some Ding Dongs, even though he knew space was limited on his racks. He wondered if he could install shelves above the cash register. Although, he didn't like the idea of blocking the view of the cigarettes behind the counter. Such choices!

He understood his job as an entrepreneur was to supply whatever his customers wanted but did not understand why anyone thought there was a difference between a Ring Ding and a Ding Dong. Marketing! It's all marketing, he thought to himself. Remember that! Always.

"Mike Kansas, come up here…hurry!" came a yell from the office loft up three steps behind the cash registers. It was Shkodran. No, Mike checked himself. It was Karl. Karl Belmont, his partner, friend, mentor, and fellow traveler in this adventure that had brought them from Shkodra, Albania to America and the sleepy town of Norwich.

Shkodran was Karl's real name, Shkodran Encheleis, just as Mirilind was Mike's given name at birth. Mirilind Pasha Bushati, a direct descendant of the Bushati dynasty that ruled Shkodra in the 18th and 19th centuries.

Karl's birth name traced his heritage from the name of their hometown and the extinct Illyrian tribe.

While Mirilind's family had ruled over Shkodran's relatives, it was Shkodran's relatives that had founded the city when it was just a hamlet. It was an interesting hierarchy they often joked about, although Mirilind understood that he could push Shkodran only so far before his desire not to be ruled turned the joking into a serious confrontation.

Shkodran could be very serious. He had been a victim of the Sigurimi, the secret police force of Evan Hoxha who ruled over the People's Socialist Republic of Albania. A wannabe Stalinesque character, Hoxha ruled with the strength of a 'no holds barred' enforcement squad. Political opposition was frowned upon. And frequently crushed, literally, at the end of night sticks and guns.

Shkodran had attempted to create opposition to the failed practices of the repressive leader in his community. Meetings were disrupted, pamphlets destroyed, and government sponsored vandalism reigned wherever Shkodran found support. The Sigurimi would not allow him to get a foothold politically. He resorted to selling guns to opposition groups across his country.

Mirilind joined him and they soon expanded to surrounding countries where conflict was never far away. Nor were dollars, rubles, and lira. They did well. Mirilind tracked the money and Shkodran tracked the weapons.

It was good, but it was dangerous. They decided to leave.

Upon their arrival in New York City eight months ago, they had changed their names to Mike Kansas and Karl Belmont, believing it would help them on their quest for the American Dream.

They quickly found that neither Mike's bushy blonde hair and quick smile nor Karl's wiry dark curls and foreboding eyebrows, coupled with their Americanized names, amounted to a hill of beans when judged by those they met. They discovered America is indeed a melting pot. Everyone came from somewhere else and hardly questioned the combinations of names, hairstyles, and nationalities. Jeans and a clean shirt were all it took. At least, for the most part. Or so he thought. Up to this time.

Mike enjoyed his new name and new life. He understood everyone is from somewhere and we all choose our friends. Social distancing was natural. People were attracted to those most like them, hoping to find understanding. The problems begin when there are so many people; you must branch out and let others into your personal circle, even if you don't like them.

Karl was another story. Darker in complexion, he was also darker in spirit, less trusting, and never at a loss for something to worry about. He saw demons everywhere. Mike had come to believe the demons must be inside Karl. How could he see so many demons unless he was possessed with demons? Or maybe because Karl was a demon? Or so Mike worried.

"Mirilind! Mike!"

The anger was clear in Karl's voice and Mike Kansas hurriedly manipulated the remaining cakes into their assigned places, crumbled up the carboard box they came from, and ran up the three steps to the office loft in the back of the store where the two men ran their small enterprise of gas, gulp and go.

He found Karl at his messy desk, littered with invoices, purchase orders, catalogs, and half a dozen copies of Soldier of Fortune magazine. Mike slipped his wiry frame into the metal chair behind his own desk which sat facing Karl's, happy to be off his feet for a moment.

"What is the problem, my brother?" Mike smiled patiently.

"The bank is stealing our money!" Karl hissed, holding up a bank statement he had covered in red markings. He obviously had been messing around with the document for some time.

"They…the American bastards…our money! Our blood and sweat! They have no right! They are no better than criminals and I am mad." He tossed the paper at Mike in disgust, reached for a pile of statements from past months, waving them with equal anger before tossing them as well.

"Who do they think they are! I have been studying them, I have been watching them, and I am ready to crush them! They have no right! They are criminals!"

Mike picked up the one statement and looked at it carefully.

"You made the deposit last week, yes?" Karl snarled, shooting Mike a sideways glance, his left eyebrow arched high, it's bushiness accentuating the vein clearly visible pumping on his forehead. Mike had seen his partner angry many times, but he seemed especially ornery today.

"Of course, I did," Mike said simply and focused on the red circles and arrows that marked up the bank statement. He found the date and saw nothing had been entered on the bank statement about a deposit on the last day of the month. It was supposed to show over $14,200, a good result for a special 24-hour period when it seemed their operation at the corner of Routes 12 and 2A was the center of attention for the gas guzzling world.

"It's not here!" Mike said in confusion.

"No, it is not there! I tell you; they are crooks. They are stealing from us! I have a good mind to go to that bank and bust some heads!"

Karl snapped his flyswatter at one of the winged creatures who enjoyed buzzing his desk and had paused on its frenetic, aimless flight to apparently seek a nibble on a half-eaten bagel sitting on a paper plate atop a stack of purchase orders. The fly's demise came instantly, and Karl expertly twirled the swatter, slipped the mesh under the crushed fly's body, and scooped it with a practiced move into the nearby trash can.

"They are criminals, I say. Criminals!" Karl's anger was not yet ready to subside.

"I will call them and get to the bottom of this. I'm sure the receipt is here," said Mike. He looked on his own desk and rummaged around for the yellow deposit slip that would indicate the amount from the day's receipts. It was not immediately visible, and he began a systematic search, first lifting and sorting through the stacks of papers, receipts and order forms, bills, and magazines. Then he went through his drawers one by one. The longer the search went on the more concerned he became.

Mike remembered making the night deposit and putting the receipt in his pants pocket, just as he had done a dozen times before. But that was when his memory ran cold. It wasn't in his pocket. Was it sitting at home? Was it in the truck? It was becoming clear it was not in or on the desk in front of him.

He did remember it was a particularly difficult night with a series of chaotic events that had left him shaken, but he knew he had put the bank bags in the night depository.

"Did I give you the receipt?" he asked Karl, as he pulled one drawer completely out to see if it might have fallen behind the opening. There was no response. "Karl, did you see it?"

Mike replaced the drawer and looked over at Karl's desk only to see he had already left the tiny office. He let out a big sigh and sat up straight in the chair, stretched out his arms and placed his hands flat on the desk as if attempting a mind meld with the wood to find the missing slip of paper.

He started to replay that night, just a few days ago, when he had bundled the cash and checks in the blue and red deposit bags and set off for the bank. It had been a busy day and, in fact, a most unusual day for them. They raked in a large amount of dollars for their humble operation. The deposit included a wad of cash that had placed them at a fork in their road to the American Dream, and now it appeared someone had tried to take it from them. Again.

4 - Dr. Z Gets Smoked

The man who became known as Dr. Z never planned to give up his career as an artisan for a career as a fugitive. It just seemed to work out that way. And he never expected to play a key role in the lives of strangers who just wanted to make a few dollars and live the American Dream. But he did.

Dr. Z was one young man who had many ideas of what he would like to be and even started out on the path to realize his own American Dream. But something always got in the way.

He once thought about being an animal doctor, owning a zoo and traveling to the deepest back o' beyond places to find, capture, and bring home exotic animals to be displayed for all the world's children. It was an easy dream for a seven-year-old with a dog. When ol' Barker was hit by a car, the dream died with the dog.

He had a knack for balance on a skateboard and liked to show off for his friends. He had the nerve and the skill to race down a section of Route One that curled around the edge of Fitch High School and down into the Fort Hill neighborhood in Groton. No one else could handle the speeds, topping 40 miles per hour. No one could make it all the way to the bottom without crashing painfully onto the concrete road and then into the trees alongside. Dr. Z loved the speed. He looked no more concerned on top of his skateboard than if he had been waiting for a bus. Some kids dubbed him the town's skatehead. Unfortunately, any dreams of a payoff for this talent were just that. Dreams. The X Games had not yet been invented, and with not much more to prove, he lost interest.

In high school, Dr. Z found a natural love for science and technology. The world was rapidly finding new ways to conduct electricity and build new-fangled devices. His mind sparked at the dream of creating a small music box. His bedroom became a workshop of transistors and solder, monitors, circuit cards, mother boards and keyboards. His vision, however, was well beyond his patience and while he did manage to build a small shortwave radio from parts, he left the serious work to guys named Jobs and Gates and moved on to other things.

Artisan and car mechanic had their day, or maybe, it would be better to say months, before the paint brushes grew stiff and the tools lay rusted. He really liked working with leather, tooling designs in the impressionable skins of dead animals. It was a talent, but not a career that drove him.

He loved cars as much as any kid. He never really felt a need to learn how to fix them because, at the age of 16, thanks to his parent's generosity, he had one that worked. He left fixing to the world of real mechanics, a world he wasn't going to join.

All was not completely lost, however, for he found success with the opposite sex.

He liked girls. He was the guy in high school who always seemed to hang with a pretty one. And never the same one. Having a car really helped, and while he never played a lick of football, he established a sizeable reputation at Fitch as a lady's man. It came easy to him, but of course, as lucky in love though he might be, it was never enough. He wanted more.

The one aspiration that did seem to find its way into his life and stick was sailing. Dr. Z always loved sailing. Growing up on Groton Long Point, a couple of tacks west of the Mystic River, the lure of the wind and the water was inevitable. The little boats were parked on the beach in front of his family home from the first days of his memories. His family taught him at an early age about balance; hiking out with his butt on the rail to keep the boat flat and fast. He took to the sport like a dolphin takes to water, a snake to the grass, a polar bear to ice. From the age of seven it seemed he was destined for nautical greatness, so well did he handle himself on the little dinghy that carried him across the waves.

Dreams about sailing around the world filled his nights, and his days were filled with racing against other kids in the neighborhood. Soon, he was entering regattas put on by the local yacht clubs, and before long trophies were overflowing his dresser and windowsills.

The quality of the competition changed from summer to summer, depending on the crop of kids who came with the families who summered in the Groton Long Point community. He was a GLP local and through his teens would start each season as the boat to beat. After the first few races, he would know if he had any serious competition that season. It was rare that he did.

However, there was one summer, in fact, one regatta over two days, when a young kid with long hair gave Z fits. It seemed as if this kid had come out of nowhere and was hell bent on keeping him from the top prize. He learned his name to be William, and Dr. Z clearly had met his match.

This William won every start, seemed to be tacking on top of Dr. Z at every turn, and showed boat speed that he just couldn't match. If Dr. Z tried to be aggressive in prestart maneuvers, this William would outmaneuver him, often leading Dr. Z into fouls. It was very frustrating to carve out a reputation over several years and have it turn meaningless in just two days!

It would be years later that William and Dr. Z would meet again. Both now adults and taking their sailing very seriously. It was a nasty February night in Mystic when the wheels of Dr. Z's saga took a new turn. He had just delivered a suitcase full of cash to On Edge Boat Company in Noank, known as OEBCo, and asked famed designer Dave Vee to build him a race boat that would compete on a national level.

"I can build you a fast boat," Dave said, "but you need a good crew to have any chance of winning. Hell, a great crew!"

"I don't have a crew," Dr. Z answered.

Dave looked at the cash stacked neatly in piles of 20 and 100 dollars bills on his wife's desk where she carefully counted it. She placed the last 100 on the right most pile and looked at her husband. With just a tick of her eyebrow, he knew it was all there.

"I do," Dave replied with a wide smile.

A few hours later, Dr. Z and Dave Vee were sitting in the Steamboat Wharf Grill alongside the Mystic River drawbridge, celebrating their new collaboration. Outside a full-on nor'easter was raging with 25 knot winds slapping at the waterside windows. Snow was flying diagonally against the pier and the storm's power played an eerie tune as it whistled through the nooks and crannies of the 100-year-old building. The raging fire in the stone fireplace gave off such a warm cozy feeling that it seemed the storm was just a soundtrack and not a gear busting spasm from Mother Nature.

The waitress had just refilled their beer glasses when a commotion along the pier burst through the back door and suddenly the storm seemed to be inside the cozy restaurant. Four men, dressed in red, yellow, and orange foul weather suits stomped their way inside. Napkins flew from the tables with the snow that rushed in and the noise of the intruders only added to, if not exceeded, the howl of the wind.

"Foking close that damn door, Freezehead!" shouted the first man through the doorway, his voice muffled through an ice-encrusted balaclava pulled across his mouth. The group moved inside and just as quickly, the door slammed shut and the storm was again a distant soundtrack.

The back entrance placed them right in the middle of the restaurant. Tables of diners sat startled and open mouthed at the violent interruption. Every man was coated in a sheet of ice. Their faces, what could be seen of them behind a variety of scarves and neck warmers, were red and raw, especially the short one who was not wearing face protection at all.

Another's glasses immediately steamed up with the sudden change in temperature and he looked like some blind Artic explorer with a ghostly sheen over his eyes.

"Dave Vee!" shouted the apparent leader of the group, at least the first one in the door. He walked directly toward the pair in the middle of the room, grabbed a chair from a nearby table and swung it backwards, plopping his half-frozen-self next to Dr. Z and Dave Vee.

The other three guys did the same, and soon the quiet warmth of this Mystic restaurant was turned into a rowdy, salty scene. Tables were jockeyed into position and the two-top was now a six-top.

"Amy, we gonna need some help here!"

Lil' Frankie Giacomo gestured to the lone waitress as he headed to the commotion in the middle of his restaurant. Nothing much fazed him anymore after 27 years in the service business. He enjoyed surprises in the dead of winter, when the tourist traffic slowed and only locals, who appreciated the friendly service and good food, bothered to show up.

His was one of the few restaurants in touristy Mystic that lowered prices in the off-season. The locals knew, from November to March, they could save a couple of dollars at the Steamboat. Frankie was no dummy and found most of them ordered an extra drink or appetizer, so, in the end, he did okay. Sure, the numbers were low, but he made enough the rest of the year when the tourists filled his place. The pace of business was so intense he hardly had time to do much more than make sure the sauces were zesty and hot, and the cash registers balanced every night.

"Billy, you dog, what the hell! I told you we allow rumheads in the front door these days!" Frankie exclaimed with glee, giving Billy Gunning a three-part handshake that involved a series of thumb grabs, fist bumps and finger wiggles. He knew them all and greeted each man by name. He loved playing the part of restaurateur and found this particular six top a favorite.

"Tank. How you doing?" he greeted them, making eye contact with each while playing to the crowd. "Brian, your toes frozen? Not! Teddy. The usual, right? No Johnny Flash tonight? What's he doing, taking voice lessons? Ha!"

The banter continued as each of the guys took off their frozen coats and unwrapped their thawing face covers. There was laughter all about. Within minutes Amy had a tray of adult beverages at the table, and the coziness of the room returned as the group focused on their drinks.

It was not unlike getting a third-grade class to focus after recess. Without the drinks, of course.

"Dave Vee, who's this?" Billy asked bluntly after taking a big swig of his Mt. Gay and ginger ale.

"Guys, this is Dr. Z," Dave Vee answered. He visualized the pile of cash sitting on his desk and a smile came to his lips. "We're building a race boat and he needs a crew. He wants to do the circuit. We start laying her up next week. 41 feet!"

Dr. Z was speechless from the moment the four came in the door. He just watched with eyes wide open as the group took over the place, settled in and suddenly, all of them looked at him.

"Where did you guys come from?" he asked.

"Fishers Island. We were celebrating Billy's birthday and went over to the Pequot House for a few." It was Tank McHale, sporting a bushy, red mustache that contrasted his receding hairline.

"It was definitely a flyer," Teddy Trumanlee joined in. "Going downhill was a lot better than the uphill grind back!"

"You guys were out on the water tonight?" Dr. Z asked in amazement. It was not a night to be out walking, much less crossing Fishers Island Sound in a small boat.

"To go drinking?" he added.

"No problem. Except we couldn't get the damn engine started," exclaimed young Brian. "Bad battery cable! Had to use my shoe." He lifted his right foot with the steel toed boat shoe showing burn marks around the metal plate that connected to the leather.

Teddy and Tank started laughing at the sight of Bellows hair standing on end when the spark jumped through his shoe, and the engine came to life while they were sitting at the Fishers Island Yacht Club dock.

"Brian, I've always thought of you as a live wire. Now I've seen you light up the night!" gushed Tank with a laugh.

"Fok you, McHale! Your foking ass would be a block of ice if not for me!" Bellows smacked him on the arm with his shoe before slipping it back on his foot.

"Ouch! It is a block of ice, asshead!"

"You guys always go out in weather like this?" Dr. Z asked, again not able to hide his amazement.

"Hey, the water wasn't frozen, so what the hell! Besides, it was a two for one night at the Pequot!" Tank exclaimed.

"I like celebrating on my birthday," Billy said with a defiant grin.

"Yeah, with icing on the cake…and everything else," laughed Tank.

Everyone had a good laugh and another round of drinks

appeared before Billy took a long sip, and then he stared at Dr. Z across the table.

"So, what do you do, Z?" Billy asked.

"I'm a stockbroker?" Dr. Z answered after the slightest pause. He gave Billy a sly smile, as if to say that wasn't all he was.

"You're a gambler, right? With other people's money?" Billy smiled.

"I'm not afraid of taking some risks…as long as the reward is good."

"So, what makes you think we want to go sailing with you?" he asked.

"I've got a fast boat…at least, I think it will be fast," Dr. Z responded. He looked at Dave Vee who just smiled.

"I'm sure it will be fast if this man is building it," Billy said with a nod toward Dave Vee. "In fact, we're the ones who will build it." He laughed hard, since Tank, Brian and he would be the guys pouring the epoxy goo, cutting the shapes, and making it right. They spent the last two winters working for Dave Vee at OEBCo. "Why should we care? There are a lot of fast boats out there."

Billy went to his best poker face because a new boat meant new money and with the sailing season a few short months away, they did not have a ride lined up yet. Flying Monkees, an Edge 36, was tired, about to be sold, and it was getting a bit small for everyone.

As good as they were, the crew was a handful. Most MFOs weren't ready to turn over their boats to them. For some, it was more than just winning. With Billy's boys, you basically were along for the ride.

"I have the resources to make a campaign happen," Dr. Z said with a touch of smugness. "I am generous…and I'm a good driver."

"Are you now?" Billy said. "Well, generous is good. You expect to drive?"

"I do."

A short burst of giggles rang around the table as the group shook their heads at this guy's naivete`.

"Well, now, Dave Vee, you didn't tell me we had a champion driver here," Billy said evenly. He leaned back. "A guy who falls for the leeward duck hook every time."

"What's that?" Dr. Z asked. He looked at Billy carefully as if a dim light of recognition was slowly turning on. He remembered a summer long ago when his starting tactics seemed to go to hell in just two days.

"You still don't know what it is, do you?" Billy said. He raised his hands and went through wave like motions simulating two boats heading for the starting line. The hand behind made a sudden turn to pass the one ahead on the right, to weather, only to duck sharply in the other direction as the hand ahead turned up to block.

On the water, the boat that tried to block slows down because it turned into the wind. The boat behind accelerates and sticks its nose on the left side, creating an overlap to leeward. It's called a hook in sailboat jargon, and under the racing rules the boat on the left side gains the right of way. The boat that was once ahead cannot turn very far off the wind to gain speed and is left at the mercy of the leeward boat.

The end result is either being forced over the line before the start signal, or trailing behind at the start, sailing in disturbed air. Both bad results. One has you doubling back to start correctly, the other has you sailing slowly. That puts you in the "land of opportunity", as it is referred to by unhappy tacticians.

"Ding any bells, Mr. Z?" Billy asked with a smile as he finished his air guitar demonstration of the start sequence.

"William?" Dr. Z asked, the hurt of losing two days in a row to the young long-haired kid in the summer regatta suddenly fresh in his memory. "From Groton Long Point?"

Billy sat back with a grin and a simple nod.

"Shit, you hooked me a dozen times…every time!" Dr. Z said in genuine disbelief.

"You want to go big time, you can't let that happen," Dave Vee chimed in.

"So, you want to drive?" Dr. Z asked.

"Ha!" snorted Tank. "Not him!"

"We've got someone better than even me," Billy said with a feigned expression of pride.

"Who?"

"Johnny Flash. All American, national champion, a natural. The Kid."

"And what do you do, then?" Z asked.

"I tell him which way to go," Billy said simply.

"And what am I supposed to do?" Z questioned. He was wondering what he was getting himself into. Isn't the point of owning a boat to drive it and lead the team to victory?

"You get the boat to the regattas, then sit on the rail, write the checks," Billy smiled. "And collect the trophies."

Dr. Z looked around the table at the four guys and the world-famous boat designer. He had just shelled out a ton of cash to build a boat with dreams of making an impact on the grand prix circuit. He knew the designer built fast boats, but who were these guys?

Hell, if he was going to hand the boat over to them! They all stared blankly back at him. The soundtrack from outside's storm raged and filled the room. They had been out in this, in February, for a birthday drink. Well, more than one. Who would do that? They were either fearless or crazy.

And then he realized. He wasn't either but would like to be both.

"Okay. Dave Vee says you're the best. You make her go fast. And I'll sit on the rail."

"Great! Dr. Z, I think we have a deal," Billy smiled, his white teeth bursting out from under his long mustache.

"There's just one thing."

"What's that?" Billy said, his hand extended over the table toward Dr. Z.

"I don't write checks."

"What?"

"I am in a cash only business."

Billy's smile brightened, along with everyone else.

"Well, that is just fine with us!"

More drinks were ordered, and the plan was set in motion. Billy and his crew joined Dr. Z and Dave Vee on a highway of opportunity that would cross the paths of other men chasing the American Dream, with unexpected consequences. These young men, who loved to race and party, thought they had found their dream with a new boat, a new level of competition, and no one to blame, but themselves. What a country!

5 - THE AMERICAN DREAM

🏁 IN 🏁

Hi, Big Mo again. It doesn't take long to understand sailboat racing is a delicate balance of humans interacting with nature – pulling and pushing lines, controlling the tiller, recognizing many different parts of the environment, all of which seem to be changing every 'then and again'. And again. Human actions impact the moment. What those actions cause lead to another action. And so it goes.

It's not unlike the chase for the American Dream.

Part of the American Dream is literally played out on highways every day as citizens of the United States of America steer their sheet metal rockets between the guard rails, following that ribbon of concrete to the next milestone, be it a trip to the store to satisfy a craving for Ding Dongs or a jaunt to nirvana with a special someone.

In the land of baseball and apple pie, free will seethes from every driveway. There is nothing to stop you from getting out of your comfy chair and slipping behind a one and half ton dream bucket and hitting the back o' beyond. No borders to cross, no check points to be checked, no patrols to avoid, save the Smokies and their radar, but we've developed a special relationship with them. We accept their cat and mouse game as part of the living, open weave of a country where you can get away with speeding most of the time.

No wonder there are so many cars to choose from, on so many car lots crowding every community! While many see a white picket fence around a two-bedroom home with a swing in the backyard as the embodiment of the American Dream, there are a whole lot of folks who will take a shiny metal machine with seven spoke alloy wheels, leather seats, 255 horses under the hood, and a bitchin' stereo with nine surround sound speakers any day of the week. Oh, heated seats? Thank you very much!

Since 1931 when James Thurslow Adams popularized the phrase "American Dream" in his book Epic of America, we have been driven by the free will that creates all our pockets of obsession. Houses, cars, boats, business, babes, and boys. Who do you want to be? Well, this is America. Go ahead! Be it! Do it!

Happier! Richer! Better!

For Mike Kansas and Karl Belmont, the "charm of anticipated success" as written by Adams, was palpable. They wanted more than just a couple of nice cars. The democratic ideals of America promoted the promise of prosperity. Self-indulgence drives ambition and creativity. Add the new imagery of MTV on satellite to make it seem that much more real.

Living near the Balkans in the middle of a seemingly endless, centuries old conflict was not good for the free will. Although it was good for free enterprise. And, as Mirilind and Shkodran, they made the most of it. The war, that is.

They found themselves in the somewhat lucrative career of gun running. They were old fashioned in many ways because it was the family business started by their grandfathers. They sold guns to whomever needed them. And that turned out to be just about everyone. It was small potatoes most of the time, selling stolen military rifles and rockets, supplied by various factions from various countries. There always seemed to be merchandise and a broker willing to make a deal.

They prospered. But the Balkan Dream wasn't as attractive as the American version. As their receipts grew, so did their worry and fear. It was all the shooting that was troublesome. Living in the shadow of tribal warfare with a state label put a crimp in any serious attempts at a high stepping lifestyle.

It took many a late-night rendezvous with unknown, nefarious persons, several ambushes and the growing presence of serious military might from the good old USA and USSR to get them thinking about getting the hell out while the getting was good.

So, they packed up their lives, profits included, in a few suitcases and found passage on a Greek freighter with a friendly captain driven by his own willingness to prosper. A few thousand dollars and three weeks later, the gun selling duo found themselves on the Brooklyn docks in New York City, the shooting behind them and their new life ahead. Or so they thought.

They bought transportation, a Chrysler station wagon, headed north to Connecticut and holed up in the Rest E-Z Motel along Route One outside Stonington until an opportunity showed itself in the New London Day classifieds.

"Business Bargain. Can't miss convenience store with gas pumps. Owner must sell. New digital operation."

Mike had read an article in Business Weekly that suggested the world of self-serve gas stations was about to explode. The oil embargo was over, Americans were on the road daily, with new horizons to conquer from the comfort of their metal chariots. They visited the location and found a remodeled gas station with a brand new, aluminum portico jutting from a decent sized storefront. The portico sheltered six pumps, each one offering two blends of gas, Regular and Premium. A seventh pump offered diesel. A two-bay service garage had been converted to expand the office and create a 1500 square foot retail space with ceiling to floor coolers built into one wall.

What attracted them the most was the newly installed remote-control technology that allowed one cashier to control the pumps. Customers could pay at the counter and the cashier would set the amount to be pumped. No need for attendants, just a need for an efficient cash register to keep track of the money. The owner was ready to sell and retire to some cabin in the woods to enjoy the rest of his days among the forest people. The two Albanian immigrants, with suitcases full of cash, paid the owner half of the asking price up front and financed the rest through him for the next five years.

Within a week, they were stacking shelves, making coffee, and dealing with Americans hungry for "Gas, Gulp & Go". Every one of them was on their way somewhere else, chasing their own American Dream. The two transplants christened it QuiKee Gs.

They hung an American flag crossed with the Albanian flag over the front door. The red, white, and blue clashed with the black double headed eagle on a red background, but no one seemed to notice. Few seemed to care enough to inquire and then just nodded their head in acceptance when they heard the explanation.

"Albania? Where's that?" they would ask.

If Karl and Mike had owned a crystal ball, they would have looked into a rosy future. They would have seen the arrival of two Native American gambling empires within minutes of their small station and store. One literally across the river within sight of their back door. They would see an increase in traffic tenfold and would have realized the kind of business volume that turns profits into American Dreams. And businessmen into leaders of men.

But they had no crystal ball, and the casinos were still years away. Out the back door they saw 900 acres of brush and forest, scattered with dozens of ancient stone and wooden buildings, with gabled roofs and Victorian arches, and an oddly shaped clock tower, all a part of the Norwich State Mental Institution. Hundreds were either being treated or locked up there. Many couldn't tell the difference.

Despite the location, it soon became apparent many of the traffic figures shown by the previous owner were the unusual days of traffic and not the norm. After a few short months they realized their path to the American Dream would involve struggling just to make ends meet, a reality that is oft the unintended realization of the chase for a dream.

So, Karl and Mike looked for other ways to make money. And that led them directly to Dr. Z, who, as it was stated in court papers years later, was engaged in a continuing criminal enterprise and always had a need for enterprising young men who wanted to make a fast buck on the wrong side of the law. And that is what led them to a second key element in our story. The rockets.

6 - BILLY & GOLDEE

Speaking of rockets, the red glare of desire burned brightly in Billy Gunny Gunning's brain as he thought of the love of his life, Goldee 'Golightly' Prescott. He was especially pleased when one of the Westmount jail deputies showed up in the concrete hallway of the jail, opened the holding cell and allowed the crew of Smoked free.

He looked for her through the thick plexiglass window that separated the processing area from the public waiting room, but she was nowhere in sight. He signed for his personal effects; a set of keys, his Kevlar wallet holding 27 dollars, his driver's license, and a small compass. The rest of the crew followed suit and they all spilled onto the front steps of the police station, collectively breathing in the fresh air of freedom.

And then he saw her. The unmistakable lithe figure in black and white, sporting boots with 3-inch heels, tight, black pants showing a slight flare below the knee that accentuated her long legs and flat belly, all topped with a loose fitting white summery blouse over a form fitting designer t-shirt. Her heels stood her eye to eye with Billy, and he swept her up in his arms and planted a big kiss on her lips, holding her close for half a minute.

"Sorry I spoiled your night," Billy was heard to say when he came up for air.

"You haven't, silly man! It's still early!" Goldee smiled. She beamed a confidence that he loved and hated. It meant she had plans and they likely didn't include him.

"Oh, shit! The Pissantheads!" He remembered the band she loved was playing that night nearby.

"The Pleasants! You stop being a piss ant!" She playfully smacked him on the head then moved closer and kissed him again. She knew he knew her weakness and tried to convince herself the individuality of their lives was part of the attraction that brought them together.

"How much time?" he asked, jumping over the barriers he accepted in his own mind when it came to her. He wasn't going to always get what he wanted, but fortunately, he got enough to make it worth his while. Plus, they had a big race tomorrow and he really had not planned to get lost in sex, drugs and rock 'n' roll this night. Maybe just sex.

"They start in an hour," she smiled, looking deeply into his eyes.

"Let's go for a walk," Gunny said, grabbing her hand and pulling her toward the park across the street. "Tank, ferry the guys back to the boat and I'll hook up with you later!"

Tank McHale caught the keys Billy threw his way and gave him a short wave to indicate he understood. He looked at the rest of the crew scattered on the lockup's steps watching their leader and his irresistible girlfriend walk away.

"Gentlemen, to the van we go. I'm driving!"

There was a sudden scramble of movement as the crew moved toward the parking lot, a few of them quicker than the others, knowing full well there was only one seat available next to the driver and the rest of them would have to share the steel floor with bits of gear and a few sails that were not already on their racing boat.

"Shotgun!" declared bowman Bellows even as his partner up

front on the boat, mastman Trip Standish, lived up to his own name by sticking his foot out, sending Bellows sprawling on the grass.

"Trip!" Bellows shouted in protest as he rolled forward. "Asshole!"

"Exactly," Standish laughed over his shoulder as he led the way to the van.

"I'm guessing that's a protest," remarked tactician Teddy Trumanlee with a mock look of seriousness on his face. "Rule 14, avoiding contact."

"Tonnage rule may come into play there," added pitman Toby Patton. "Standish has easily got Brian by fifty pounds."

"He'll never outrun him," laughed Teddy. He knew the hard floor of the van was his destiny and was not in a rush. Five minutes later, they were loaded and heading to the marina.

No one was running across the street in the park where Billy and Goldee were alone walking hand in hand toward a circle of benches.

"Who do I owe?" he asked.

"My brother. He ponied up the $1000. I didn't tell him what you guys did."

"Wow! Thanks for that! I guess he's not such a shithead after all!"

"Billy!"

"I'm kidding! Just kidding! You know, we battle pretty hard on the water. I'm glad Monty's there. Good competition for us. I mean, we do like beating up on him regularly. LykytySplyt this, Babe!" Billy flashed a big grin, which drew another playful slap from Goldee.

He sat there shaking his head, the proverbial Cheshire cat, sitting with the beautiful and sexy sister of his biggest pain in the ass competitor, Commodore Montgomery Fillmore Prescott III, who had made him angry enough to lead his crew into a flagrant act of criminal vandalism that landed them in jail, only to have the cause of it all bail them out!

"He really wanted to make sure you guys were racing tomorrow," Goldee laughed. "He is committed to winning and it wouldn't have been the same if you guys couldn't sail because you were in jail!"

"I love him, and I hate him!" Billy cried out in a mock shout. "We will be there, and we will give no quarter!"

He then led her to a bench, sat her down next to him and whispered in her ear. "Tonight, no jail, no sail. Just you and me. Simple and free."

She felt his warm breath on her ear, his strong arm around her shoulder, and his fingers gently caressing her neck. She responded in kind and they shared a half hour of open erotic passion, their consensual joy an escape without care, except how wonderful it was to be with each other.

Later, after dropping her at the club a few blocks from their park passion, where she was to likely lose herself in another part of her world, he wandered slowly toward the marina, the full moon low in the sky, leading him to his crew and the racing sailboat that gently rocked at the dock, awaiting their leader and the championship finals on Sunday.

He felt the northwesterly breeze on his face and smiled, expecting it would hold through tomorrow. That would be a good thing because there was one thing he loved as much as holding a woman. It was the power of a sailboat in a stiff breeze and the touch of a talented crew bringing her home to victory.

7 – ZCCE

Dr. Z took his own road to the American Dream and it involved engaging in a continuing criminal enterprise. Or so said the indictments handed down by the Federal Prosecutors who concluded a seven-year investigation by indicting Dr. Z and three dozen of his compatriots.

It all started rather innocently.

As a young man out of college he signed on as a deckhand for a yacht delivery from Jamaica to Annapolis. Big yachts and little yachts are always moving from one sunny spot to another, depending on the season, and not always with the owners on board. In fact, the larger the yacht, the more likely the owner is not there when it comes time to leave the winter warmth of the Caribbean and head for the summer shallows of Chesapeake Bay, or the small town charm of Long Island Sound, Cape Cod, or the Gulf of Maine.

At first, he was a bystander, a gofer crew, helping the skipper of a 60-foot cruising yawl calmly load several 10-pound bags of marijuana in a marina after dark.

"You are a new face, Mon?" asked the man they called the Dock at the Wharf in Jamaica who was running the supply side of the deal. Dr. Z thought him a pleasant enough fellow after the initial fear of being called out on his first appearance in this type of transfer.

"I'm here to learn the business," Dr. Z remembered responding. He shook hands with the guy. "I'm Z."

"Delroy. That's me. Nice to meet you, Mr. Z," the Jamaican answered. They both went about their business without saying anything else, but soon they were communicating every few weeks. Z's innocence quickly melted at that moment with the $500 he was handed for the least amount of assistance and a strong admonishment to keep his mouth shut.

DO THE MATH AGAIN!!!! The numbers were mind bending. $300 a pound wholesale for Jamaican weed, twice that on the street. But how do we get away with it? He wanted to know more. The math was easy to figure, the logistics much more complex.

Just about the time Billy, Darts and Tank were up to their elbows in fiberglass and varnish working at On Edge Boat Company, Dr. Z delivered his first 500 pounds of marijuana fresh from Jamaica by sailboat to the Connecticut River. His story grew over the next few years, built around bar talk turned into rumors, wrapped around eyewitness accounts, and supported by the occasional "surely they can't be lying" news reports, all spread by his many helpers, some of whom were sailors. Dr. Z's passion for sailing and golf connected him with many who didn't care about his job, just the good ol' ganja he had available. Most didn't have any idea how large his enterprise became.

"We thought his family was involved with Nintendo," remembers one racer who was around for a few of the big regattas and was handed a pocket full of cash from Dr. Z when the time came to settle up expenses.

The law enforcement agencies of the United States noticed and started tracking his movements, but they never pulled the arrest trigger. The law wasn't specific enough and frankly, the mafia was more the focus for any concentrated task force searching for organized crime. Advantage Dr. Z. He took to his enterprise like a pro.

Moving tons of marijuana required a logistical plan involving dozens of sailors, big boats, humpers, drivers, unloaders, distributors, sellers, and bookkeepers. Patience was important, as is a certain amount of brashness to drive a sailboat with bales of marijuana stuffed in the bilges, under mattresses, and in every nook and cranny that would hold them.

While some cartels were using high speed cigarette boats, high-capacity trawlers and airplanes, Dr. Z was happy with a lumbering, 7-knot cruiser sailing its way to Connecticut from Jamaica or Colombia over a few weeks, taking a roundabout way to avoid the heavily patrolled waters off the east coast of America. Nothing to see here, Coasties! We just cruising! Enjoying life at sea!

Dr. Z would send his cargo carriers east toward the Canary Island, then north toward Newfoundland and eventually into the eastern passages of the Atlantic Ocean, arriving south of Martha's Vineyard, sailing between Block Island and Montauk into Long Island Sound and finally, the Connecticut River. It added an extra week or so to the journey, over two thousand miles, but it was safer. Or so he thought.

Usually only one boat was involved with each shipment, and he built the enterprise from several hundred pounds to one or two tons each trip, and never more than a couple of trips a year. There were two or three crew on board to sail the boat because there was no stopping along the way. You sailed through the night, through the storms, the waves, and the changing winds. Nothing better than a love of the sea with a big payday at the final destination!

The humpers would meet the boat when it arrived in one of the many inlets up the Connecticut River. These "gunkholes" are shallow, narrow and rarely used. The mud on the bottom never got on your head, but it did limit where boats could travel. And that limited nosey DEA agents as well.

Dr. Z would pass the word to his shore crew that a boat was arriving at such and such a time, maybe at "Digger's" or "Baloney's", the code names for the gunkholes where the bales would be off-loaded. The crews would sometimes load up smaller boats, take the stash to shore and transfer it to pick-up trucks or vans for delivery to several warehouse locations for storage and then into the distribution system across New England and New York City.

The money, in small bills, went the reverse direction, from man on the street buyers to the sellers to distributors and eventually to Dr. Z where it was literally stashed in boxes, jars, Tupperware containers and drawers in a residential neighborhood where he and his wife lived. Some of it was buried in their backyard.

The cash became a problem because there was so much of it. He smuggled much of the cash back to the Caribbean where the banking laws are more lenient, and the prying eyes of the banking regulators are less interested. Dr. Z understood his local bank branch in Glastonbury wasn't going to take suitcases of tens of thousands of dollars in small bills without a question or two that might end up with the IRS sitting across the table.

St. Barts became a favorite haunt. He invested in a home there and became a good customer of a locally owned bank. While the stories have died down a bit in recent times, the numbers kicked around by those who were aware of the good Dr. Z's efforts suggested as much as 20 million dollars went through his continuing criminal enterprise before it came to an end.

But let's not get ahead of our history here. An event that would have a major bearing on our story in the quest for success in the ESYRU championship connected Dr. Z with our two immigrant Albanians hot in pursuit of their own American Dream.

As I mentioned earlier, Mike Kansas and Karl Belmont at the QuiKee Gs on Route 2A, just outside Norwich, realized shortly after they bought their business enterprise that they would need some extra income to make ends meet. By happenstance, Dr. Z was getting gas at their station one afternoon and noticed a shiny white box truck parked next to the small store. A hand painted "For Rent" sign hung on the back door. "$150/day" boldly written across it. Dr. Z pulled his car up behind the truck and started checking out the vehicle's heft.

He spotted an air hose and followed it around the cab, finding a man bent over the front wheel. He was either making expert fine tunes or bumbling his way through injecting air into the tire. The nozzle would not lock onto the tire valve stem until several movements by the man's fingers, accompanied by under the breath cursing, only to be followed by a quick smile as the connection was secured.

The man turned his head suddenly, realizing someone was standing behind him. Dr. Z admitted later that he was initially frightened by the man's darkish face, day old stubble and his curly, no, wiry black hair. He took a step backward.

"Can I help you?" asked the man without easing his grip on the pressure hose. He flashed Dr. Z a smile.

Dr. Z thought it odd the smile seemed to click on, as if someone had thrown a switch. In a moment, he responded.

"You rent this truck?" Dr. Z asked, nodding toward the vehicle.

"150 a day."

"I'm good with that," Dr. Z answered.

The man looked back at the hose, cocked his head to read the tire gauge and, satisfied, disconnected the valve. He stood up, coiled the hose, never once taking his eyes off Dr. Z. Once coiled, he slapped the hose on its bracket and, only then did he respond.

"Hi, I'm Karl. What you planning on hauling? How far you plan on traveling?" He stuck out his hand and they shook in greeting.

"You can call me Z. And I'm wondering how much this truck will carry. In pounds."

"Well, according to this sign here, 1000 kilos...ah, that's 2200 pounds. About a ton, right?" Karl gestured to the manufacturer's plate inside the door with the truck's specifications inscribed on the metal.

"Even more. Good!" responded Dr. Z.

"So, I ask again. What you planning on hauling? How far you plan on traveling?"

Dr. Z studied Karl for a moment, choosing his next words carefully.

"Does it matter? Just want to use your truck."

"My truck. I like to know where, when, even what."

"Okay. I get that." Dr. Z shook his head, walked a few steps, and patted the sign on the side of the truck that described the rental fee.

"Just a day, a quick trip from the river to Rhode Island," Dr. Z answered with a shrug.

"You fishing? In what river?" Karl cocked his head.

"Connecticut River. Harvesting. It's agricultural. Boxes and bags of plant stuff, about so big." Dr. Z held up his hands about two feet apart.

"Agricultural? From the river?" Karl looked Dr. Z straight in the eye. Z held his gaze, then pursed his lips, stepped closer and whispered to the dark-haired man.

"Look, I pay cash. Off the books, no papers. And I could use some help driving, loading, and unloading. Maybe you can hook me up with some muscle guys to make it a full package."

Dr. Z reached into his pocket and pulled out a roll of money, the outside wrapped with a $100 bill. It was quickly apparent they were all $100 bills. Karl watched him peel off ten and hold them up.

"Cash deposit. You drive the truck, load, deliver. I'll pay you, in addition, three dollars a pound."

"Three dollars a pound of what?" Karl asked.

"A ton of it, at least. How many trucks you have?"

"Just the one."

"Well, I could use two maybe."

"A big harvest, yes?" laughed Karl. He looked at the money in Dr. Z's hand.

"It's a good harvest, yes!" Dr. Z laughed in return.

"Just you?" Karl asked. The look on his face hinted he had been in this conversation before, with others, about using trucks and moving stuff. Boxes and bales.

"A couple other guys, all friends. Unload, load, haul and get paid."

Dr. Z offered him the ten hundred-dollar bills and Karl took them.

"We can do this," he said as he stashed the bills in his pants pocket.

"We?" asked Dr. Z, caught up short. "Who is we?"

"My partner, Mike. It's his truck, too."

"Mike. I see." Dr. Z looked at Karl, cocking his head again, a trait Karl was beginning to believe was activated whenever this Dr. Z had to think about something.

Dr. Z was thinking about this new wrinkle in his impromptu encounter with the man and the truck. Too many wrinkles spoiled the brew, he worried. He finally shrugged his shoulders again, as if it wasn't a clear violation of something his mother warned him about, so what the heck. He knew he was still working out the details of his latest venture. Technique comes with practice.

"Okay, you and Mike. I will need you soon. I will get in touch, here and tell you the time." He pulled an index card out of his back pocket and handed it to Karl.

"You know Hamburg Cove? My guy will meet you there. Look for a big sailboat named Calyopy."

"When do we get paid the rest?" Karl asked. Dr. Z pointed to the address on the card.

"When you drop the load off there, at this address."

Karl read the two handwritten addresses on the card. One said Elys Ferry Lane and the other a street address in Charlestown, Rhode Island, a small town along Route One about 10 miles east of the Connecticut border.

"We good? You understand?" Dr. Z asked, reaching out his hand to Karl.

Karl took it and flashed a thin smiled, nodding his head. "We good. You call, we go."

Dr. Z smiled back. They shook hands and he turned away. He walked only a few steps then turned back to look at Karl once more. Dr. Z was an optimistic kind of guy and he felt his new acquaintance was a positive thing on his road to making the money flow his way.

He couldn't help adding, just in case, "Karl, no one has to know about this, right?"

Karl looked back for a moment before answering.

"We know the procedure." He waved his hand in front of his mouth, in a motion normally used across the throat. Dr. Z turned away and slipped behind the wheel of his red sportscar and drove off. His mind shifted gears to the pending arrival of Calyopy. He estimated she should be approaching the outer shoals of Nantucket at that moment. She was scheduled to layover in Cuttyhunk for the night and then continue on, at a leisurely pace, for the planned arrival at the mouth of the Connecticut River in Old Saybrook around six tomorrow evening.

He calmed any doubts that naturally ran with this continuing criminal enterprise by thinking of the payday in the next few weeks from this shipment. Just then he passed a state cop set up for a speed trap and decided to get off the interstate at the next exit and take the back roads home.

8 – Z Rents Crew

"Mike, do you miss the old country?" Karl Belmont pushed his question as he climbed up the three steps that led to the back office behind the sales counter in the QuiKee Gs. He stopped at the top and realized that Mike was not at his desk.

He shrugged his shoulders in surprise and sat down at his own desk, swung his feet up on a nearby shelf that held quart-sized plastic containers of motor oil and folded his hands in front of him, not moving once settled. He allowed his mind to take another meandering trip that had turned into a recent habit when he was feeling pleased with himself.

The stark dolomite peaks of the Dinaric Alps that stretched across Northern Albania from Montenegro to Kosovo filled his mind this time. He felt the chill of the high mountain air as clearly as if he was back there again. He remembered the aroma of an exotic mix of wildflowers, gun oil and donkey dung. He could hear the grind of the engine from that old Chinese truck struggling to make the grade under the weight of boxes filled with AKMs, destined for the Kosovar insurgents in Pristina or the Serb rebels up north.

The tense quiet of hiding alongside the road, fearful of the Serbian patrols, filled his ears with a deadly silence. He felt the memory as if they were still around the corner.

A moment later the sound of a toilet flush from the bathroom in the back corner of their small office announced the reappearance of Mike. He was busy wiping his hands with a paper towel as he came around the rack of motor fluids and sat at the desk facing his partner. He picked up a half finished Ring Ding sitting on his desk and bit into it.

"Mikey likes it!" he smiled, making a conscious effort to sound like the funny men he had recently seen on TV. He looked at Karl who didn't respond to the comedic effort.

"Mirilind, do you ever miss the old country?" Karl repeated his question after a moment, a wistful look on his face.

Mike thought immediately of several things, mostly bad. He thought of the things that drove him to the United States. He also saw the dark hair of Rovena Salaku, a girl who he seemed to love but regretfully left behind when he and Karl decided it was time to get out of the chaos that was Albania. He still harbored hopes of her coming to join him, although they were never closer than boy-girl drinking buds in the war-torn environment.

He didn't miss the shooting and the unknown dangers when they would go on a deal to move guns. Or the painful rides up steep mountain trails and the lugging of gun boxes from truck to donkey and then back to more trucks on the other side of the Kural Pass. It was mostly the danger he didn't miss. However….

"My rakia!" he finally spoke, a slight smile on his face as he thought of the tangy refreshing taste of the traditional homemade mix of grapes and alcohol. "I missed my afternoon drink at the San Francisco Bar in Shkodra. With Rovena. And sunshine." He looked quite satisfied that he had answered his friend's question completely.

"I miss the rakia, too, but I'm learning to deal with the rum here," laughed Karl after a moment. Mike smiled back at him, nodding his head. He also had developed a taste for rum.

"I do miss the danger," Karl continued, turning serious.

"Oh, no, no, Shkodran…Karl," protested Mike. "You cannot mean that! Why are we here in America? No danger. No bullets!"

"As you know, Mike," Karl smiled, speaking his friend's adopted name with a sarcastic spark, as if making fun of the very origin of the name. "I come from a long line of lions. Proud and strong! We were born to fight, not to laze away our days pumping gas and stacking bags of chips and cookies!"

Mike Kansas just sat and watched his friend's growing energy, the early venting of a volcano leaking steam before it blows its top and spews lava everywhere. He had seen it before. Karl's lava was a streak of viciousness that flowed from his hatred for the Orthodox Serbians who tore up his family and their village during the nasty bit of confused fighting that plagued their country of birth. If anything, Shkodran was as ornery as the doubled headed eagle that symbolized all things Albanian.

"There is no fight here, my friend!" smiled Mike.

"Well, maybe I have gotten us a fight. And some money!" Karl answered.

"What have you done?"

"It's a delivery. A simple one from what I have been told, but it is a job that no one can know about." Karl smiled tight lipped and pulled the roll of 100 dollar bills he had received from Dr. Z, tossing it on the desk.

Mike reached for the money and counted it, then looked up at Karl with a question. He was sure this was not a legal arrangement and assumed they would have to deal with cops and crooks, just as they had done in the old country. Still, he wasn't comfortable with the idea.

"That's it? $1000 to risk our business? Our future? All we have worked for?"

"There is plenty more where that came from. Maybe $5000

more."

"We certainly can use the money," Mike admitted after a moment, holding the bills fanned out in hands. Five thousand dollars sounded much better. "It's drugs, yes? Marijuana? Coca?"

"Agricultural product," smiled Karl. "Ganja, I'm sure. Pick up, deliver, collect. And no mountains to cross, no donkeys to herd, no Serbs to avoid."

"And who are we doing this for?" Mike asked.

Karl described his encounter with Dr. Z, the location for the pick-up and drop off. It was clear that Karl was excited about the prospect of pushing the boundaries of the law again, possibly hooking up with other like-minded persons and adding a little tension to his current life.

"We should maybe acquire another gun or two, just in case," he suggested with enthusiasm as he wrapped up his story. Mike could see the gleam in his eye as the appeal of intrigue and danger pulled at his friend.

Mike didn't like guns, but he knew how to use them. What convinced him in the end was the money. He liked the money. And they had done this before in their homeland, under conditions far more horrendous, difficult, and dangerous. This sounded simple, surely "a drive in the park", he thought.

"When does this happen?" Mike asked.

"Soon, maybe later this week, early next. He will contact me, and we'll be ready to go," Karl replied.

"Okay, Karl. Let's do it! But I don't think we really need more guns."

Karl shrugged his shoulders, as if to say "whatever". He apparently wasn't going to push the issue and Mike knew his friend well enough to understand that if Karl felt like getting a gun, if he could figure out a way to get a gun, he probably would get a gun.

Mike smiled and offered his fist to Karl, who at first wasn't sure what he wanted. Then he smiled and banged his fist against his partners, and even added an exploding hand with a "whoosh" sound effect, just like he had seen the kids doing it in the school yard down the street where he went to shoot baskets.

Mike smiled and scooped up the dollar bills, stuffed them in the blue bank bag sitting on his desk and stashed it in his lower drawer. That would be banked with tonight's deposit. And we'll be a touch closer to our American Dream, he thought to himself.

9 – Delroy

It was going to be a good spring for Delroy Lawrence. The box of cash was safely in his special hideaway and the first of two loads was nearly all on board. The second was scheduled a couple of weeks down the road, but it was already paid for. Hell, it was going to be a good year. Still, Delroy was not happy.

He knew something was wrong with the load. It was too light. He had been watching his men carry the 15-pound bales of ganja from the back of the Jamaican Defense Force truck festooned with the red crosses of the ambulance corps. The only thing injured here, Delroy thought, was his pride! He never expected Lieutenant Arlo Raines would try to slip a fast one by him…after all his years running the docks? He was the dock broker, wasn't he? Everyone knew him as "Dock". The name spoken with the same reverence as one might address a surgeon.

Everyone knew he was way too smart, with way too many years invested, for anyone to try to shortchange him. Especially when it came to goods the "Dock" was brokering for a regular customer. And yet, it appeared there were no more bales of Lambsbreath, the popular strain of marijuana grown at nearby Orange Hill, coming from the back of the truck. The load was definitely light.

It was an exceptionally hot day in Jamaica and Delroy did not feel like chasing down the lieutenant, so he sat quietly in the porch shade in front of the Martnick Wharf office, located on the western side of the Port Antonio Harbor, and waited. A cloud of smoke swirled around his long white dreadlocks stuffed under a rainbow beanie woven from hemp. Waiting would not have been an option for others who supervised the transfer of illegal weed, but Delroy had been here before and he wasn't about hurry. Hey, Mon, we movin' ganja in Jamaica. There is no rush.

Since the banana market began its decline, the freighters that had loaded up with Jamaica's number one fruit four times a week were down to just one boat, one visit, one load. Consecutive hurricanes had messed with the crop and the pace at Martnick Wharf, just off the A4 on the western edge of Port Antonio, had slowed considerably. As had the available work for the locals.

A handful of cruising boats nestled against the cement wharves were all that were left and provided a minimum of paying jobs for the few locals who wanted work. The boats used the East Passage between Cuba and Haiti to reach the Caribbean and then to North America. The access to ganja and the rest of the world made this an ideal place from which to smuggle. Navy Island, once the home of movie star Errol Flynn, protected the Northwest Channel with Folly Point Lighthouse shining its beacon on the eastern side. Titchfield Peninsula split the harbors in half and Martnick Wharf sat along the western shore of the horseshoe shaped bay. No police, no hassles, no serious efforts to speed things up. But the lieutenant was in a rush. He stepped quickly out of the cab of the ambulance that doubled as a weed hauler and rushed over to Delroy.

"Heard on the radio comms just now; there is a command unit in the area; I've got to get going!" said the lieutenant apologetically.

Delroy looked at him silently at first. He took a long drag on the blunt between his fingers and let the smoke billow around his head. The lieutenant, a young man about 24 years old, shuffled his feet uncomfortably, clearly intimidated by the older man with his shock of wild white hair matched by his full beard, and the well-known reputation as the go-to "there's-only-one-Dock Broker-with-a-capital-D". They both understood they needed each other.

Lieutenant Raines had control of the government run force that made periodic raids on the local farmers and distributors who grew and packed the ganja. He was as enterprising as anyone and made a decent supplement to his soldierly salary by carving off a portion of the confiscated marijuana and selling it to the Dock Broker. He liked the man, and he couldn't help marvel at how much smoke poured from the Dock's mouth and nose.

"Did I make a mistake in paying you first?" Delroy asked calmly when he finished puffing. "Did I piss you off, Mon, the last time we made a deal?"

Arlo automatically shook his head, spreading his hands, a clear act of denying there was a problem.

"What are you talking about, Dock?" he said in as friendly a manner as he could muster.

"I'm talking about the eight bales you shorted me, Lieutenant!" Delroy said calmly, with the rank dripped in sarcasm. "We are going to have to do something about that, aren't we?"

"No way, Dock! Come on, I didn't shortchange you. I don't know what you're talking about! No way!"

The two of them stared at each other. Delroy leaned forward then slowly stood up, never taking his eyes from the lieutenant. He moved in close. The smell of ganja filled the young man's nose, strong enough to get him high if he just kept breathing.

"Here's what you're going to do, Lieutenant Arlo. You're going to head for that JDF truck parked over by the shed and pull out the two boxes in the back. You know the two. And then I want you to haul them onto that there sailboat my men have been loading for the last twenty minutes. I'll speak to the captain and hopefully, if he understands, he won't pull out a gun and shoot you. Then you are going to get back in your ambulance and get out of my sight."

Lieutenant Arlo stood defiant at first, but soon his head moved slowly backward and the force of Delroy's demonstrative presence pushed him back even further until they were four feet apart.

"How many bales short did you say?" he asked after a moment, as if he had merely misheard him the first time.

"Eight bales of Lambsbreath!" Delroy smiled. "About $2400 worth by my calculations."

"Copy that, Delroy. Ok. Ya. Ya. Eight bales. Ok. We'll be making that good next time." He started backing away toward the truck parked near the shed, apologetically gesturing that he was happy to carry out the requested task.

Delroy sat back down and smiled at one of his men who stood nearby listening to the brief conversation with a grin on his face. He knew the old man well and enjoyed his antics.

"Smile away, Redbone! Smile away!" Delroy laughed. Then he pointed after the lieutenant. "Go help him! He'll need another pair of hands."

Redbone laughed and sauntered off, calling to the other two men who worked for Delroy at the marina. They were conversing with a thin but fit fellow in a thatched, broad brimmed hat, cutoffs, and boat mocs. He was shirtless with a hairless chest and a well-developed set of pecs. He walked over to Delroy when the two men followed Redbone.

"Delroy, we good?" said the thin man.

"We will be, Captain Tom. You know me, value for value." He offered him a hit on the blunt in his hand.

"No thank you, Delroy. I'll wait until I get out of the channel," Captain Tom responded, waving his hand.

Delroy took another big hit, filling the air with the pungent smoke. He rolled his head and looked right at the captain.

"I got a 'make good' for you this time."

"A 'make good' for what?" asked Tom.

"For my man screwing up! It appears you are short, somewhat. But not a problem."

Just then the lieutenant walked up with Delroy's men, two wooden crates between them. The logo of a company called Dynamit LTK was branded on the side of each box, along with a pair of logos, one gold, black and red resembling a German crest and the other the red, white, and blue Union Jack of the United Kingdom.

"Whiskey Tango Foxtrot?" questioned Tom. "Where did those come from?"

"The JDF, my friend. They have stashed trucks with gear and guns around the island. Just in case the natives get restless!" Delroy let out a sharp laugh, remembering the riots from years back that had brought out the strong arms of his normally placid island.

"What are they?" Tom asked.

"Rockets. Shoulder mount. British surplus from the Germans. Called a PXF 44. A "Panzerfaust". Been here for a bit, maybe five years, but they are in working order. Powerful, accurate and pack a wallop. Stop a tank! Bust a wall! Very valuable!" The lieutenant practically gushed.

"What the hell am I going to do with those?" Tom was incredulous. He was just a pothead captain who enjoyed getting high on the ocean while making good money ferrying someone else's boat around.

"Sell them, Mon!"

The Captain looked at Delroy.

"I'm not a gun broker! I smuggle grass!"

"My child could sell these. Even my nine-year old!" Delroy laughed. "Tell your partner in crime, Mr. Z, that the value far exceeds the ganja. Think of it as a gift!"

He didn't wait for the captain to approve, instead waved his men to load the boxes on the sailboat tied to the wharf. The captain wasn't sure what to do, but he wanted to get underway, and it appeared there was little choice left for him.

"We will have more product as a bonus to make good our mistake next time," Delroy told him, more a command than an explanation. Even as he said it, he was staring directly at Lieutenant Arlo. After a moment, the captain nodded toward Delroy. They shook hands and bid farewell.

"It will be Captain Tony next time," Captain Tom noted. "Probably next week."

"I will be ready for him, whenever he show," Delroy nodded with a smile, blowing a big cloud his way.

The captain turned and walked straight to the Shannon 50 sailboat with the name Calyopy embossed across its stern, sitting at the dock, now laden with nearly a ton of fresh Jamaican ganja and two shoulder mounted rockets. He started the engine and with help from his two American crewmates, slipped the lines and eased into the channel. It would take them about ten days to make the trip from Port Antonio to a small harbor along the Connecticut River nicknamed "Baloney's" where the Captain Tom's boss, Dr. Z, would be waiting.

10 - AUSA NEOCDETF

Molly Fitzgerald never sailed a day in her life. Then one day her whole life became devoted to one sailor. His name first appeared to the authorities a few years back when the U.S. Coast Guard stopped a sailboat carrying a load of marijuana off the coast of Massachusetts near Falmouth. For some reason, lost in the history of legal paperwork, the sailor was not taken into custody, but his load was seized, and he was chastised by the Coasties. They did put his name into an official database where it joined many other names filed away in her neatly organized desk, each occupying a folder that detailed their involvement with drug trafficking in New England.

She arrived at that desk in Bridgeport with a smattering of experience, but none focused on drugs. After graduating from Mt. Holyoke College, where she studied Law, Public Policy, and Human Rights, Molly passed her bar exam and joined the legions of legal beagles in the prestigious Benson and Drole, LLP law firm in New London. Three years later, tired of defending petty crooks and emptying the wallets of cheating husbands, Molly turned her moral compass to the laws of the United States by joining the Justice Department as an Assistant U.S. Attorney for the District of Connecticut. A fastidious young woman in her late twenties, she loved the detail of the work. In short order she was the lead prosecutor for the newly formed New England Organized Crime Drug Enforcement Task Force. NEOCDETF for short.

Potheads and crack smokers may have thrived on the streets, but they were of no real interest to Molly. That social disease was not her battle. She felt removed from that day-to-day smoke festival even as she wished someone could and would do something about the seemingly insatiable appetite for mind and mood altering drugs that fueled a multi-billion dollar international trade.

Instead, she was focused on those at the top of the big picture, the smugglers and sellers who fueled the disease with regular shipments. The suppliers who moved large quantities of product, earned large quantities of money, and involved many partners, over a period of time. It was the 80's and the government had shifted gears in the war on drugs by going after the big fish and their operations. She wanted to be a part of that fight. It was an exciting time for a young go-getter.

Molly's job was to find evidence and bring charges against individuals operating a Continuing Criminal Enterprise. Those who violated 21 U.S. Code 848, the Kingpin Statute; the bosses who strictly moved drugs. Bosses like the sailor known as Dr. Z.

When Molly got on the Z case, it was the first time the 848 statute was enforced in Connecticut and the effort was groundbreaking. No one had gone about it in quite this way. It would prove a tough case to build. She pulled out his folder and began the planning, enlisting many of her human resources, all ready for the hunt. She needed a win. She felt the pressure from a previous investigation of a local motorcycle gang suspected of running drugs. It had turned up nothing.

Sitting in her office in Bridgeport, she had access to the Department of Justice's entire arsenal of law enforcement weapons; wire taps to search warrants; surveillance stake outs, and classic gumshoe detective work from the best agents of the DEA, FBI, and the IRS. Her mandate included strategic partnerships with state and local law enforcement agencies. She had the connections to get the job done.

One of those connections paid off and started the ball rolling downhill. One night, a Connecticut state cop on I-91 picked up a young man and his girlfriend, allegedly on their way to Vermont. A bad taillight, the best friend of all law enforcement, led to a trunk full of marijuana. The young man called the found product Z-Weed. Molly connected that thread to another suspect who had been arrested in Bridgeport on a drug possession charge and requested the same attorney connected to a Dr. Z when he was arrested, but never charged in a possession incident several months before. She found herself lapping up breadcrumbs.

She quickly ran a search for Z-Weed, Dr. Z, and the boat Calyopy, compiling a list of leads connected with the mystery sailor from Noank. She was studying the papers spread on her desk when the office door opened and in walked a familiar face, preceded by his distinctive cologne. By design, the cologne had a chemical effect on her and she turned to greet her secret lover, momentarily lost in the memory of her own sheets from that very morning.

If a workplace affair could be revealed by a sly smile, she projected it at that moment. Though alone in the room, that was as far as it went. Neither of them were ready to spoil what they had been enjoying for several weeks.

"You are just in time," she said, genuinely happy to see his scruffy face.

"For what?" he responded with a big grin, ready for anything. Her curly blonde hair and deep brown eyes focused his gaze as he slipped comfortably into the chair opposite her desk. He fought hard to dismiss the memory of her naked flat belly as he took the list of incidents from her.

"The guy who owns the sailboats we've been tracking on the Connecticut River shows up again in a traffic stop on I-91," she reported by way of explanation. "Well, not him directly, but references to Z-Weed. He's got a crew out there and I want him tracked; him, his phone calls, bank records, whatever he's doing."

"Z-Weed? Like the shit I turned in last week?" he laughed. The motorcycle gang investigation had allowed him to learn their habits. "Might as well carry a sign, right?"

"I need to find that sign maker and connect these other names with him. This is a first-time, big time deal for Connecticut and the boss wants to burrow deep and come up with a connection." She looked up from the documents and laughed at the sight of her new boyfriend.

He wore a black leather vest, a white t-shirt that revealed tattoos on his arms and a gold medallion hanging from a silver chain around his neck. The contrasting colors drew her eye right to it. A bear and a monk shared the oval shape, inscribed with "St. Columbanus Pray for Us" around the circumference. St. Columbanus, the patron saint of motorcyclists as proclaimed by the Catholic Church.

"Jimbo, should you be here dressed like that?" Molly asked. "What if one of your biker gang sees you coming into the building where the DA works?"

"No one saw me," he assured her. "Besides, I thought we were done with them."

She shrugged and gestured to a pile of folders on her desk. "Not if this Z-Weed you bought is the same stuff coming in through the Connecticut River."

"Look, these guys can party with the best of them, but they're just bikers. Like to ride. Their supply is coming out of the Bronx and goes no further that I can see. They're certainly not growing it, storing it, moving it. They're just smoking it!"

Molly looked at him for a moment. He was one of her best assets, but not until that moment had she thought about the toll deep undercover work must take on a human.

"You look like shit," she said softly. His eyes were alert, but they sat in a sunken face, dark circles under his eyes, his week-old stubble covered pallid cheeks suggesting he really needed a dose of good old, sunshine producing, Vitamin D.

"I didn't think you cared," he laughed.

"I do, but it was dark last night." She rolled her eyes, embarrassed. "I like when we don't talk sometimes."

She remembered the first night she invited him to her apartment. He gave off a sense of danger and trouble. That struck a chord in her belly and chest. It was the antithesis of what she had been taught, but that learned attitude seemed to fuel her need to cross a line. An impulse to be with him became an open invitation for sex. She felt wicked when she offered. Then he called and she left the door open. It was the middle of the night and they never turned the lights on. And now she sat there, caring about how he looked and worrying about how the drugs he must be taking, as part of his job, were affecting him.

She wondered if this was the first step on the road to discover how their relationship was affecting her. Did she actually care about him, beyond his thin, yet muscular body, and how well it fit with hers?

"I have a counselor you can call. Someone to talk to, help you cope," she offered, trying to sound like a friend and not a boss.

"I am coping," he answered defiantly. Then he softened, with a big smile on his face.

"You help me cope!"

She smiled with a glimmer of understanding, and they held each other's gaze for a long moment. Then he was gone out the door, and she turned to her folder strewn desk, happy to take on the balancing act between her number one undercover asset and her midnight lover.

11 - GANJA, MON!

First and last encounters are important benchmarks in a person's life experience, including me, your humble storyteller, Big Mo. One started a chain of events that changed my life and the other made me realize how passionate Dr. Z was about sailboat racing.

The last time I saw Dr. Z was in the middle of the night during "The Fuller", an overnight sailboat race. I was on the competition, Madcap, and we were sliding along on a reach at hull speed, maybe 9 knots, with a solid 25 knot push from Mother Nature. The fresh breeze was coming over our right shoulder and the sails were filled and straining. The rush of water along the hull was invigorating and the fact we had torn the mainsail at the top batten about 20 minutes earlier didn't diminish the thrill felt by all six of us on board.

There had been some talk of reefing the mainsail to shorten the amount of Kevlar catching the wind, thus making it easier to control the boat as she surfed off the waves coming from behind.

"It won't move! Up or down!" yelled Dutch at the halyard controls which held the sail in place on the mast. He tried to see the rip, but there was nothing to see in the darkness sixty feet up. "Someone's got to go and check it out," he yelled above the noise of the wind and waves, pointing to the obvious over his head.

"I'll go up," came the response from our dynamo MFO,

Stoney Bullard. The diminutive Bullard, a quiet man who carried a monster reputation on his 5 foot 6 inch frame, grabbed a handful of halyards hanging along the mast and proceeded to free climb up to the second spreader.

"Wait, Stoney! You're going to need…." yelled Dutch. It was too late. The owner was already up and moving quickly, leaving Dutch reaching for a knife while Stoney was climbing up the aluminum shaft. The angle of heel allowed Stoney to walk up the side, like climbing a flagpole bent by the wind, pulling himself with the halyard. He reached the top spreader in less than a minute. Dutch aimed a flashlight up at him and we watched him poking around with one hand while the other held tight to the halyard and his shoes clung to the mast.

At one point the boat lurched forward, lifted on a big wave from behind, and Stoney swung wildly away from the mast, holding onto the halyards to prevent being launched into the briny darkness. A moment later he was back on the deck, letting his weight drop him quickly down the halyard. Dutch swore later Stoney's gloves were smoking when he reached the deck.

"Damn bolt rope is jammed, track is bent, sail is ripped," Stoney explained, gasping for air. "Need a knife!"

Dutch just stood there holding the knife he had pulled too late from his pocket. Stoney looked at him, shrugged and smiled.

"And maybe someone else to go up there, because I sure as hell am not doing that again!"

"Leave it!" shouted Dutch.

"Hey, Jimmy! You got control of this tub?" Stoney yelled at his helmsman behind the wheel.

"Stoney, she's doing 9 knots and I'm holding on with one hand. We're good!" came the response from Jimmy. We called him the "Oakman" because he drove standing straight, as effortless and firm as a tree, only his arms moving with the wheel and his eyes with the wind.

So, we hung on. Jimmy seemed quite content. The rest of the crew hunkered down on the starboard rail and enjoyed the ride. We thought we were on top of the world until we heard a distant cry coming from behind.

"Sheeett! Look at that," shouted our mainsail trimmer, Lenny Kane. His arm nearly poked me in the eye as he pointed behind us. Every man on the rail looked as one.

"Aiiieeeeaaaaooooouuuuu!!!" came a repeat of the earlier sound. I followed Lenny's finger in front of my face and could just make out the port bow light of another boat overtaking us. The eerie glow of red cast a dim circle on the water and on the hull of what was clearly another racer moving twice as fast as us.

Within seconds they were abeam. I felt the next wave lift our stern and give us another push forward, tickling the speedometer over 9 knots. I watched the same action on the other boat, looking more like a ghost thanks to the gradient color scheme from grey to white that gave the impression in the dimness they were floating above the water, even as their hull gushed ahead on the combined power of the wind and wave.

Again, a wail from our competitor, louder and more distinct than before, six voices huddled on their own starboard rail putting out a choral soundtrack for the power delivered when Dacron and Kevlar push fiberglass through the ocean. Speed kills, but for these guys, speed thrills.

"Aiiieeeeaaaaooooouuuuu!!!"

Just as they slid off into the darkness ahead, I caught a glimpse of Dr. Z sitting calmly on the edge of the cockpit, his feet braced on a crossbeam and his two hands calmly holding the steering tiller. The quintessential helmsman in charge of the night. At least for the moment.

"Pig Pen," said Lenny with a shrug of his shoulders,

identifying the name of the boat. "Damn Edge 32! We're not catching them tonight." He went back to trimming the big main overhead and gave a little laugh. The rip in the sail hadn't increased, so that was good. The speedo was still toying with 9's and the boat felt fast. That was good. However, Dr. Z was, once again, in a different zone.

"Aiiieeeeaaaaoooooouuuuu!!!" came again, well in front of us and barely above a whisper lost in the howling breeze. I never saw him again.

The first time I met Dr. Z was much different. I was sitting on my favorite barstool at the Seahorse and in he walked, all preppy-like in a suede jacket and cool shades. He stood by the door for a moment and surveyed the room. It was quiet except for four women in their sixties, regulars from Noank, laughing over an early dinner. To their left, a couple of college-aged kids sipped beer and watched a Red Sox replay on the screen over the bar.

I turned to look at him and gave him a nod. Up till then, we had never actually met, but he and I had been at the same regatta parties, on the same racecourses, frequently trading nods, but no words. I was surprised when he walked directly over to me.

"Big Mo, right?" he asked. "Dr. Z." He stuck out his hand and I shook it.

"Look, I'm going to be straight forward with you," he started in earnest, his voice down a tick or two. "I've seen you about on the circuit and I trust you're a card-carrying member of this community." He gestured around the bar with a big smile.

"We don't have cards," I smiled. "Just barstools." I pointed at the one next to me. He slid onto it and bellied up to the bar.

"So, I'm in a bit of a situation here and I could use some help. I suspect you might like to make a fast buck."

I nodded in agreement, smiling at the classic come on. I never knew what a fast buck was because in my experience all of them had come slowly and not without some effort.

"I find myself short a guy for a moving job. I need a humper. Nothing too heavy, just some discreet transfer of assets. I can pay you $5000, but I need you tonight for a few hours."

"Assets?" I asked. My ears immediately perked up when he mentioned the dollars involved.

"Some bundles, bags, boxes. Important stuff to me and I need some muscle for about an hour. What do you say?" He held up five fingers to punctuate his offer.

It was a good sales pitch that struck my "yes" nerve pretty quickly, especially when he opened his jacket and showed me an envelope in his inner pocket with a thick layer of what appeared to be one-hundred dollar bills.

Now, I'm a great believer in escape and find it often out on the porch of the Seahorse in my favorite chair. However, as far as I must go to escape, I always need something to escape from, like an adventure, especially one with a hint of the unknown. This one sounded perfect. What could go wrong? $5000!

So, two hours later I was cruising along with Dr. Z in his sleek Datsun 280Z, feeling the wind ten times as fast as on a sailboat. And the thrills just kept on coming!

He turned off I-95 at the last exit on the east side of the Connecticut River and headed north up Route 156. I mentally ticked off the passing of Goose, Mink and Rat Islands along the way. The water was nowhere to be seen in the darkness, but I have this chart that never goes away in my mind. I could see a hint of wide lawns and mansion-like homes lit up, mixed in with classic New England cottages built over the last four centuries on the edge of the marsh land that extended a few hundred yards beyond the edges of the river. We suddenly dipped toward the river on Elys Ferry Road and followed its twists and turns, rolling up a couple of miles later in front of what I would have to call a palatial estate on the edge of the Connecticut River.

A stone gate welcomed us to a gravel drive that ended in a darkened circular parking area next to a stone wall that apparently separated the property from the river.

Dr. Z skidded to a stop next to a pickup truck and a box van backed against the opening in the stone. Through this gate was a two storied boathouse with a wooden dock. Tied to the pilings floated a splendid sailing yacht I recognized immediately as a Shannon 50. The rollbar over the transom gave it away, as well as the distinctive two cabin bumps on the fiberglass deck. Judging from the lights across the river, I positioned us almost a mile south of the entrance to Hamburg Cove. The tide was up, and the boat sat quietly, though low on the waterline. Two fingers of light bounced back and forth from a pair of handheld flashlights, dimly illuminating the dock.

Suddenly, there we stood in a small huddle as Dr. Z detailed our game plan. Captain Tom was introduced with two crew guys from the boat that had just come up from the south, two came with the box truck and Hank, who owned the pick-up truck. Hank raced on Wednesday nights and frequented the Seahorse where we had traded nods and chat. He was the only one I knew besides Dr. Z. At first, I felt exposed to strangers, but realized we were all exposed in the same light.

"Gentlemen, we have about one hour before the tide is gone and Captain Tom's boat here is resting on the bottom and stuck until daylight. I don't want that to happen, so let's start moving the product into the trucks. Karl and Mike here will take the first 150 bundles and Hank's truck gets the rest. We have one hour!"

It was quickly apparent what we were hauling and why we had to hurry. The smell of marijuana filled the forward cabin where the 2-foot by 2-foot bundles were wrapped in plastic and tape. It was like a photo out of Grass Weekly magazine. Or Smuggler's Daily.

We quickly set up a chain gang to hoist the bales up through the forward companionway and onto hand trucks. A piece of plywood covered the four feet of beach between the end of the wooden dock and the path leading to the trucks. Without much chatter, we set to the task and had both trucks loaded in 50 minutes.

The last thing Dr. Z wanted was daylight showing off this beautiful boat tied up to the dock unable to move. Of all the places he had used over the years to off load his product, this one was the riskiest because it wasn't some gunkhole hidden up a channel or buried in the back of a cove. Instead, it was sitting right on the east side of the Connecticut River. The boathouse was a well-known landmark to boaters who motored up and down the river daily.

From what he told me later, the moonless night and the tide played out in his mind, trumping the out in the open location. Sure, easy to see, but you must be around to notice anything. He admitted he might have over thunk it, but he rationalized somehow the police would not expect smugglers to be playing near a well know spot where the water is not deep enough for a big sailboat. Except for a short time when the seasonal high tide allows the seven-foot keel to get in and get out without crunching on the river bottom.

On the plus side, the dock and path were close to the trucks so the process of carrying nearly 200 bundles was less labor intensive and worked with the short time span. No need to double load, from big boat to small boat to trucks on land.

Just as we finished, two unusual events occurred I had the good fortune to observe. First was the transfer of five storage boxes about the size you would expect to see in an office holding extra files. They came out of Dr. Z's sportscar. I hit the edge of the companionway in the bow as I handed my one box to Hank and the cover slipped off revealing tight little bundles of cash stashed in a garbage bag. Lots of bundles. I saw 20's and 100's and, if the other boxes were filled the same way, well, Dr. Z was doing okay! At least as far as money was concerned. I didn't ask and Hank just looked at me as if, hey, all part of the game. He quickly put the cover back on the box and we finished up the loading job.

Within minutes, Captain Tom turned on the engine, his two crew tended the lines and they backed off the dock into the river, turned south and disappeared into the night, destination unknown. Hank nodded at me and took off in his pick-up truck, a tarp secured over his load.

A moment later I caught up to Dr. Z and the two fellows called Karl and Mike. They stood by two long boxes that had come off the sailboat with the bales of marijuana and been set aside.

"So, look, fellows, you're square with this, right?" Dr. Z was telling them. "The value is probably twice the cash I'm shorting you, but you can do with them as you wish. I don't want to see or hear about them again, got it?"

"We know what to do with them," answered the shorter one, with the dark bushy hair and mustache. "We good."

"Good," answered Dr. Z. He shook their hands and walked off toward the car. I offered my assistance and grabbed one end of the two skinny crates. The three of us walked them to the box truck and loaded them up. The fellow named Mike threw a tarp over the crates, closed the roll down door and in seconds they pulled away. Z wasted no time, waved me to get in the car. He wasted no time slipping it in gear and the 280Z powered its way passed the loaded truck leaving them in the dust.

"You've got some interesting assets," I laughed as Dr. Z drove back onto the highway heading for Mystic.

He looked over at me, all serious like, and then broke into a big smile. As if the tension of the last couple of hours had broken and he was feeling good.

"It is a nice enterprise, Morris. Nobody gets hurt, everybody gets paid and there's no trouble." He reached in his jacket pocket and pulled out that envelope I had seen earlier in the day and he handed it over.

"And there is plenty more where this came from. You did a good job tonight; I'd like to call on you again if I could."

I took the envelope, feeling its heft and nodded.

"I'm ready to help out. I can be a humper."

"And Morris, remember. You talk, the money walks. Just our game."

"I was at the library tonight, Z. Don't know nothing."

And we drove on at speed, the conversation shifting to sailboat racing and the upcoming events for the rest of the summer. He admitted he was pretty excited about the regional regatta at Westmont Harbor a couple of weeks away and the chance to tackle Smoked's rival Montgomery Fillmore Prescott III and his yacht LykytySplyt.

I listened, laughed, and enjoyed the banter, and this loosie goosey guy who apparently was a major weed smuggler. I admit I got caught up in the moment, and pretty soon, I had forgotten about the envelope that moments before had been burning a hole in my pocket.

I'm sure my carefree soul would have been spinning a very different tune if I knew that night what I now know. Seems a few short miles north of where we had unloaded the boat, a small task force of DEA and FBI agents were hiding on the edges of Hamburg Cove waiting for a boatload of dope from the Caribbean. The tip they had received was either wrong or an intentional misdirection. In the end, their night was far less productive than mine.

12 - Bridge Down

The Gold Star Bridge spans the Thames River between New London and Groton, the lynchpin of commerce that keeps the trucks and cars moving on the I-95 corridor between New York City, Providence, Boston, and the communities in between. Its imposing superstructure of steel and concrete spans over 6000 feet and the roadway rises about 150 feet above the water, depending on the tides.

Everyday about 120,000 vehicles travel north and south on the 11 lanes of traffic. There are people who have a fear of crossing bridges. Business entrepreneurs worry about how far their potential clients are willing to travel to sample the goods they sell if there is a bridge in the way. Be that as it may, the rest of the logical thinking world gets on with their life and depends on moving across the mile-wide gap between New London and Groton at 75 miles an hour.

But not this night.

As Karl and Mike approached New London on the western edge of the Thames River with a load of marijuana in their box truck, the I-95 traffic suddenly slowed in a forest of red taillights and then they came to a complete stop. It was straight up midnight and there were cars all around, not moving, as if it was rush hour in downtown Big City, USA. The approach to the Gold Star Bridge was at the edge of their vision ahead, but dominant in the sea of taillights was the flashing blue, white and red of emergency vehicles. Clearly an accident of some kind blocked the road completely.

The bleep of a siren from behind startled them and Karl eased the box truck a few feet to his right to allow an ambulance to pass by in the breakdown lane to his left.

"Accident on the bridge," Mike said, stating the obvious.

"You think?!" snarled Karl, slamming his hand on the steering wheel.

"Maybe a good time for you to take a walk around the truck. Cool down." Mike spoke in a calm voice despite the heated argument the two of them had shared for the last 20 minutes since leaving the river where they had taken on their illegal load of Jamaican ganja. But it wasn't the agricultural contraband that concerned Mike, it was the last two crates loaded into the truck.

Mike had seen the crates sitting there while they were loading the marijuana bales. He knew what they were right away and that just kept stewing in his mind as they humped the load out of the sailboat and into the trucks. He had to admit to himself that a couple of years back, seeing two crates like that waiting for delivery to some unknown rocket cowboy would have made him salivate. He was over that, wasn't he? He was in America to find the "dream" and not chase the deadly dollar that was always buzzing around firepower.

"Damn, man, I thought we had agreed we were done with smuggling weapons! No guns! What are we going to do with a pair of rockets?!" Mike argued silently to himself.

He and Karl had exchanged glances in the darkness as they focused on the task of humping the bales at hand. Mike could see Karl's familiar tight smile, as if he couldn't wait to get the final bale loaded and then begin to haggle on who gets the rockets. Mike knew somehow, someway, the powerful shoulder mounted weapons were going to end up in their care. In their truck.

"I thought we were in this for the cash, which we need!" Mike opened up verbally as soon as they hit the road. "And you know we need it!" Mike knew his pleas were not going to convince his partner, his buddy, to turn back. It was too late because the guy they called Dr. Z had already explained, even apologized, that the load was short so, he would give them the rockets in lieu of cash.

"I have absolutely no interest in keeping them!" Dr. Z had declared. Mike remembered how emphatic he sounded. "They are as good as cash!"

Karl interrupted the memory, his eyes focused on the highway ahead. "With the right connection we will make twice what that pot pusher was going to pay us."

"What connection?! Karl, we don't have connections anymore! Brother, we are thousands of miles from our connections. We are literally in another world!" Mike laughed to himself as Karl stared straight ahead. He had seen that look before when they were crossing the mountain gaps through Plav and Peja on the way to Prishtina in Kosovo, next to their native Albania, with a load of Kalashnikovs and a big payday ahead.

The tension, the excitement, the anticipation and, surely, the fear generated by the act of delivering firearms to a desperate people fighting for their lives against a relentless force bent on destroying them, was very real back then. People who believed their only salvation was at the end of a gun barrel. Many gun barrels lying neatly and quietly in the back of a truck, awaiting the touch of humans and a clip of bullets. Karl wasn't a fighter so much, but he lived for the joy expressed by those fighters when their weapons arrived safely with him at the wheel.

There was no enemy now on I-95 as they were heading to Charlestown, Rhode Island to deliver the weed of escape to folks who surely had better things to do than fight. Their only fight was to get the cash to buy the weed and enjoy the clouds of relaxation, the smoky creativity or mind-numbing defocus that took them away from the reality of their lives. And wasn't that part of the American Dream, Mike wondered?

So, on they drove and argued until the flashing lights signaled the major stoppage in the concrete artery and for several minutes the two of them sat there. It was Mike who eventually got out and walked around the truck, surveying the scene of idling vehicles. He wandered behind their truck and checked the locking latch. He couldn't help glancing around as he had done so many times before when smuggling weapons, always on the lookout for the police or the passerby who showed too much curiosity. Nothing like that was evident, only impatient commuters trying to get somewhere. The pause button pushed on their lives.

He walked up to the driver's side window and stood quietly looking at his friend at the wheel.

"I like the routine of our QuiKee Gs!" Mike smiled, shrugging his shoulders, as if he had to apologize for slipping into another life in America that was very different than Albania.

"We knew America was not going to give us anything except an opportunity, right?" Karl responded after a moment. "And opportunities mean choices and that is what we can make here. Choices. And then take the opportunity, match the right choices and make it work for us."

Mike nodded.

"We know guns. We can make them work for us. For our dream!"

Mike nodded again in agreement and understanding.

"Now, get your ass back in the truck, I know an alternate route."

Mike jumped in and Karl deftly maneuvered the truck across two lanes, foot by foot, with Mike hanging out the passenger side window gesturing and cajoling other cars to let them get to the side of the highway where Karl proceeded to drive up on the curb then 30 yards on the grass to a small opening protected by bushes that separated the interstate from the parallel service road. He crashed through them with a forestry thump and continued across another grassy divider into the Coat Factory Plaza parking lot which led them to Coleman Street. A couple of lefts and rights and they were soon on Route 32 heading north out of the city of New London.

Behind them, the irritated drivers, who at first objected to the guys in the box truck trying to bully across the tight lanes of clogged traffic, realized what they were doing and soon a steady line of cars was bumping through the bushes, squeezing over the grassy dividers, and escaping to the side streets.

Karl knew Route 32 ran north to I-395 toward the sleepy old mill town of Norwich and then to the Route 2A connector that ran west to east to Route 12, which fed them back south to rejoin I-95 on the Groton side of the river, allowing them to continue their trip northeastward toward Providence and Boston. The connector had its own bridge over the Thames River. It was a 20-mile detour but the only way to go.

Reports were coming in on the radio about a tanker truck and a bus that had an unfortunate meeting leaving two dead, several injured, including children, and a few thousand gallons of diesel fuel spilled on the roadway, not to mention the mangled steel and glass from other vehicles involved. The highway was expected to be closed for several hours according to the CT Department of Transportation. Maybe longer.

Right away, they were moving faster, but not as fast as normal because word of the chaos was out and drivers back to the west were diverted onto I-395 several miles before the stoppage at the Gold Star Bridge. The effect of the roadblock was to eventually send several thousand cars right past Karl and Mike's QuiKee Gs gas station and food mart now conveniently located on the Route 2A connector.

It had not been their initial intention to stop at their place of business. They were heading to Rhode Island to unload the weed. However, when they arrived at their gas station, they were amazed at the mob scene created by the detour ten miles away. Two lines of cars were stretched into the street as drivers took the opportunity to fill up on gas, snacks and lottery tickets and all the other finger distractions that made the gas, gulp and go business model look very smart.

"We have to help!" laughed Mike as they pulled up alongside their building. Both jumped out and set about to ease the crush of people inside the store. Karl opened the second register, smiling broadly at his overnight cashier, Phillip, who only nodded and punched buttons on his register. He threw his hands up at the people waiting. The expression on his face like he had been swarmed by bees.

"We need more coffee!" was all he could say as he stashed another twenty in the cash drawer and returned change to a woman customer.

"Coffee is me!" waved Mike and set about refilling the row of coffee urns against the wall. He didn't bother worrying about the French Vanilla, the Cinnamon mocha, or the decaf Hazelnut. He just grabbed the first bag of beans and started grinding, filling the filter bags, and brewing as many pots as fast as he could.

The madness continued for several hours. At one point, Mike called in his morning shift and the twin sisters, Betsy and Jacqui, arrived two hours early. The lines were steady, and the cash flowed as the world seemed to be on the ultimate gas, gulp and go frenzy.

At one point, Jacqui came up to Mike with a smile.

"You guys are losing big time! Bump the price!" She gave him a thumbs up motion, and repeated it a couple of times, followed by a head nod as if he was being dumb.

Mike looked at her for the briefest of seconds and then smiled, grabbed her by the shoulders and planted a big kiss on her cheek, much to Jacqui's surprise.

"Stupid me!" he moaned and ran to the storeroom where he proceeded to pick up a container of metal number placards and an orange cone. One at a time, with deft placement of the cone, he reprogramed the pumps and changed the prices to bump the price by 5 cents. No one seemed to notice except the half dozen or so customers who happened to be the last ones getting gas at the old price.

"Any more Ring Dings?" came a call from among the disheveled piles of gooey chocolate cakes as Mike returned to the store. He waved and brought fresh boxes from the storeroom and made several more trips to replenish the "Crunchy Aisle" as he called the chips, pretzels, and dip delights in the middle of the store.

At one point, Karl stood watching the steady stream of cars lined up at the six pumps out front and thought about calling the gas broker for an unscheduled delivery of fuel.

The tanks held about 18,000 gallons in two blends plus diesel. That usually lasted a week, but at this rate it would be gone in a day or so. Karl was never driven by the chase for money, but he had to admit to himself that cash flow at three times the normal rate was appealing and while Mike had always been the money guy and had pushed for their escape from the war in Albania to chase an American Dream feathered by dollars, Karl was seeing that dream much clearer right in front of his face.

He made the call with the sunrise, waking up the owner of Crescent Oil Products, Alex Veron, an immigrant from Turkey. In the few months that Karl had done business with Crescent, he never liked talking to Alex because he was part of an old culture that did not like Albanians. Thanks to centuries of conflict over religious, ethnic, geopolitical, or whatever the reason; there was blood spilled, land stolen, battles fought during the Ottoman Empire seeking access to Europe, with Albania in the middle, in the way. An atmosphere of animosity existed that one could not help but absorb while growing up. If nothing else, as a child, Karl had developed a healthy suspicion of anyone of Turkish descent.

And yet, they did business because no one else seemed open to the idea of supplying QuiKee Gs with fuel. Karl and Mike did not know the reason for that just yet.

"Alex, I need gas as soon as possible. I've had a run and we are going through gallons at a record pace." Thus, Karl began when Veron answered the phone.

"I hear the bridge is out," Veron answered sleepily. "How soon?"

"Today. Immediately! I could be dry by tonight!" Karl didn't try to hide his concern.

"Hmmm…not sure I can do that. I've got a full schedule today, short on trucks…." Veron protested, his voice trailing off as if distracted.

"Alex, damn it! No games, okay! What's it going to take?"
Veron was silent for a moment.

"I might be able to send over a truck, but I got to go outside the network, it's going to cost you." Karl could hear the smile on Veron's lips and that kicked his blood pressure up a notch beyond what the press of business had already created. Pulling money in hand over fist was fun, but it created its own kind of issues.

"Probably 3 cents on the boost," Alex answered.

"You are a prick, Alex. You know that!" Karl spit into the phone, but he had no choice for the moment. "Send a full load. I need it today."

The cleanup on the Gold Star Bridge took longer than expected and the inspections revealed damage to the roadway that required new pavement. It was as big a mess as Southeastern Connecticut had seen since the bridge opened during the Eisenhower administration. Today, the detour had turned Karl and Mike's QuiKee Gs into an extremely popular spot, at the elbow of exposure, a cash machine. Karl wasn't ready to wake up.

Later in the day, Mike and Karl were sitting in the office counting money when Jacqui stuck her head up the short stairway.

"Karl, you have a visitor!" she yelled.

Karl met her at the bottom of the stairs, and she whispered. "I don't think he's very happy!"

13 - Z Comes Looking

I admit I grew to like Dr. Z after he began trusting me, even asking me to accompany him on some appointments. I admit I'm a big man, but not the fighter type. Nevertheless, standing next to the thin Dr. Z, I apparently fulfilled the need for "imposing". So, I stood tall when I got out of Dr. Z's sports car at the QuiKee Gs on Route 2A and the two of us walked up to Karl, of the Karl and Mike partnership that runs the store and humped the weed.

"Act big and tough," commanded Dr. Z just before he greeted the man with the wiry, coiled black hair and stubble on his chin. I recognized him as the driver of the box truck.

"Karl Kansas, I see you are busy."

"Accident was a good thing for us. Suddenly the trout are running."

"Trout?" asked Dr. Z.

"We are catching a lot of the fish in the creek. They were all forced to take this creek because it's the only creek. Fortunately, it's my creek and they were thirsty."

Karl smiled, hands on hips, looking happy as could be, embracing the distinct emphasis he had given the word "creek" each time, as if it was a particularly important possession. I couldn't help thinking Karl was feeling pretty American with his use of the metaphor.

Dr. Z seemed unimpressed, stepped up real close to him, almost cheek to cheek and he whispered in Karl's ear. "You have something of mine, don't you?"

Karl took a step back, but Dr. Z wouldn't let him get away, following him with his own step, moving right back cheek to cheek.

"Karl, man, it's the money! You get that, don't you? The money is why we are all here and you are killing me by holding onto the load! That's money that is nothing when it is sitting on your lot."

Dr. Z gestured off to the east side of the station where the box truck was parked. It had brought a sigh of relief when we pulled up next to it. At least it wasn't missing.

"Z, I get the money. You don't think I get the money?! That's why I'm here! We've been swamped! Your shit is safe, but my shit is flowing right now." Karl pointed at the traffic filling the gas pump lanes. The store was clearly still enjoying the fruits of the detour caused by the deadly crash.

"I need that load in Charlestown now. It's my shit, and it needs to get flowing!"

"I am needed here!" Karl stood firm.

"Okay, my friend. You don't want to play hardhead with me. You have two choices here."

Dr. Z put his finger in the air as if instructing a dog.

"You get in that truck with my man Morris here and the two of you deliver the product right now! Or you give me the keys and Morris will make the delivery, I'll make the appropriate adjustment to your promised pay and we'll be done with our little effort here!"

Karl looked at Dr. Z and for a moment it appeared he was thinking hard. He stood pretty solid with fists clenched, easing back away from the drug smuggler as if preparing for a fight. Then he relaxed, as if a switch was flipped.

"You're right, Man! That's your shit. I'll move it."

Just like that he seemed to understand exactly what Z was saying. He nodded at me and beckoned with a quick wave of his hand.

"Let's go, Big Guy!" and he moved toward the box truck parked on the other side of the lot.

I looked at Dr. Z, who just smiled and moved his arms like a matador pointing the way for me to follow Karl and deliver the product.

I was halfway across the front of the store when Karl came roaring at me in reverse, moving the truck to the west side of the lot. He expertly spun the wheel and eased the truck down the side of the building to the rear where he stopped in front of a narrow garage door. It rolled up with an iron rattle to reveal the storeroom and twin number one, Jacqui.

"You guys need any help?" she asked, still holding onto the chain that controlled the metal door. The room behind her was filled with racks of goods waiting to get on the sales floor and a section with plastic strips hanging in the opening that led to the standup coolers that allowed resupply from behind.

"We got this, Jacqui!" Karl smiled at her. He stood for a moment at the rear door of the truck, not moving. "Can you check on the coffee urns? And I'm thinking maybe we have to rearrange the beer stacks…make sure all the 12-packs are slid forward in the cooler."

Jacqui looked at me as if she wondered what this stranger was doing with her boss, but then turned back to address Karl. Her curiosity left her hesitant to move right away.

"I did that yesterday with the beer, but sure, I'll check again."

Then she turned with a nod and headed back inside toward the coolers. I thought it best that she did not see what was in the truck. She snuck one last glance anyway.

When she was gone, Karl opened the truck and we removed the two crates of rockets that had been sitting on the beach during the grass hump. Karl splashed a tarp over the boxes where they sat under a rack of hand sanitizers and sponge wipes. Out of sight for the moment. We then hit the road with over a ton of Jamaican ganja destined for Charlestown, Rhode Island.

Karl eased the truck into traffic on Route 2A, made the right on red onto Route 12 and twenty minutes later we were back on I-95 heading northeast. We could see the flashing lights on the bridge and the empty highway behind, but around us was the rest of the detoured world, their lives back on full speed ahead. Karl stayed within the speed limit and we shared a few stories during the ride.

"You didn't scare me, Morris. Not one bit." It was not a boast from Karl, simply a hard fact.

"Not even a little bit?" I returned.

"No. You may look like a bear, but I see Teddy Bear."

We both laughed. "Well, he's right, you know. Weed turns to money only when it's moving, not when it's sitting turning into… well, weeds."

"I know," Karl nodded. "I understand about the money. I'm just a hothead! Ha!"

In twenty minutes, we pulled into a gravel driveway that led behind a comfortable farmhouse and stopped by a two-car garage attached to a barn. As we pulled up, the door opened closest to the barn and a man in a baseball cap appeared, quickly gesturing for us to back in. Karl smoothly made a half circle and eased the box truck into the building.

"Thought you'd be here last night," was all the man said as he plugged an extension cord into a socket on a post in the middle of the floor where the wall between the garage and the barn should be. The open space had a workbench in the middle of the floor. As we got out of the truck, an electric motor kicked in and the bench began to slide, revealing a six-foot long opening in the floor. A head popped up in the opening. A metal ramp followed from the hole and was muscled into place, one end on a sawhorse next to the truck. It was a gravity roller, conveyor ramp designed for moving boxes and that's what we did. The guy in the ball cap gestured to Karl, as if to say "let's get it going!" Karl opened the load door in the truck and, pretty soon, the four of us had a chain gang moving the bales of ganja out of the truck, onto the ramp where they rolled noisily into the hole in the floor.

In short order the task was done. The hole apparently held a shipping container that handled the load. I was surprised and impressed with the facility. It wasn't just some guy's garage used for storage. It was an underground hideaway.

The guy in the ball cap went to the opening and said something to the fellow who was in the hole. He disappeared for a moment and reappeared with a paper bag which he handed to Karl. I could see the bundle of cash as Karl opened it and gave a cursory glance inside. He nodded and got back into the truck. I followed and we headed back to Mystic.

"Well, your Dr. Z seems to have his shit together," Karl finally broke the silence about fifteen minutes into the trip. "A real life drug smuggler!" Karl was smiling and shaking his head in disbelief.

"We thought his family owned a piece of Nintendo!" I added with a laugh. Around the docks, and in the bars there was plenty of buzz from the crew sailing on Smoked with Dr. Z, stories about payments in cash for all the boat's needs, be it a new sail or travel expenses. It wasn't all games, apparently!

We drove on, trading tales about sailboat racing and smuggling. I talked about lobstering from my boat and the quiet coves that came with freedom on the seas. Karl dropped me off at the Seahorse and went on his way. I ordered a Mt. Gay and tonic and contemplated the rabbit hole I hardly knew existed just a couple of days before. And here I was, riding shotgun with cash in my pocket, willing to go deeper!

14 - THE SNITCH

It seemed every day Molly came to work she added new details to her calendar. "Meet with snitch" came this day. She had never met up with a snitch before and had a flock of butterflies in her stomach. The breeze felt nice, however, blowing in across the New Haven Harbor. It carried the pleasant smells of grilled meats, tangy sauces and seagulls.

The foot-long hot dog sitting on the table in front of her wasn't doing her demeanor any favors either, but there it sat, covered in onions and sauerkraut, with two biggie drinks and a paper boat of Italian fries. It was more a code signal than her favorite lunch and the food was a lot closer to going stale than satisfying her hunger.

She saw her contact before he saw her. He shuffled across the parking lot between the harbor and the interstate, heading for the snack shack on wheels called Larry's. It was an Elm City landmark of sorts and it served delicious cheeseburgers and hot dogs to travelers and locals who made it a regular stop in their daily wanderings.

The debate about who created the first cheeseburger raged among the hoi polloi between Larry's and Louie's, a similar joint a half mile away in the middle of downtown. Everyone won that argument because both places served up a wicked good meal of meat on a bun.

She looked at the photo sticking out of her pocketbook on

the bench next to her and confirmed it was Hank, the Confidential Informant. She watched him pause near the open service window cut into the side of the shack, to look around the half dozen tables spread out in the small park that served as the eating area. Molly smiled at the man with the cherub face, encircled by hair, curly and thick on top, spilling over his ears and seamlessly sprouting around his chin in a beard. All of it distinctively reddish brown, punctuated by a toothy smile right in the middle. So innocent, she thought.

He walked over toward her table, eyeing her carefully and then stopped a few feet away.

"Is one of those for me?" he asked, pointing to the supersized paper cup filled with soda.

"Do you have something for me?" Molly answered with a smile.

He paused for a moment, not sure how to answer.

"I've got something for Sam, but you're not Sam, are you?"

"No, I'm Molly. I'm Sam's boss," she answered. "Why don't you sit down?"

He thought about it, then nodded and sat across from her at the picnic table. She pushed the drink toward him, and he readily accepted it, immediately taking a long pull on the straw.

"Where's Sam?"

"He's busy. I wanted to meet you myself and see how things were going. You kind of left us high and dry last time."

Hank shrugged his shoulders defensively and shook his head.

"Hey, I didn't mean to give you the wrong info. The Z man changed the plan at the last minute. Literally!" He sounded apologetic and angry at the same time. "I got the radio call 30 minutes before from the boat captain. I had no chance or choice."

Molly remembered the good feeling she had when the initial tip came in that the boat Calyopy was heading for Hamburg Cove with a load of weed and her team was deployed, hidden, and waiting. No one showed.

"Well, you know the deal here. You give me something good, and we make something good happen for you."

"Yeah, yeah, I know. Say, mind if I grab a couple of fries?" He pointed at the order of Italian fries, another Larry specialty with pesto mayo and Romano cheese. Molly pushed the paper container toward him.

"Help yourself, Hank. Then help me, okay? What do you know? Tell me how this Z character contacts you? How often?"

He grabbed the fries and started munching. Molly wondered if he had eaten that week.

"I see him, run into him at the bar sometimes. Sailing stuff. He will come over and let me know a day or time. Sometimes he leaves a message on my machine."

"How often?"

"Not often. Maybe once a month, maybe every couple of months."

He looked at her as if he had something else to say then decided against it. Molly picked up on his reluctance.

"What's coming up, anything? Another load?" she pressed.

"So, look, if I tell you, you make my DUIs go away, right?"

"Hank, that was the deal, but you have to deliver, right? I need good information, or you will find yourself in deep ka ka, not only for the DUIs...you have three, right? Jeez, you know you're looking at jail time! And this - smuggling? Please! How would you like to spend the next ten years?"

Hank had a heartsick look and suddenly wasn't so hungry.

"Inside or outside? 10 years?" she asked as if the answer was easy.

"Man, I'm so screwed. All I know is there has been some chatter about a big boat, another 50-footer, under a German flag. Maybe next week, Friday or Saturday. Heading for Deep River."

"Friday or Saturday? Which way is it coming?"

"I don't' know, probably like the others, past Block, Montauk. From the east. You're going to dump the unregistered car charges, too, right?"

Molly sensed Hank was not used to snitching. He clearly felt trapped.

"Tell me something, where do you take this load?"

"Jezzus, how much you want from me?"

"Everything, Hank. I want everything! What the hell you think we're doing here? I'm trading the power of the U.S. Attorney for information. Hank, if this pays out, you will be outside. Walking free!"

She looked right at him with a tilt of her head and a small smile, as if she was about to dispense the kind of advice that everyone knew, but it still had to be said.

"You can't sail in jail! Duh!"

Hank rolled his eyes, nodded his head and gave her what she wanted.

"Probably seeing Luiz in the Bronx. He's the guy down there. I just drop some bales and go home."

"Anyone else?"

"I don't know anyone else. There were a couple guys in a truck last time, but it changes. Different guys, different trucks. I know where I go, that's it."

"Okay, good info, Hank. You're doing good."

Molly reached over and touched Hank's arm, adding a friendly smile. She felt emboldened to use her womanly charms on this young man who was in way over his head.

"There is a guy up in Maine near Kittery," Hank smiled as if another piece of info was ignited by her touch. "I think they use their art association as a front."

"That's good to know. Sounds like he has a lot of tentacles

out."

"There's a lot of weed coming in. Gotta move it to make it work!" he chuckled. He was feeling good but suddenly a thought crossed his mind.

"And nobody knows, right? You're not using my name for any of this right, no publicity, no mention to Z, right?"

"Does he frighten you?"

"Not really, but you know, he's not going to be happy! Ha! He's going to be pissed!"

"Hank, I'm counting on that!"

Molly got up with a smile on her face. Hank sat there, quietly, accepting the fact he had just sold out the guy who had been paying him good money. A guy who did not have the power to keep him out of jail.

"Hey, Molly, you going to eat that?" Hank pointed to the untouched hot dog sitting on the table.

"Go for it, Hank! Fill up!" He pulled it over and began eating it.

Molly walked away toward her car, pleased the butterflies were gone.

15 – TIFFANY & TUCKER

Tiffany and Tucker led a weird life for a couple of yuppies who had already lived the American Dream. They were both seniors at Brown University, she beautiful and smart as a whip. Him? Maybe not so smart, but handsome as a cool breeze. Their real connection was a mutual obsession with robbery. It was probably more Tiffany's fault than Tucker's because he didn't need money. Nor did she, come to think of it, since both their parents were successful - his father a Mercedes-Benz dealer and her mother a bank vice-president.

The key factor, as it often is with young folks, was sex. Tucker was totally smitten with Tiffany and would do anything for her. And she liked to rob people. It clearly turned her on and Tucker liked how sexually demanding she was afterwards.

So, one night, at her urging, they borrowed a couple of handguns from his father's collection, donned ski masks and held up a gas station. She could hardly keep her hands off him as they sped away from the scene. A few weeks later they did it again, and then again. Their mantra was Rob, Rut, Repeat. Before long, there were stories appearing in newspapers in Providence, Hartford, and New Haven. The local TV channels started talking about the 'Preppy Perps'. Grainy surveillance photos accompanied the stories of two lanky adults dressed in black, including ski masks and black framed glasses, one clearly a female in a tight-fitting outfit.

The preppy tag was conjured up by a young reporter who focused on the variety of school logos emblazoned on their masks each time they pulled a job. And the variety of Mercedes-Benz they used for getaway vehicles. Tucker apparently used his father's connections to obtain knowledge that allowed them to steal a different car for each of their adventurous efforts which they considered simply 'foreplay'. Police found the cars abandoned and tracked down the real owners which led to a dead end.

"I think tonight we actually will see some real money for a change," Tiffany whispered sitting next to Tucker in a black SL450 parked in a commuter lot just off Route 2A about a quarter of a mile from the QuiKee Gs.

"Hmmm," was all Tucker managed, his mind focused on her hand gently drifting over his inner thigh.

They had seen the stories about the traffic accident on the Gold Star Bridge the night before and decided the QuiKee Gs might be a good target. They confirmed it by driving past it several times earlier in the day. The line of cars stopped for gassing and gulping was encouraging. Most of their previous heists had netted a few hundred dollars at most, barely enough for a trip to the mall. Tonight, however, was a busy one on the gas line and both thought about the money for the first time.

"Let's do it!" she said with a final squeeze of his leg. She pulled down her Yale ski mask, checked her look in the mirror and clicked the safety off her Smith and Wesson Model 57 with the classy wooden handle. She had loved it at first sight when they rummaged through Tucker's dad's gun collection. He checked his new Glock 17, slipped the car in gear, and headed for the QuiKee Gs down the street.

Mike Kansas had gone without sleep for nearly twenty hours and had just emptied the cash drawer for what seemed like the tenth time since the accident induced rush had started at his now booming gas station minimart. He stuffed the bills and receipts in a bulging blue bank bag while silently thanking his partner, Karl Belmont, for coming up with the two cent per gallon cash discount weeks ago. Although it was originally designed because business, frankly, sucked, before the accident, he didn't regret their impulsive decision to keep the discount, in spite of the increased traffic over the last 24 hours. Their five cent price increase eased the pain of the discount.

They were now running at four times their normal flow of traffic, pulling in the green, and that was the whole reason they had come to America. Mike was hoping the bridge repairs would take forever!

"Coffee change, Mike. Can you watch the register?" came the call from Jacqui who was pulling double shifts as well. He nodded at his trusty worker bee as she slid out from behind the counter and went to attend to the coffee urns along the back wall of the store. He found himself staring at her as she walked, admiring her youthful gait and form. Yeah, he admitted to himself, he liked her. Then he had a moment of confusion as he wasn't sure if that was Jacqui or her twin Betsy.

"No complaints, Mike," he admonished himself as he threw the blue bag under the counter and stepped behind the register to deal with the next customer.

Suddenly two people burst through the front door dressed in black, brandishing handguns.

"Nobody moves! This is a stick up! Don't move and you won't get hurt!"

The unmistakable high pitch of a woman's voice cut through the store. The three customers in line all turned in shock. The woman aimed her weapon, waving them to stand close together on one side of the register.

She shouted again, "This is a stick up! Don't move and you

won't get hurt!" Mike thought it odd to see the face of a bulldog on the forehead of the mask she wore.

The man, with the letters "B.U." stitched on his facemask, walked right up to the counter and aimed his gun at Mike.

"Open the cash drawer and stuff everything right in here," he ordered, snapping open a cloth bag like you might take to the beach. Mike didn't move. He had faced gunmen before, albeit on mountain trails in the Albanian Alps. He had learned that if they don't shoot first, they usually don't want to hurt anyone. Their focus instead was to just grab the goods and go.

"Stay calm, Buddy!" Mike smiled. "I'm going to open it up here and stuff the money in."

He couldn't help flashing a smile because he knew the cash draw held only $100 in change. A couple of twenties, four fives and four tens, plus a few dollars in singles and coins of varying denominations. He threw it all in the bag only to draw a sharp rebuke from the masked man holding him at gunpoint.

"What the hell, man! Are you crazy? You want me to fok you up? Where's the rest of the money!"

"I just cleared the cash drawer, that's it. You got it all!" Mike responded holding up his hands like he had nothing to do with it.

"Mother f…." The man in black looked over the counter into the empty cash drawer. He then jumped up, landed his butt on the counter, swung his legs over, landed next to Mike and pushed him away. He slammed the drawer shut in frustration then looked around behind the counter and spotted the blue bank bag that Mike had just stuffed and stored.

"Oh, yeah! Now we are talking!" He reached for the bag just as he heard a loud shout coming from the side. He looked over in time to see a woman, dressed in a blue uniform shirt, throw a coffee urn directly at Tiffany.

It was Jacqui. She never expected to be involved in a robbery when she came to work for Mike and Karl several weeks back. Her plan was to learn retail from the ground up and build her practical knowledge to add to the business courses she was taking at Three Rivers Community College up the road a few miles. She was an industrious, well-meaning, young woman. She was prepared to accept her heroic toss of a ten-pound coffee urn, half filled with hot French Vanilla, as a part of her training.

"Arrgghhhh!" she shouted, the sound giving voice to the energy she put into the toss, swinging it with all her might and letting it fly right toward the woman in black holding the three customers at gunpoint against the counter. Fortunately for Jacqui the rack of soups and cereals between her and the gun toting woman hid her from view. The coffee urn's launch went unseen until it appeared flying over the rack of goods, catching Tiffany by surprise. It smashed the gun out of her left hand, spun off her arm and smacked her in the face, the top flying off and hot coffee spilling everywhere, including into her eyes.

"Tiffany!" screamed Tucker as he watched her tumble to the floor. The customers scattered when he jumped over the counter and ran to her. He reached for her and in doing so, dropped the bank bag instead of his gun so he could help her up. She lay there stunned for a moment against a rack of Ring Dings and Yodels. Her face felt the sting of hot coffee, and it hurt.

Betsy, Jacqui's twin sister, had been stocking the shelves with quarts of oil on the other side of the store and the sudden intrusion of the two would be robbers froze her, but only for a second. She quickly grabbed a quart of oil and tossed it over a rack of chips at the fallen women, hitting her squarely in the back.

The male customer who had been next in line went to kick Tiffany's revolver, which had fallen to the floor when the coffee urn connected, but he slipped on the spilled liquid, missed it, and instead, kicked the blue bag stuffed with money lying next to it. The bag skidded along the floor for fifteen feet and stopped under the newspaper rack near the front door.

Jacqui wasn't finished. She grabbed a second coffee urn, this one filled with decaf, and flung it toward the two in black. At the same moment, Mike reached under the lower shelf of the counter and pulled out a double-barreled shotgun that Karl had insisted they hide there, "just in case". It was a special weapon that had been Karl's grandfather's, old but effective, with two shells filled with buckshot, loaded and ready to go.

"Karl, do you really think we need this?" Mike had asked when it turned up one afternoon shortly after they opened the store. Mike had always been the money guy and Karl had always been the weapons guy in the many years they traded on the black market in a war zone. He wasn't afraid of them, but his American Dream had not involved shooting.

"I think there are bad people everywhere," Karl had answered.

The second coffee urn came flying over the soup rack and bounced in front of Tiffany and Tucker, then up against his leg. Tiffany struggled to her feet and Tucker aimed his gun toward the coffee racks, even as the hot decaf spilled from the second container.

"Son of a bitch!" he shouted. He never got off a shot because Mike swung the shotgun toward his intended target. Fortunately for Tucker, it was a light trigger; it went off prematurely and shot a cloud of tiny pellets toward the ceiling. The loud blast was enough to wake both Tucker and Tiffany up to the dire situation they faced. They ducked back to the floor. In a moment of amazing timing, Betsy's second quart of oil reached the peak of her toss and caught the buckshot from Mike's gun blast. The container split open above Tiffany and Tucker, sending buckshot and pieces of plastic container into the ceiling, and oil down onto the Preppy Perps.

Neither was thinking about a sexual adventure as he grabbed

her arm.

"This is no good, let's get out now!" he yelled in her ear.

Tiffany didn't hesitate. Together they scrambled for their footing, slipping on the oily floor, and finally tumbled outside. They jumped into their stolen Mercedes SL450 and sped away, hardly raising an eyebrow from the gassers filling their tanks at the pumps.

It was quiet inside the store as the three customers picked themselves up from the floor where they had scrambled when the blast from the shotgun rang out.

"Holy crap!" exclaimed Jacqui. "Mike, you okay?"

The gun in his hands was still smoking when Mike raised his head up from behind the counter. The blast surprised him and knocked him down. He looked at Jacqui and shook his head.

"They got the bank bag!" was all he could say. She could see he was crushed. Betsy poked her head around the racks with a shocked look, worried more about the oil on the floor than the attempted robbery.

"Oh, sorry! I made a mess, didn't I?" she apologized.

"Oh, jeez! That's a good mess, Bets! I'll call the police." Jacqui picked up the phone and dialed 911. She looked around at the two coffee urns and the pools of coffee on the floor mixed with the splash of oil. She couldn't help but smile at the accuracy and timeliness of their tosses.

Two of the customers looked around for a moment, thinking about why they were in line. They also did a double take seeing the twin sister on either side of the floor. Then the customers, as one, decided they had paid enough in excitement and danger for the night, and booked out the front door to their cars and away.

The third customer, the man who was waiting next in line, dropped two twenties on the counter much to the surprise of Mike, who immediately pushed them back.

"This one's on the house," he said.

The man smiled and took back his money. Then he pointed over his shoulder at the doorway and the newspaper rack next to it.

"I think you'll find what you are looking for under the papers," he smiled and then waved goodbye and left.

Mike wasn't sure what he meant as he watched him walk out the doors. He stowed the shotgun and wandered out from behind the counter. He was a bit numb, stunned actually, by the encounter with people who were bent on robbing him. The same attraction of making money that drew him to America must attract everybody, he thought, even if their approach to attaining that dream involved taking it from others. What a country!

He absently went about pushing the product racks back into place, picking up fallen Ring Dings and Yodels. Jacqui grabbed a mop and Betsy went for some rags and both worked on cleaning up the spillage that had disrupted the whole event.

"You are some crazy ladies!" Mike playfully offered.

"I guess so," Betsy laughed, shrugging her shoulders. "I just reacted. That tall piece of cheesecake in black was going to disrupt our store, Mike! What's wrong with her? She must be the crazy one!"

A few moments later the approach of a siren shifted the atmosphere and Mike was suddenly introduced to the local police procedures for investigating a robbery. The first officer was from the City of Norwich who introduced himself as Officer Kalinowski. He was as polite as pie, patiently asked the right questions, jotting down the answers in a notebook. He made sure everyone was alright, and while eyeballing the store layout, he noticed the blue bank bag under the newspaper rack by the front door.

"Well, this maybe turns into an attempted robbery," he smiled toward Mike as he brought the bag up to the counter and plopped it down. Mike was ecstatic.

"Oh zot, mahnitess!" he shouted in his native Albanian,

grabbing the bag. "Oh my god, amazing!"

Mike took the bag immediately upstairs to his office desk and stashed it in the bottom drawer with the other bags, also stuffed with money and receipts from several hours before. When he returned to the floor a second policeman, this one a State Trooper, had joined the gathering and he was getting a rundown from Jacqui, Betsy and the Norwich cop. Seconds later Karl walked in the front door, fresh from his marijuana delivery trip after dropping Big Mo off at the Seahorse. When he opened the door the sound of a dog barking filtered in from the parking lot.

"Mike, what the hell happened!?" exclaimed Karl. He had already experienced an instinctual pause when he saw the blue lights flashing on the police vehicles out front. He looked at Mike as if to say, "what are these guys doing here?"

"Well, you were right. 'just in case' happened," Mike answered. "But they didn't get away with anything. Jacqui and Betsy saved the day with coffee and oil!"

"And you scared the hell out of them with that shotgun!" Jacqui chimed in, happy to feel a part of the family.

"Shotgun?" asked the trooper as another customer came in the store to pay for his gas. The dog could be heard barking again and the trooper seemed torn between the dog and getting an answer to his shotgun question. He decided to hold off on the dog, who was his partner, Scramble, safely secured in the back seat of his police car. He looked at Mike, as did everyone else, awaiting an answer.

The Norwich cop tapped the state trooper and pointed to the ceiling, where the burn mark and the circle of small holes were plainly visible from the where the buckshot and pieces of plastic from the oil container had penetrated the white panels.

"Protection," said Mike emphatically.

"It's strictly for defense," Karl stepped in, reading Chiarelli on the trooper's nametag.

"Mind if I see this shotgun for protection?" trooper Chiarelli asked.

"And we'll need to see the security tapes as well. I assume you have tapes?" added Officer Kalinowski. Betsy nodded and pointed to a camera mounted in a corner over the counter.

Before Kalinowski could react, Mike reached under the counter and pulled out the shotgun, much to the consternation of the customer who was paying Jacqui nearby. He took his change and watched as the gun was handed to the trooper who examined it closely. He spread his fingers and walked them once along the barrel measuring its length.

"Italian design, a classic over-under from Beretta. It was my grandfather's." Karl couldn't help but gush about the nicely polished model called a 668 Pigeon. He had spent many afternoons shooting ducks with it as a young man.

"I see you modified the barrel," the trooper smiled as his apparent appreciation for the design evolved into a bad news shake of his head. "I'm going to have to confiscate it."

"What!" Karl shouted. He grabbed the shotgun from the trooper's hands. "No one takes this baby!" He stepped back.

"Sir, that gun barrel is less than 18 inches. It's been sawed off! You can't do that in Connecticut unless you have a Federal license stamp for it. It's a section 53 A-112 violation." The trooper reached out his hand and gestured for Karl to hand it over.

"53 A this, Storm Trooper Chiarelli, Sir!" Karl stood defiant. Mike was afraid his partner was going to point the gun at the officer and that would just complicate everything. He quickly stepped up behind Karl and put his hand on his shoulder.

"Karl, you have to relax. We can work this out." Karl didn't move.

"There is nothing to work out, Karl," interjected the trooper.

He didn't move either, his voice registered in the octave of 'authority'.

"Please hand over the weapon. That is an illegal weapon. You must turn it in. It's the law."

"No. Not going to happen." Karl stood defiant.

In an instant, a struggle ensued. The state cop grabbed the shotgun and for a moment, he and Karl danced with the sawed-off weapon between them, two pairs of hands holding on tight. The Norwich officer stowed his notebook and moved in, timing his approach to wrap his arms around Karl from behind. The trio spun about, staggering for balance against each other, all the while slipping on the still moist floor, until finally Karl lost his grip as they bounced against the counter.

The customer watching the chaos turned and sprinted out the door. The trooper stood back with the shotgun in his hands, while Karl remained pinned against the counter by the Norwich officer.

For the third time the dog's bark penetrated the store as the customer left, causing the trooper's eyes to look toward the sound. He was clearly torn between the action in front of him and his partner outside.

"Leave him alone," shouted Jacqui behind the register, even as Mike reached in for the weapon in the trooper's hand.

"Stand back!" retorted the trooper, holding it away. He looked at Mike as if to say don't be stupid. He focused back on Karl. "Sir, you are under arrest!" The shotgun was placed on the counter and the trooper pulled out his cuffs. In seconds, Karl was shackled.

Karl might never admit this, but at one point in the evolution of his desire to come to America with his friend Mike, there was surely a picket fence in his imagination. It has always been a part of the lore of the American Dream - a yard, a house, a white picket fence.

A picket fence is a contradiction. It sets a border, but it's open, breathable. You can pass food between the open slats in a picket fence yet the sharp pointed peaks of the vertical slats suggest protection from invasion. Make your neighbor think twice about attempting to climb over it.

The irrefutable dynamic of the American Dream is that the picket fence always separated your dream from someone else's. And over the development of the free society called America, there were always lines - around your property, in the sand, on the street, or in the law books. And when you came up against those lines, they created separation and often conflict by their mere definition. What's yours? What's mine?

Karl had just met his picket fence in the form of Trooper Chiarelli. He was the enforcer of law. And despite the heritage of the Beretta shotgun and the wonderful memories that Karl may have experienced as he and his granddad helped build one dream, it had been turned into an illegal weapon when his father sawed off a few inches to transform it from a duck hunting tool of recreation into a defensive weapon, to protect his family from the vicious Kosovo police squads that ravaged Albania. This night, thousands of miles away and even light years beyond, those squads appeared again, albeit a bit less vicious, but none the less, just as definitive, turning a dream into a nightmare.

Karl and his gun on one side and the law of the local constabulary on the other. A picket fence between them!

"Officer Kalinowski, would you be so kind to take this man to your car?" the trooper ordered, not an ounce of kindness in his voice. Kalinowski nodded and led Karl away. The trooper ordered Mike and Jacqui to stand down and stay right where they were. He then followed Officer Kalinowski to the door carrying the shotgun.

"What the hell are you doing?" Karl was shouting. "I'm the victim here! I did nothing wrong! You can't treat me like a criminal! It's a family gun! It's tradition! It's protection!"

Outside, Scramble barked steadily, adding to the uproar of the complaining coming from Karl. People looked up from their gas pumping duties a few feet away wondering what all the commotion was about. An argument between man and dog?

Trooper Chiarelli knew otherwise. His partner was a trained sniffer, certified in bomb and drug detection using the powerful range of a dog's olfactory nerves. Scramble, a black and grey German Shephard, clearly had something up his nose. He was doing his job, alerting his partner that one of those two smells, hell, maybe both, were in the air.

Chiarelli walked up to the opened window of the cruiser's back seat and held up his hand in front of the dog's face. Scramble responded with attention, letting out one more definitive bark. Chiarelli stashed the shotgun in the front seat and opened the back door. Scramble leaped from the car barking and immediately sprinted past Officer Kalinowski as he helped Karl into the back seat of his Norwich cruiser.

Reaching the box truck Karl had just parked, the dog held his ground, pacing and sniffing and barking. Trooper Chiarelli looked it over quickly and realized it was a rental. He gestured to Kalinowski to bring Karl over to him.

"Whose truck is this?" he asked the handcuffed gun owner.

"We rent trucks," Karl answered simply.

"Were you driving this earlier?"

Karl nodded slowly.

Trooper Chiarelli looked at Officer Kalinowski. "My partner Scramble likes this truck for either a bomb or drugs. I'm going to open it up for cause."

Kalinowski nodded, holding Karl by one arm. "Go for it."

Chiarelli opened the latches and rolled up the rear door. It clattered loudly and revealed an empty truck. Scramble jumped up into the box at the urging of his handler and sniffed around.

"What do you have, boy?" Chiarelli cooed at him, but there was nothing. Scramble did a couple of circles around the perimeter inside and then stood at the back end. His barking stopped as he sniffed the truck edges. Then he suddenly looked up and bolted out of the truck, leaping past Chiarelli.

"Scramble!" shouted the trooper but to no avail. His K9 partner scampered to one of the cars at the gas pumps and sniffed around, finally focusing on the passenger door of a VW beetle. The woman sitting there rolled up her window even as Scramble reached up on his hind legs and scratched at the glass. Then he sat back down and looked expectantly at his partner who was running toward him

"Scramble! Good boy!" the trooper congratulated him and reached in his pocket for a bite sized treat. The woman and the trooper made eye contact and he ordered her to roll down the window. The smell of marijuana was evident as she slowly rolled the glass halfway down. The sheepish look on her face would have been comical if it weren't so obvious.

"You are lucky tonight, young lady," Trooper Chiarelli admonished, his look scaring the woman stiff.

She was clearly in possession and using, but he didn't have time to deal with her and her pot smoking at the moment. "Don't let me see you again like this!"

She blankly nodded and rolled up the window, turning over her shoulder to get the attention of her companion who was finishing up filling up. The VW sped away, a hint of smoke trailing from the window.

Trooper Chiarelli hooked Scramble's leash and led him to the cruiser's back seat. He then returned to Karl who was standing patiently with Officer Kalinowski by the rental truck.

"More dope than bombs, Chief?" Kalinowski smiled.

"Looks like it," was all he said as he lifted his hat and ran his hand through his hair. He moved up close to Karl and stood eyeball to eyeball, inches away.

"So, look here, Karl. You have a choice. Tell me where that truck has been, what you've been hauling and maybe a name or two and you can spend the rest of the night collecting money here at your nice little gas and go. No cuffs, no bother. We depart as friends and you stay on the list of law abiding citizens of this great community."

Karl just stared back, waiting for the alternative. The trooper moved closer.

"I've got a nasty detective sergeant and some agents from the DEA who would love to sit you down for a nice long chat at the police station. You might get a piss break every few hours, but in between they will grill your ass, dig into your life and, eventually, they will find out who you have been dealing with. And you'll probably spend some time with a bunch of nasty asses who don't particularly like foreigners."

Karl didn't move, even in the face of Chiarelli's spittle splashing him. The trooper's bullying approach did nothing but dig Karl deeper into his bunker. He had seen it before, seen it worse, and was ready for the intimidation. Trooper Chiarelli nodded at Officer Kalinowski after a quiet moment, where Karl stared straight ahead, his eyes focused deep inside himself, as if he saw nothing in front of him.

The two policemen grabbed Karl and roughly dragged him to the Norwich police car and literally tossed him in the back. There was no gentle hand on the head of their prisoner. No effort made to insure no contact with the hard edge of the doorway. Just a sack of Albanian potatoes being hauled away.

Mike and Jacqui stood at the store entrance as the two police cars drove off. Karl's face was stoic from the back seat, his arms clearly pinched behind him in handcuffs. He did not look at the two. Mike didn't move until the cars were out of sight and suddenly realized he was standing in the way of a customer who was trying to enter his store to pay for gas.

"Karl will be okay," he said aloud to no one in particular. Jacqui knew the two partners for only a couple of months but had to agree.

"They'll work this out, I'm sure," she said. "The gun is not the issue here! We were robbed!"

"Almost robbed!" Mike corrected her with a smile on his face. He turned to the sisters. "Thank you again."

"What about the money? It's not safe here. There is no safe here." Jacqui laughed to herself. She was learning a lot about business in this little world.

"I'll take care of that now. You mind the store, okay? You'll be alright, yes?" Mike asked. He couldn't help but smile, confident of his young worker.

"I'll refill the coffee pots, then we'll be okay!" Betsy laughed heartily.

16 - The Real Heist

Tiffany was not feeling well. She had a bag of ice on her face, soothing the lingering sting from the hot coffee. Worse, their robbery was a bust! That was the real pain for this woman of confidence, woman of means, brought up in a suburban household with a successful mother who had provided all she could want. All but the time a daughter wants and needs to spend with her mother. She felt the hole in her life and, for reasons she didn't understand, it was filled only when she took from those who had something they wanted. A doll or a bankroll. If it was theirs, if they had it, she wanted it.

Was she dumping it all on her mother's neglect and how that made her feel? Did she steal to make the victims unhappy? So they could feel the unhappiness she felt? She didn't know the answer. However, the thrill of the steal was enough to make her not care. That's what turned her on. But damn, her eyes hurt!

Tucker was lying next to her in the bed they shared mostly on weekends. It was over the two-car garage that was set next to the lovely home in Pachaug where her mother had raised her. When she went off to college at Brown, just 40 minutes to the east, it became her apartment and provided a personal space that many of her classmates would have envied. It was an important place as she set off on her own path of hedonistic fun and adventure. Tucker's familiar hand was on her and he stayed close, like a good sheepdog, concerned about his master. His hand told the real story because it had been slowly creeping up her thigh since he handed her the ice pack.

"We are not finished!" she shouted, pushing his hand away and throwing the ice across the room where it clattered against the dresser. "Get the car," she ordered and jumped up slipping into her sneakers. "Wait in the driveway, I'll be right back."

"My car? Or yours?" Tucker asked. "Or shall I steal another one?"

"We'll use your car. No one is going to see the car. Hurry, I've got to run into the house. And, Tuck, be very quiet. I don't want to wake up Mother."

He nodded and pulled on his own shoes, retrieved his keys, his ski mask with the Brown University logo on the front and followed her out the door and down the outside staircase. She headed into the house through the backdoor while he turned the car around and sat waiting. He felt the purring of his Shelby Mustang and wondered if Tiffany would be purring later. He also wondered if he should argue that someone would see his car because it was a unique, special car. Five minutes later she rejoined him and waved him to go.

"To the bank," she ordered. Tucker nodded and drove, wondering what was on her mind. "On Maple Grove, Shoreline. I need to feel the steal!" He looked at the focused eyes and the thin smile on her face. He could feel the building excitement in her and knew it would build in him as well, because there was nothing sexier than this woman charged up after a robbery. He picked up speed in anticipation. At that moment, he didn't care who saw them.

Fifteen minutes later they drove by the QuiKee Gs gas station they had left a couple of hours ago and two miles later arrived at a large shopping plaza where a branch of the Shoreline Bank sat in one corner, little more than a kiosk with a drive-up window, an ATM and a night deposit box inside a glass enclosed structure.

"Park on the side street over there," she pointed, and he pulled behind several parked trucks of the furniture store that anchored the mall. A casual passerby from the street, like a cop, could not see the Mustang.

"Wait here!" Another order, but this time Tucker shook his head.

"No, let me come with you. I'll cover your six. Your sexy six!" He smiled as he handed her the Yale ski mask. They locked eyes and she nodded. "Okay, but all I need is this!" She held up a small key that was on a ring with the fob from a Lexus. He recognized it as belonging to her mother's car. He reached up and lovingly tugged down one side of her mask which was riding just a tad high on her face.

"Now you're covered," he smiled. She tapped him on the cheek gently and headed off.

They moved quickly between the trucks and across the 100 feet of parking lot, approaching the bank structure from the only side that had a solid wall. Then around the corner to the doorway which normally opened with the swipe of a bank card. She used the key instead and they entered the lighted lobby. Another door next to the pair of ATMs against the wall opened to a small room behind the machines where the bank employees could load the money. She ignored the key lock on the ATM back panel and bent down to an obvious safe built low in the wall. She pulled a piece of paper from her pocket with numbers written on it and calmly spun the big fat dial on the lock to the right, then left, then right again, and the safe opened revealing the contents of the night deposit box.

Tucker couldn't help but admire the way she crouched, her left leg bent holding her weight and her right leg angled straight to the side for balance. She quickly pulled out four leather money bags, a red one, a brown one and two blue ones. She passed them to Tucker then closed the safe, spun the dial and they left, moving quickly through the small lighted lobby, across the parking lot and back to the car.

Tiffany slipped into the driver's seat and Tucker balanced their bootie on his lap. As they sped away, she let out a yelp and reached over to caress the leather bags filled with the daily receipts of local businesses whose owners were likely sleeping soundly, confident their hard-earned money was safely deposited in the bank.

Businessmen like Mike Kansas who lay back on the cot in his cluttered office, closed his eyes for the first time in 24 hours and worried about his friend Karl Belmont spending the night in jail, but at ease that all that cash pulled in from the last hectic, crazy day was safely locked in the bank. He savored the latest step taken on their quest for the American Dream.

Tiffany's hand wandered off the bags to Tucker's thigh and she never really let go as they raced back to her hideaway. In the end, it was Tucker who did not get much sleep because he was holding on for one of the wildest nights of passion he had ever experienced with his crazy, exotic girlfriend who couldn't seem to get enough of him, and the cash spread out on her bed.

17 – Karl Ain't Talking

Nothings spoils a dream quicker than waking up in jail. Karl opened his eyes, felt the hard bench under his back and sat up to his new reality. A flood of thoughts shook him. The bars in front of him filled his vision. The 10 x 10-foot room made it clear he wasn't free. His first thought was remembering being so angry that the mere fact he had woken up from sleep surprised him. He couldn't have imagined sleeping, yet here he was awakening. A nightmare in the flesh.

The rule of law ruled the state he was in. Literally and figuratively. The shotgun was an illegal firearm, a class D felony, and though on the low end of the felony list, it was enough to have the authorities confiscate the weapon, and set him up for a court date. However, his arraignment didn't happen last night. Instead, and he believed this to be true, under the pretense of waiting for the judge, they sat him in a room with a table and chairs, and asked him about his truck, his whereabouts, and what could have caused the reaction of that trained, drug sniffing, police dog. State Trooper Chiarelli pushed Karl's buttons as best he could. Karl remembered he said nothing. His buttons were numb.

"You are doing yourself no favors by keeping your mouth shut!" the trooper had snarled at Karl, slamming his open palm on the table in frustration. It brought the slightest of smiles from Karl and that seemed to anger Chiarelli further.

Karl didn't know the law or police procedures, other than the ones used by the Sigurimi, the secret police of Albania. Despite all his political activities back in the day, he had never been arrested before. He didn't like it.

"My dog is not a dumb animal, Mr. Belmont," Chiarelli boasted during the brief interrogation. "He has been highly trained to sniff out the goods and you, Sir, smelled funny. Right in his wheelhouse."

Karl felt powerless and accepted it for the moment. He just sat and looked at his questioner, offering no hint that he knew, or even cared about what he was being asked.

Chiarelli also was bound by certain rules, though he had been known to push the edges at times; treating people he arrested as if they were already guilty. It was a game to him. He knew suspicion could only take him so far and his powers came to their limit until they had proof, and a judgement was made by the judge and jury. He sighed and stood up, gestured with his hand for Karl to follow him and led him off to his night in jail to await charges in the morning.

The sun was up, but Karl's was unaware of the time of day. He could hear his grandfather's voice and see his smile.

"This gun will get you into trouble someday," his grandfather had promised.

Then things happened quickly. A jailer in uniform showed up in front of his bars, opened the cage and led him to a small room where an official looking man passed judgement on him.

"Mr. Belmont, due to the circumstances surrounding the attempted robbery on your store last night, I am going to waive your arraignment and let you return to society with the admonishment to keep yourself clear of the law. No more struggling with police. Regarding the possession of a sawed off shotgun, I will waive the fine and the six month jail time. However…."

The judge looked directly at Karl, turning on as judgelike a face as he could muster, as if to maintain his ultimate power to decide who and when someone goes to jail, a power that required strength rather than the clemency he had just displayed by waiving the fine and jail time, and spoke in an octave lower than his previous pronouncements.

"I am confiscating the shotgun and it will be destroyed!" With a quick rap of his gavel and a quick signature on the papers sitting in front of him, he nodded his head and said, "You are dismissed!"

"You can't do that. It is a family heirloom!" Karl protested, uttering his first words since he had been shoved into the police car. The judge looked up at Karl with the same judgelike face and held his gaze. "I can and I have. Now, you may go."

A uniformed bailiff moved toward Karl from the side of the judge's bench and gently directed Karl toward the exit. Realizing he was free to go, Karl turned and moved toward the door. He saw Trooper Chiarelli sitting along the wall and they traded empty gazes as if they had never encountered each other.

Half an hour later, Mike rolled up in the station wagon and took Karl back to the QuiKee Gs. Mike sensed pent up anger from Karl's sullen mood.

"We found the money! They got nothing!" he offered trying to cheer him up.

Karl nodded his head and looked at Mike with a thin smile. Mike could see he was in a dark place.

"We need to find another gun," was all Karl offered.

18 – ISHKOODAH

It was always about the cash with Dr. Z. He grew up with enough of it to want more. He understood how it opened doors and brought things into his life. How it made life more enjoyable, created a sense of freedom even as it presented a path that could enslave him. The more he wanted, the more he needed, the more he had to find it, create it, build it.

Grass seemed an easy way to satisfy his needs. And, at first, it was. The cash flowed as he hoped. And it kept flowing - to the point he had to reckon with the concept of too much of a good thing.

The enterprise he built began to tax his capabilities and put him at greater risk of discovery. Sure, a few folks already knew of his project. Most of them were intimately involved and shared the same risk. His wife, Camille for one, who doubled as his best friend. Her brother, Tony. A couple of sailing buddies. Over the six years of smuggling, all of them did a good job keeping their horizons in check. They had access to money but contained their exuberance. He liked to call it comfortable consumption.

Z didn't drive the most expensive cars, or have the biggest house. They were nice. He did have a second house, of course, and a few sailboats, but that was all a part of the business. He certainly wasn't hurting anyone. In fact, he was providing a solid service to his many customers. And he had grown in his personal development. His golf game was as good as ever and he could relish his adventurous spirit for unique experiences, like diving from the cliffs of Acapulco. And he did love fast cars and would never have been able to immerse himself in that drama, if he had stayed the leather artisan he once was.

Bill McCoy came to mind before Scarface. Two scoundrels who flaunted the law. The bootlegger supplied the Southern New England coastline with undiluted rum during Prohibition. The cocaine crazed crime boss fed the frenzied fever of drug fiends, real or imagined. He preferred to identify with, and lived, as the friendly, heroic idol of thirsty thousands who would travel offshore in the 1920's and 30's, beyond territorial limits to secure their taste for the week. He liked to think Z-Weed was the rum du jour. And yet, he had to feed a fever of some kind because there was so much in motion. And the cracks were starting to appear.

Stronger still was his love of sailboat racing and the need to compete. He often cursed the out-of-balance game and especially felt the power of the ESYRA Championships drawing him this weekend. His boat Smoked was in the thick of the competition, ready and capable of winning with his Billy-led crew poised for another title. And here he was being chased by the law…or, about to be.

The cops didn't know where he was this Saturday morning. While his boys were prepping for day two of the regatta, he found himself indulging one of his other passions, flying. His mission: to keep his enterprise afloat. There was a problem. Ishkoodah was missing. It had been two months since her last delivery, only two weeks since her last pickup, and she was scheduled to be in the Connecticut River at "Esties", the drop-off rendezvous near Deep River, on Friday night. He had waited there but no one showed. Repeated efforts on ship to shore radio had gone unanswered. Now he was piloting a rented Cessna out of Hartford's Brainard Airport to look for her.

It wasn't the first time he had been forced to hunt out an overdue shipment of Z-Weed from Jamaica. Marine radio communications were unreliable unless you were close to the boat you were calling. There was also a certain sense of privacy that he attempted to maintain when it came to dealing with a boat that was smuggling hundreds of pounds of illegal weed into the country. Schedules were tenuous, based on a plan rather than a reality. A plan that had to be flexible as the reality played itself out.

So, once again he was in the air, trying to keep a low profile at 2000 feet under spectacular VFR conditions, just another lucky pilot flying south through one of the prettiest sections in all of Connecticut with green forests below, blue sky above and a million-dollar payoff gone missing.

Dr. Z had left the airpark literally on a wing and a prayer. He figured Ishkoodah had to be out there along the river somewhere. Airborne for a half hour, about 25 miles downriver, he spotted the missing sailboat south of Deep River. Suddenly, the anticipated discovery was not so pretty. What caught his attention first were the flashing blue lights attached to a pair of small motor craft that were obviously manifestations of officialdom.

"Crap!" he muttered as he circled above the drifting flotilla. He could see the unusual roll bar of the Alubat 50 over the stern section, the auto pilot wind vane and radar dome, all obvious giveaways that this was his missing sailboat Ishkoodah, now fully found. A third boat joined the group, this one larger and more menacing. The flotilla was just south of Chester Rock at the end of Eustasia Island, a couple of miles from the planned drop off point near the Pratt Creek. And Dr. Z, once again, experienced coming face to face with his worst nightmare.

The entire Connecticut River flood plain south from Middletown was a marshy haven of back creeks among the reeds and weeds, that led to docks of all shapes and sizes, ideal for off-loading product without drawing a crowd. At the heart was Deep River, a town known for smuggled elephant tusks in the 40's and still a favorite spot to drop off illicit goods.

As long as no one was looking for you.

For whatever reason, and his deep brain was working overtime to try to determine where he had exposed himself, the authorities had chosen this moment, this boat, this 2500-pound load of ganja, to exert their powers.

The third boat was black, sporting a red stripe around its hull, the signature logo of a U.S. Coast Guard vessel. Z guessed rightly that it was the Guard's 82-foot Point Class workhorse. Normally used to service navigational buoys, it was playing squad car. He could see the unique wheelhouse surrounded in glass with a solid window frame that extended aft along and above each side of the lower cabin before abruptly stopping as if there was no need to further protect anyone beyond the driver.

A crane sat in resting position at the stern, normally used to lift buoys from the water. However, it was the gun placement on the bow with a .50 caliber machine gun under the guidance of a blue uniformed sailor that changed the tone. Maybe out of place, but clearly in the middle of the action. It had been modified to handle the USCG's expanding mission of drug interdiction. He guessed again it was the Wicopesset stationed in New London.

As he watched, a hard-bottomed inflatable, an HBI, all business looking with twin engines hooked on the stern, and five armed soldiers squatting on the sides, launched from the larger Coast Guard boat, sped toward the surrounded sailboat. The small boats with the blue flashing lights had to be the DEA or maybe EnCon Police. They stood by in front of the sailboat, blocking any forward movement. There was no hi-speed chase in anyone's future, he thought. A moment later, Dr. Z noticed a small single engine airplane circling the gathering on the river, probably 500 feet below him.

"Crap, crap, crap!" he repeated. He had seen enough. Time for plan B. He increased the throttle and started to climb, turning back to the north toward Hartford. He knew he had to get away as quickly as possible before anyone thought to connect him with the scene on the river. And connect him they would, he knew, because his brother-in-law, Tony Fangioloni, was captain of the sailboat. It wouldn't be long before the phone would ring at his house in Glastonbury and his wife would find herself up to her earlobes in authorities who would begin asking questions and she would have to deal with another worst-case scenario. Lie or come clean.

They had discussed the possibility, but both dismissed it way too lightly. Both had pledged to say nothing when asked, but they knew they were kidding themselves. Too much money, too much fun, they were in it to win it, enjoy it, live it. It had been woven into the fabric of their lives. They always knew it would end but were convinced they could end it on their own terms, in their own time.

Z and Camille knew they were classically naïve, but too much money, especially easy money, had a way of building great walls. His wife liked to laughingly call it their "room of ignorance". She couldn't help but admit to him that "…I like it here!"

On the water below, Captain Tony cut the throttle on Ishkoodah and looked at his two crewmates, as if to say we are foked! The trio had sailed about 6000 miles together during the last five weeks, but all they could share at that moment were looks of dismay and chagrin. The freedom of the open ocean seemed so far away. All three stood quietly in the spacious cockpit of their boat, unmoving, as the HBI pulled up with the squad of armed soldiers.

Captain Tony couldn't help but think they looked like a squad of ivy league cheerleaders, all with closely cropped hair, neat blue uniforms emblazoned with "USCG" across their flak jackets, combat boots with pant legs tucked in and blue ascots. The M-16s in their hands and helmets on their heads were also very uniform and brought a smile to his face as he imagined them suddenly breaking out in a choreographed chant, complete with weapons spinning and legs kicking.

"You're under arrest! Here comes the judge! It's the end of your sail! You're all going to jail!"

"Squadheads!" Tony muttered to himself as he watched the HBI slide up against Ishkoodah. There was no dancing. Instead, the lead soldier, with three stripes on his sleeve, and a .45 caliber pistol on his belt, jumped on board with a big smile.

"Afternoon, Captain! Chief Colby at your service. We are here for a safety check! Mind if we look around, check your papers?"

Captain Tony numbly nodded from behind the wheel and gestured toward the front of the boat as if to say, "Have at it!". Chief Colby motioned two of his squad on board and they slipped below through the companionway. Less than 30 seconds later one of the men appeared through the opening.

"Chief, you're gonna want to see this!"

Chief Colby went below and the first thing he saw at the bottom of the stairway ladder was a neatly kept galley area on the left with a coffee pot locked in place on a small portable burner. To the right was an equally neat navigation station displaying a chart of the Connecticut River. Looking forward he saw two mattresses right in front of him, but unexpectedly, both sat at chest level on top of bales of something carefully wrapped in plastic that filled the cabin from side to side and as far forward as he could see. If one wanted to get forward on the boat, there was just enough room for a body to crawl on top of the mattresses and under the ceiling of the cabin, but there appeared to be no reason to do so because the entire space had been turned into a large storage room.

Chief Colby's experienced nose easily identified the strong

aroma filling the main cabin.

He turned toward the aft cabin and found it also filled with the same tightly wrapped bales and one mattress on top with just enough room for a body to fit under the cabin ceiling. For Chief Colby, a 12-year veteran of the Coast Guard, his earlier suspicions had played out as if he was dealing the cards himself. Two hours earlier he had spotted the Ishkoodah entering Long Island Sound and noted the German flag it was flying. Something didn't seem right.

He knew there was an international sailboat regatta underway in Newport, Rhode Island, about 30 miles to the east and it was known to draw yachts from all over the world for the semi-annual event. However, this particular yacht, an all-aluminum Alubat 50, was familiar to him. He was absolutely sure he had spotted it in the spring cruising near Block Island, but it was flying an American burgee at that time.

Add in the most recent directive from Command to be on the lookout for large boats smuggling drugs in the region plus a tip from an informant, solidified his expectations that this was the reason their radar had been up and turning. He reached in his pocket and pulled out a folding knife.

"I am checking for contraband here, Danvers." He looked at the young seaman next to him and received a nod in response.

Chief Colby poked the sharp blade into the plastic wrap and it popped. A quick twist and a slice revealed the contents. As expected, it was marijuana. The dried clusters of brown buds growing from the center stalk left no doubt. Their robust appearance brought a smile to the Chief's lips. "This was a good crop!" he thought to himself.

"Contraband here!" Colby announced, loud enough to be heard topside where the HBI was tied up to the side of Ishkoodah.

"Copy that, Chief. Contraband!" came the response. The

three remaining soldiers smartly shifted from a state of casual readiness to guns pointed at the three crewmen huddled behind the wheel.

Colby appeared in the companionway, stepping up a couple of steps so half his body was visible on deck. "Captain, I think it's time to see your papers. I am seizing this vessel and placing you and your crew under arrest for smuggling a Schedule One controlled substance in violation of 21 US Code 812, 841 and 952."

Colby held up a handful of weed like a prized trophy. The buds were thick in his hand, as if he had been scratching around in someone's garden and found a prize winning display at a local fair.

"I'm sure you don't need to be a lawyer to know what all those numbers mean. You guys are in deep shit! As we like to say, 'Busted'!" Colby couldn't help but smile at his three captives.

"It's actually pretty good weed, Commander," Tony laughed as he reached in the waterproof locker next to the helm and pulled out a pouch with the boat's papers inside. He handed them to Colby with a grin, grim as it was, as if he had expected this moment but wasn't expecting to feel so hopelessly helpless.

"I'm pretty sure I'm going to need some of that before the day is over," Tony said under his breath.

"Where you're going, all of you, there isn't going to be any of 'this'. Of that you can be sure," Colby answered. He placed the handful of pot he was holding in a plastic baggie pulled from his pocket and handed it to Danvers.

"Mark it and keep searching."

Colby then took the pouch of papers from Captain Tony and began examining the boat's documents. The breeze gently ruffled the pages as Colby shifted from one to another. For a moment it was quiet on the river, the gentle rumble of the big Coast Guard boat's engine and the faint sound of a plane overhead the only noticeable sounds. Captain Tony wondered how his life was about to change. He preferred the open solitude of the ocean, rather than being the focus of so much effort by the government.

"Weapon here, Chief!" came the shout from Danvers below. He quickly appeared on deck with a shotgun in his hand. Colby looked at the weapon and turned to look at Captain Tony. The Chief shook his head and raised his eyebrows, almost in disbelief that this bust was so textbook, then turned back to the documents.

A few moments later Colby took back the bag of confiscated pot from Danvers, grabbed the shotgun and moved to the aft deck of Ishkoodah so he was in full view of the 80-foot Coast Guard command ship behind him and the two vessels watchfully idling nearby.

The US Coast Guard is unique in the law enforcement world in that they don't need cause to stop, board and search a boat. Under the guise of a safety check, they have the government granted right to board virtually any vessel in the waters of their jurisdiction. As part of that grave responsibility, Guardsmen are trained to act in a polite and respectful manner when they do step on board a strange vessel to conduct their duties. There are clear procedures to follow and ways to act, and each bit of training includes the steps from boarding, searching, maybe finding contraband, and then dealing with the physical interaction that may come with attempts to arrest the captain and crew of a vessel that is in clear violation of the laws as set down by the rulers that be.

Chief Colby, after a long summer of searching under newly issued guidelines that shifted the focus from laisse-faire to direct action, at that moment, felt a sense of relief, justification, and plain old satisfaction that he and his boys had scored big. He stepped outside the protocols of professionalism and raised his arms over his head with the dope, the weapon and the papers held high as symbols of victory and celebration.

The Coast Guard boat responded with three long blasts of its air horn. The crew of Ishkoodah turned toward the sound and saw the machine gunner behind the .50 caliber return the salute with a fist pump in the air. And the two other small boats chimed in with toots of their own. The horns were a rare display of celebration that Captain Tony had never seen before, albeit he had never been arrested before. Amid this brief outbreak of joy, the squad of gun toting cheerleaders stood ominously in the HBI, any expressions of victory hidden behind the barrels of their M-16s pointed squarely at him.

A few moments later, in the plane that was circling overhead, Colby's voice came over the VHF radio on Channel 26A. It continued making tight turns a few hundred feet above the flotilla guided by Connecticut State Trooper Bill Cantor, newly assigned to the New England Organized Crime Drug Enforcement Task Force. Next to him was Jimbo Hurley, DEA and Chief Investigator for Assistant US District Attorney Molly Fitzgerald.

"Eagle Eye One, this is Bravo Two, we confirm contraband. Repeat. Confirm a boat load of contraband. We are enforcing 952 and have suspects in custody. Enroute to Essex Marine. Bravo Two out."

"Bravo Two, this is Eagle Eye One. Copy that. Good job, Chief. See you at base." Agent Hurley smiled as he replaced the microphone. He was grinning ear to ear as he looked at Trooper Cantor.

"Home, James…ah, Bill. Back to Hartford and let's get us a warrant or two!" Agent Hurley was pleased to be near the seizure of the sailboat Ishkoodah, even if several hundred feet above the action. He was an undercover guy. He loved the down and dirty of stakeouts, and mixing it up with the bad guys, literally under their noses. He knew it wasn't all down and dirty. At that moment he was looking forward to sitting in a judge's chambers making sure the "i's" were dotted and the "t's" were crossed so he could break down

some doors with warrants in his hand and dig deeper into the heart
of this drug smuggling operation.

He looked forward to seeing Molly and the look of excitement
that would surely cross her face when she got the news. He laughed
at her need to do the job ordered and get the bad guys. That's what
he loved about her. As Trooper Cantor aimed their plane north,
Jimbo formulated the next steps in the plan to make this bust turn
into jail time.

Down below on the Connecticut River, jail time was on
Captain Tony's mind as well. He focused on the cliffs of Selden
Neck to the east, rising 200 feet above the riverbank, and marveled
at their geological beauty. He wondered if this was the last time he
would relish that view for a while.

"So, Captain, you know these waters, right?"

Tony turned back toward his captor and nodded.

"I know them well, yes," he answered.

Chief Colby produced a chart and pointed to the Essex Island
Marina, three miles downriver in the heart of the historic town.
"We are taking you there. You will drive this boat. No tow, but
we are right here, escorting you, and we expect you will maintain
speed at six knots. One of my guys will be right on board with you.
Let's not make a fuss about this, just let us do our job. We don't
want to hurt anyone."

He sounded quite reasonable, and Tony just nodded his
head. A few moments later, the procession of boats turned south,
the blue lighted police craft in front and the HBI with the armed
cheerleaders alongside about 30 feet away. The Coast Guard cutter
brought up the rear.

As promised, one of the armed soldiers traded positions
with Chief Colby and sat himself on the cabin top facing aft to
keep the three crew in his line of sight as they huddled behind the
helm at the back of the boat. His M-16 lay across his knees and he

impassively watched Tony steering.

"Can I offer you a doobie?" Tony asked him about 15 minutes into the quiet ride, trying to suppress a big smile. "Just trying to be hospitable."

"I don't think you are in position to offer me anything, Captain," came the quiet reply from the guard. Tony nodded in rueful agreement and focused on maintaining his speed and direction. His thoughts turned to his sister, Camille, Dr. Z's wife, and wondered how upside down her life was about to get.

19 - Run Hide Chase

"Who is Eddy?" Camille asked thirty minutes later when Dr. Z called her from the Brainard Airpark.

"Eddy? I don't know any Eddy."

"He said he was waiting for the money and would call back. He really wanted to talk to you." He could hear the worry in her voice.

"Crap, it's started already!" Dr. Z muttered under his breath. He was suddenly suspicious of anything that didn't make sense. Had the police already tracked his contact information? He imagined the boat's papers and the listing for Islip Products Inc., the company that owned Ishkoodah.

"What's started?" she asked.

Z looked around him at the small office of the Fixed Base Operator (FBO) whose desk he had commandeered after landing at Brainard. He rented planes there often, had learned to fly with their flight school in a nearby building, and was friendly with the office manager, but he wasn't so comfortable talking about his business with folks who could still be called strangers.

He didn't know an Eddy and the only one who might be calling about money was Luiz from the Bronx. He was going to have to see him for sure to let him know the shit might be hitting the proverbial fan. Was Eddy some cover voice from the cops,

136

sniffing out the first contact they had? Hard evidence being an address and a phone number. "Z, are you still there? Honey? What's going on?"

"Yes, I'm still here, Babe. So, remember that conversation we had about a month ago?"

"About the good, the bad and the ugly?" Camille laughed. He loved her laugh. He had come to recognize it as the moment when husband-to-wife conversation turned into lover-to-lover chat. On that sunny day a month ago, they went off on a laughing jag that grew in intensity as they dug deeper into the worst case scenarios of what could happen, one day, when their little smuggling operation attracted the authorities. They found themselves making a serious attempt to paint the worse picture possible, each one taking it to another level, trying to outdo the other. It became a ridiculous game to push the limits of how far they could fall from the world of cash in which they were living and loving. They enjoyed the game immensely.

"We are the good, aren't we?" he laughed into the phone as he remembered them falling into a quick love making session because the deeper the fall revealed itself, the deeper they saw in each other's eyes that their love for each other was the only life preserver they would have. And maybe the tens of thousands of dollars they had stashed away.

"No, we are the bad!" she laughed again, this time with a hint of a growl in her voice. He felt connected with her, remembering, and he felt a stirring in his loins. Then just as quickly, quiet filled the phone line.

"Today, maybe the ugly," he said simply.

"Crap," she responded.

"I found Ishkoodah, but so did the Coast Guard and I'm sure DEA. There were boats around her and even a plane."

"Tony?" she asked about her brother.

"Yes, he was skippering her. I'm guessing everyone is in custody."

"Where did they take them? Should I call Nick?"

"I didn't hang around to see, but I'm sure they are in some jail somewhere, probably on their way to Hartford. Probably DEA."

"I'll call Nick," she said confidently after a few seconds. He could hear that take charge attitude that he loved about her. Sometimes just doing something was better than playing the helpless role. "He'll know how to get them out of jail. Bail or something."

Nick Cardman was their lawyer, a nice enough guy who didn't know much about what they did but was very good with the paperwork that came with buying houses, cars, and boats. He did it with a minimum of questions when they delivered his fee in cash.

"Maybe we should wait," Z suggested. "We don't know the situation. Tony has his own lawyer, right? Let him do the reaching."

"Z, I think it is ugly time. Nick should be alerted."

He knew she was right. In a flash, his mind zipped through a list of half a dozen people he would have to contact to warn them of possible impending doom. Or at least a police raid. He had made extra efforts to keep things private, but he was sure there were gaps where the effort to conceal was lost in the joy of success. Money talks, nobody walks.

Camille interrupted his thoughts. "I've got some clean-up to do here."

"You should call Brooks and ask her to store a few things. The garage needs to be attended to. She won't mind, will she?"

"No, she won't mind and won't ask."

Dr. Z knew Camille's good friend Brooks was out of their "bad loop". The sort of friend no one knew about. Part of another life. The friend who shared a love of plants with Camille, but nothing else. Brooks' farmhouse in Manchester would provide a safe spot to stash the containers of cash that were sitting in their garage awaiting transport south to the friendly banks in the Caribbean. He cursed the complications of success in accumulating the very thing he coveted in the beginning. Cash. Money. Moola.

"Are you coming home?" Camille asked.

"Can't. Have to see Luiz."

"What about the race? The Championship is tomorrow, right?"

He thought about Billy and the crew on Smoked. Of all the problems he faced, he felt the greatest loss not being with them, on the water, locked in battle with Mother Nature and the other competitors he loved to vanquish. It had been a long, dry summer watching his boys win while he was not there.

He remembered lifting the trophy high over his head, filled with beer and rum, the first year they won with the new boat. The feeling was one of the great moments in his quest for success in competition. They had beaten some world class crews and could find no reason not to celebrate in classic POTRAF style.

"Glasses to the wall! Rum up to your balls," he remembered and laughed, then he lamented. "I'm sure they are going to win it."

"Of course, they will, Babe, but…you can't be there, and I know that pains you." She understood where his heart was and fully supported the racing program. It was not the first time they shared the disappointment of missing out on what was really his true love and had been since they met six years ago. She didn't like to sail and let him do his thing that he had been doing since long before they met. She had her plants and then they had each other and the cash.

"Pack up what you can and go to Brooks'. I'll meet you there sometime tomorrow. I think you need to lay low for a while." He tried to sound hopeful as he laid out the hastily thought up plan.

"I'm not going to run far, but I'll hide and wait for you. Be careful."

There was silence for a full ten seconds before he answered her. It was as if their dreams were getting their last sizzle before they went as dead as the line sounded.

"I love you," he finally said.

"I love you back," she answered. "We'll get through this. I'll be fine." With that she hung up. He did the same and gazed out the window of the FBO office as a single engine plane taxied past and pivoted smartly to a tie down position right in front of the hanger.

Dr. Z saw two men and realized the pilot wore a uniform. A khaki state trooper blouse with badge and shoulder patch. The second man looked scruffy with a toss of curly dark hair and a mustache. He was dressed like he had slept in his clothes. He suddenly recognized the plane as a Cessna 172, the same type he had watched circling over the flotilla of ships and his marijuana haul.

He refused to believe they had followed him. How could they know? They couldn't see him 1000 feet above them and were clearly five minutes behind. He wasn't taking any chances and turned away from the window, slipped down a side hallway, and out the back door of the office. He walked the 50 yards to his car, breathing easily, walking casually, just a happy go lucky guy. He forced himself to ease the car out of the gravel lot and toward the main gate of the airport, glancing back several times. To his delight, no one seemed in a hurry to follow him. Within minutes he was on I-91 heading south toward New York. It dawned on him that he was officially on the lam.

20 - Preppy Perps

Tiffany's mother, Gina, knew she had a problem. The video clearly showed two robbers in black stealing from the night depository safe, their faces covered by masks with college logos and black framed glasses. Their body forms the only visual evidence showing them as a man and a woman. However, there was an obvious tell that crashed into her mom's existence and brought to fore all the guilt she had been feeling about not spending enough time with her daughter. It was the characteristic way the female form crouched down by the safe, low to the ground with one leg bent and the other angled straight out to the side. She knew immediately it was her daughter because she had seen her in that position many times before.

In fact, she had taught her the Warrior's Crouch. It allowed her to be nimble on her feet, even when bent over. Shifting from one leg to the other was second nature. Weeding in the garden, sweeping up crumbs from under the couch, varnishing the wooden floors in their living room, effortlessly balancing, shifting, moving like a cat. A cat burglar apparently!

There she was, a grainy image comfortably crouched on the floor, spinning the combination dial of a small safe built into the wall of the Shoreline Bank and Trust kiosk at the Maple Grove Plaza. She hit the numbers with effortless precision. Numbers that she probably stole from her mother's own pocketbook, thought Gina with disgust.

She turned away, unable to look, and bumped into Karl Belmont who was standing directly behind her, his eyes focused on the TV screen.

"Sorry!" she murmured and moved past him to the back of the room. Karl didn't flinch.

"That's the bags! Both of them! Blue and red ones!" exclaimed Mike Kansas, standing right next to Karl. The colors did not show on the black and white screen, but they were clearly bank bags. He was pointing at the screen as they were pulled from the safe by the woman in black next to the similarly clad man standing over her. He took the bags from her and in seconds the two of them left the room.

"That's them! The faces, the masks!" Mike pointed. "I could have shot the girl!"

"Yale and B.U.!" said the regional bank manager, a tall, young man named Rex. He saw the college facemasks as the two thieves ran out of camera range.

"Damn! The "Preppy Perps" the TV's been talking about!" he exclaimed. Rex was well aware of the big embarrassment banks faced when folks came to realize their money wasn't safe even when they put it in the safe!

Rex turned and looked at Karl and Mike with a timid smile. For a second, he wished he had seen the tape before the two men came to the bank office. He looked at Gina, standing against the back wall of the small room.

"Gina, are you okay? You look ill?" he asked her.

She put on a smile and shook her head. Like throwing a switch, she shook off the emotional shock of seeing her daughter in the role of bank robber and jumped back into her own role as Vice-President of the bank.

"I'm fine, Rex. I'm upset and angry. We have been violated and that's just not right! Gentlemen, Mr. Kansas, Mr. Belmont, I am truly sorry this has happened. I assure you the Shoreline Bank and Trust will take care of this and make sure the police bring these criminals to justice."

"What about our money?" Karl asked with a snarl.

"You have insurance, right?" Mike said with confidence. He had read the bank brochure. He believed the tag line "FDIC insured" answered any questions about the bank's reliability. He didn't know that meant nothing in a robbery.

"There was $14,000 in those bank bags!" Karl was still pointing at the screen even as the volume increased in his voice. "Even more!"

Gina knew the two men were angry. She was angry too. She looked at Rex who just stared back at her. She couldn't tell if he was angry as well or just didn't care. Or was he waiting to see what she was going to do. Who was going to fill the void? After all, she was the senior staffer here.

"$14,000?" Gina asked with exaggerated disbelief. Mike heard it as a mocking tone.

She picked up several sheets of paper sitting on the table between the two gas station owners and very carefully read off a list of numbers.

"3,300. 4,750. 4,735. 6,240. 3,565. Gentlemen, these are the recorded daily deposits from the last several weeks. Look at the dates. Some of these are for two-day totals. Your business has not come close to $14,000. Even half that!" She waved the papers in front of their faces.

"Do you take the bank for fools?" she continued, seemingly warming to the rant. She looked at Rex as if seeking his approval of her performance or at least his support. She wondered if the young man realized FDIC doesn't cover direct bank losses due to robbery.

"We keep track of this stuff! You can't expect to come in here and make up a number and steal from us! We need some proof!" She kept pushing back, taking the hard road, even as her mind sizzled with the uncertainty of how to deal with her daughter.

Mike pulled a piece of paper from his pocket, a folded carbon copy receipt from the bank deposit he had made the night of the robbery attempt at the QuiKee Gs. The same piece of paper he was looking for at the beginning of our story. It had apparently fallen between the seats of their station wagon and gone missing until he found it before this scheduled appointment to question the fact their deposit bags had not shown up at the bank.

Mike handed the paper to the bank VP.

"$14,235 right there on the receipt!" Mike exclaimed. He sounded vindicated. Gina took the paper and shrugged her shoulders. She handed it to Rex, the bank manager, who glanced at it and handed it back to Mike.

"Well, ah, Mr. Kansas, I hope you will understand the bank needs a paper trail…." Rex stammered, clearly unconvinced. This was his first foray into bank robbery and wasn't sure how the bank should be positioned.

"Yes, we do," stated Gina. She sounded certain. "Anyone can present a piece of paper, but please understand…."

"No, you understand!" interrupted Karl. He took a step closer to the Vice President. Mike thought he was going into his volcano mode. "We got lucky. Someone died! There was a crash and the blocked road sent traffic our way. We took advantage and then we brought the extra money to your stupid bank and expected it would show up in our account. Now, we have been doing that for about six months and I think we have proven we have a viable, for-real enterprise!"

Karl took another step forward and was now only a foot from Gina's face. He held her stare.

"You want proof? You don't believe us? Let me tell you something, I see a big problem at your bank. A big security problem because someone was loose and fancy with the combination to that safe." Karl moved right in on Gina and stuck his finger right in her face an inch away. Rex stepped in between and put his hand on Karl's chest to push him back.

"I can't imagine who has that combination!" Karl snarled mockingly.

"Mr. Belmont, please!" he urged. Rex held Karl in place, stopping his advance on VP Gina Sands.

"Karl!" Mike called and reached for his friend.

Karl brushed Rex's hand away roughly and held his ground face to face with Gina.

"You are supposed to be in charge? You know who has that combination, and I suggest it would not be a good thing if the word got out that your bank is careless with security. Money in a safe that's not safe is bad for business. I have learned that!" He gestured at the monitor where the security footage was just displayed.

Mike tightened his grip on Karl's shoulder and started to pull him back. Mike was concerned about the low, guttural tone he heard. A vicious sound from an angry Karl, a few inches from Gina's face, more threatening than anything he was saying. He had seen that tone turned to fists.

"You better learn that – quickly! I will not…we will not… stand for being ripped off!"

"Karl, we go now!" Mike pulled him back.

"$14,235, Miss Gina! You hear me? That is the number. That is the truth! That is our money!"

Mike pulled his friend out of the room and down the hall.

"Karl, we go home now. Settle down."

"I will not settle down. These bastards! I want to blow them up!" Karl shouted back toward the room they had just left.

Mike pulled him away and outside into the parking lot.
Karl was agitated and kicked at a handicapped parking sign by
the entrance walkway. The sign was already loose, possibly from
another attack by another person at another time. It moved,
prompting Karl to realize it was responding to his kick and he went
at it again, showing the world he could handle the sign. He attacked
it with his hands and after a few shakes and tugs, coupled with a
mighty grunt, he pulled it out of the ground and flung it to the
pavement.

It clattered in front of the row of cars, the noise sending a man
and his young daughter scurrying into the bank.

"Jesus, Karl. Settle down!" Mike pleaded.

"They better not fok with us, Mike. Not with us!" Karl spoke
with quiet determination. He stood very still over the sign, the
exercise of killing it had dissipated some of his rage.

Back inside the bank, Rex looked at Gina and rolled his eyes.

"You were kind of tough on them, weren't you? Is that what
the bank wants? Pissed off clients?"

"Those boxheads can kiss my ass, Rex!" Gina felt a mix of
anger, frustration, embarrassment, and failure. She knew she was
lashing out at the victims here, but after a decade of hard work,
she could see her career spilling down the drain. It was her own
daughter who had pulled the plug! She couldn't handle that. She
took a deep breath, then another.

"We need to keep this quiet, and I think that means believing
their story," she said to Rex quietly, a complete shift of gears. "Give
them the $14,000 and in return ask for their discretion to keep the
news out of the press. And NO cops."

Rex held her gaze. He could see she was conflicted for some
reason. He wondered about the comment from Mr. Belmont
regarding the safe combination. He was the only one with it at the
Norwich branch and it was locked up. He knew she also had the

combo for his branch and three others in the region.

Rex thought he saw the slightest movement of her pupils, as if she had been awoken from a wide-eyed sleep.

"Rex, you handle this as you see fit. I have to take care of a personal problem." She abruptly turned away, left the room, and walked down the hallway to the outside door. Rex followed her.

"Gina!" he called, but she did not turn back.

Gina was busy thinking about her own brother, Boz, Tiffany's uncle. Desperate to do something to 'fix' her daughter, she began to formulate a plan to send Tiffany to Vermont to work on Boz's goat farm. A couple of months of living off the land with a healthy dose of hard work might shake that spoiled brat veneer she was obviously projecting. Her thoughts took an uglier turn as she realized she herself might be asking Boz for a job, if word got to her bosses Tiffany was involved in the robbery!

Rex followed Gina outside and watched her walk right past Karl and Mike without a hint of recognition. She climbed into her car and sped away. Rex watched her leave then turned to face Karl and Mike standing there with puzzled looks on their faces.

"What gives, Mr. Banking man? Are we getting our money?"

It was Mike this time, turning to face Rex straight on.

Rex made a snap decision.

"Yes. Yes, you are, Mr. Kansas. We will credit your account $14,235. I ask that you let the bank investigate this outrageous act and keep it just between us. In other words, we don't need the police on this."

Mike looked at Karl, who nodded.

"No police. Agreed," Mike said, reading the thoughts of his partner.

The three traded handshakes and Rex walked back into the bank, debating how he could explain Gina's behavior to his boss. Which was her. Did he have to go higher? Clearly, she had something else on her mind.

Karl and Mike drove back to the QuiKee Gs and both had a visceral reaction to the fact only two cars were at the gas pumps. It was the first time in several days there was no line. They had heard the repairs to the Gold Star Bridge were soon to be finished. It now appeared that had, indeed, happened and the roadway was open again.

"Well, the trout have stopped running, looks like," Mike suggested wryly.

Karl was silent as they parked the car and walked into their store. He stopped just inside the doorway to step around the ladder where a workman was replacing the ceiling panel destroyed during the robbery attempt a few days ago. Karl picked up the damaged square of wood fiber and cardboard laying against a rack of sunglasses. The pellet holes from the shotgun blast were significant. The holes spoke of power and destruction. It had a surprisingly calming effect on Karl.

"Mike! Mike!" he called after his partner who was heading up the stairs to their little office. "I've got an idea!" he shouted as he scurried around the counter. "We can bring the trout back!"

21 - Gunny and Z at the Bar

Billy Gunny Gunning enjoyed drinking alone as much as he enjoyed drinking with his crew. He never saw it as a problem. He especially enjoyed drinking alone in prestigious yacht club bars like the one at the Westmont Harbor Yacht and Tennis Club where he found himself savoring his Mt. Gay and ginger on Saturday night. The crew had gone to bed, hoping to get some sleep before the final race of the ESYRA Championship Regatta on Sunday and he needed some alone time to contemplate the life that was running around him at that moment.

The Westmont bar was one of his favorites for a variety of reasons. The bar itself was a classic long wooden run of walnut edged on one side with marble. The swirls of the wood grain ran from smooth waves to tight circles. The patterns seemed to change as the number of drinks he consumed increased through the evening. He felt as if he was watching a tree grow from inside the trunk.

The marble was a perfect clean edge connecting the smooth dark counter with the business end of the bartender's world. The inevitable splashing from mixing and pouring stayed in its own zone, separate from the working flat top where the glasses stood in front of each customer waiting for the next elbow maneuver.

He also liked this bartender, Jerome, whom he knew from his two or three visits each racing season. Yacht clubs are famous for not taking cash. They expect you to provide an account number to tally up your drinking bill. An account number that belongs to members only because, after all, this is the Westmont Harbor Yacht and Tennis Club bar for members only.

Of course, during the racing season, the bar was often overcrowded with friends of friends of club members. The Parasites of the Rich and Famous. The racing crews who worked up the thirsts by manhandling the sails, navigating the courses, and spotting the wind to make the calls. The owners drove, served baloney and cheese sandwiches, savored the competition, or pissed and moaned about their ratings. Sometimes they yelled, but only in the heat of battle! So, those who knew their way around the club bar had no problem fudging the truth when it came to a splash of post-race refreshment.

The very first time they met, Gunny threw out a random four-digit number and mentioned the name of a boat owner he had done some work for. Jerome nodded and poured. Billy had not paid for a drink since. The benefits of being a POTRAF. Billy had taken it to an elite level.

Billy also loved the structure of the bar at Westmont. The long straight run of walnut had been interrupted by the insertion of a classic small sailboat with a lineage traced to famed designer Olin Stephens. It appeared as if the boat had sailed out of the back wall, smashed through the bar and stuck there, creating a 15-foot, pointy ended extension that jutted into the dining room. A careful bit of surgery removed the wooden stern and bottom, then a touch of varnish on the gunnels and deck, some bar stools and the small dinghy became a unique peninsula for hanging out with your favorite buds.

He believed his fascination with old watering holes qualified him as a genuine barhead.

The last two sailors in the room at the far end of the bar started to move, their deep discussion on the finer points of rounding the leeward mark finally over. Billy couldn't help but overhear the high points and low points of their verbal battle, forcing himself several times to focus on his drink rather than join the fray. They stumbled out and the room fell quiet leaving Billy alone with Jerome.

"Last call?" Jerome asked with a hopeful smile. He wanted to get home after dealing with a room full of fired up sailors who had two days of competition under their belt and were ready for the big final day tomorrow. Billy nodded.

The new drink slid in front of him at the same moment Dr. Z entered the bar, resplendent in a patch work sport coat that reminded Billy of those cowboy riding coats with fur sticking out of the stitch lines where the cloth was joined. This one was lightweight, however, designed for summer wear in the flatlands rather than on the big horn range

"I figured you'd still be here!" Z called out in a friendly tone. He slipped onto the bar stool next to Billy at the bow of the jutting dinghy.

"Isn't it kind of late for the MFO?" Billy responded as he shook Z's hand.

"This motha'fokin' owner needs a night cap!" Z laughed. He gestured to Jerome to indicate he would drink what Gunny was drinking. A twenty-dollar bill followed onto the bar and Jerome nodded, picked it up and went off to get Z's drink.

"Where the hell you been, Z? We've been kicking some ass out there! As usual, Prescott's got his panties in a bind, throwing red flags around and shit. He's ripe for the taking and we should be able to win the trophy tomorrow." Gunny smiled at the boat owner.

"I expect nothing less, my friend!" Z answered in mock

seriousness. "Great design, new sails, hot crew. Best that money can buy!"

"Well, we miss you sitting on the rail, papering the way! Where the hell have you been?" Billy repeated. He realized that as much as he loved being in charge and as easily as he slipped into the role of leader, he did enjoy racing with Dr. Z and his easy-going attitude, coupled, of course, with his open wallet.

"Things have come up." Z said as he sipped his newly arrived drink. He raised a toast to Billy and took another sip.

"You coming out tomorrow? Final race. One win. Big moment! You know you love that part!"

Z shook his head. "Not possible. Something's come up."

"What's come up?"

"Remember what happened at Key West last winter? That's what's come up." Z looked at Billy and shrugged his shoulders as if the inevitable had finally arrived.

Billy flashed back to the winter when the crew had taken Smoked to Florida for the Southern Ocean Racing Circuit. Two events were permanently etched on his mind from that week of hard racing against pros on factory teams from the top sailmakers, boat builders and designers in the country. They were among the youngest crews but surprised everyone, including themselves.

The first event was during the Fort Myers to Ft. Lauderdale race, a gear buster around Key West and up the east side of Florida. Smoked was in the Gulf Stream about fifty miles from the finish and leading the pack.

"I remember it was the middle of the night and Dave Vee stuck his head out of the hatch from down below and announced out of the blue, 'Tornado warnings in Dade County!' then disappeared back into his hole," Billy laughed at the memory.

"Yeah, and I remember you saying, 'Dade County? What the fok is Dade County?'" Z returned the laugh.

"Two minutes later we were nearly upside down when that blast of air smacked the whole fleet pretty hard. Must have been 50 knots!" Billy gushed.

"Hell, it could have been 100 the way it laid us over!" Z exclaimed, continuing to laugh.

"Tank saved us that night!" Billy stated, tipping his glass in a toast to his good friend and crewmate. Z followed.

The story as told by Tank found him underwater when the boat tipped over, hanging onto a double grip winch handle locked in the big drum that controlled the spinnaker sheet attached to one corner of the three-sided parachute-like sail. The blast of air filled the chute and overpowered the weight of the boat's keel, laying her on its side.

"Ease the guy!" shouted Billy from the tiller. The guy controlled the second corner of the sail and Tank climbed his way up the now vertical cockpit, eyeballed the locked winch with the guy wrapped around it to make sure the tail was clear, and then unwrapped it. The pressure from the sail pulled the line from his hand and whipped it off the winch to a sizzling sound of wire on metal through the end of the spinnaker pole, looped crazily like a jumping jack line and disappeared into the night.

"Seconds later, the halyard snapped at the top of the mast, which was probably a good thing because it released the third corner of the chute and it spilled open, letting the air out. As Tank tells the story, he watched the chute floating toward the water, but it never got wet. It began to float a few feet above the waves, anchored to the boat by the lone trimming sheet which could not be released because the double grip winch handle was bent and stuck in the drum.

"Tank was always impressed with the beauty of the chute waving like a gigantic flag, a few feet above the water, 50 feet off the boat!" Billy sipped and shook his head remembering the moments of panic mixed with pure awareness of what was happening.

Other boats were knocked around as well, including one who lost her mast. A third boat rendered assistance to the dismasted boat. The crew on Smoked, unaware of other boats' problems, got going again with a new sail and went on to finish.

They would have won the whole thing, but a jury's ruling granted another boat a time allowance for helping a third boat in distress during the squall. They got redress. Safety first and all, no one complained, but the boys felt the allowance was excessive and it created a time difference of one minute, pushing Smoked back to third. The "us against them" attitude made the sting of that loss hurt more, even though it did bring the crew closer together.

What Gunny remembered most from that week, however, was the photos that he was shown by Dave Vee's wife, which showed Tank and Billy hauling sail bags to and from the boat between races. Photos taken by law enforcement who apparently had the crew of Smoked under surveillance for suspicion of smuggling drugs.

"Can you imagine?" Vee's wife had laughed.

The sail bags were filled with sails not weed, but it had created a good laugh. "We wish!" he remembered Tank commenting. Admittedly, there was never a want for weed, but not while racing. They were there to race on the water. The partying happened after the racing. What was more attention getting to Billy was the availability of the cash that Z handed out to pay expenses. Everyone had dope, but Z had the cash.

The fact the law was interested in the boat, the crew, whatever, it opened up a whole world of speculation about Dr. Z that had gone unnoticed up until that time. He had told them the seemingly ever present money that financed their racing campaign was from a video arcade chain his family ran. No one questioned, no one cared, if someone else was paying for exotic locations to race fast sailboats.

"The DEA?" Billy asked, looking at the man next to him at the bar, half not wanting to believe the rumors. He had always taken the attitude that he didn't want to know, but every time he took that road, he only longed to go the other way and learn all the dirty little secrets.

Dr. Z sipped and nodded quietly.

"Whiskey Tango Foxtrot, man! What happened?" Billy asked. "Tell me everything!"

"Let's just say the statees, the coastees, the drugees…the foking bustheads, confiscated a boat that I own and the cargo it carried," Z offered.

"Cargo, as in weed?" Billy asked.

"Z-weed," came the answer. "How much?"

"About a ton or more." Z finished his drink.

"Holy fok noodle, Z!" Billy was astonished. Suddenly, everything was clear. The cash, the dope, the missing owner. He was sitting next to a true to life god damn drug smuggler. Hell, he worked for him!

"Shit, are you on the run? Should you even be here? Should I be worried?"

Billy couldn't help himself, but he glanced at the bar door expecting SWAT teams to burst in at any second. He imagined himself up against the wall, dogs sniffing, cuffs clanking, young dudes in flak jackets with rifles pointed at his head and yells of "spread 'em" and "hands up" filling the quiet wood paneled sanctuary of prestigious sailing culture.

"Jerome! One more last call, please!" Billy waved at the bartender who checked his watch, offered a look as if to say 'seriously', then reluctantly poured more rum.

"No worries, Billy. They don't give a shit if you just smoke it. Not really. Just don't try to move it."

Billy looked at the man who paid the bills when it came

to sailing. The MFO! He suddenly felt sorrow for him and what appeared to be his impending doom.

"So, you couldn't do a slip into the bushes thing? Like you did at Block a few years back?" Billy's question brought a big laugh from Z.

"That would be nice! But no. I don't think we are dealing with a couple of summer gendarmes who are two joints short of being on our side." Dr. Z remembered the night during race week at Block Island. A bunch of the crew crammed into a late 60's Buick station wagon, rumbled along after closing the famous bar called Captain Nick's, heading for the boat and a few hours' sleep before the next day's race event. One of the guys decided it was a good time to unload his pocketful of cherry bombs and began launching several out the back window of the overloaded wagon.

A pair of headlights pulled in behind them and rather than discouraging the fiery playfulness, it became a real target. After a couple of relatively harmless flash bangs bounced off the car, another set of lights joined the small parade, this time from the car's roof. Unfortunately, they were blue and flashing and sitting atop Car One of the two car Block Island Police force.

"I remember they had us get out and lined us up right alongside Ocean Avenue by Harbor Pond. The cop couldn't believe how many bombheads were in the car!"

"I thought we were all going to jail for the night," laughed Z, "but they didn't even have a jail back then."

"If I recollect, you disappeared into the night, didn't you!"

"I did. Standing in line, it was dark, the cop was flashing his light at the other end and I just stepped back about three steps and into those tall weeds that grow along the road there. You know, tall like 6 feet tall! There's still no lights along that stretch!"

The two of them laughed hard and clicked a toast with their new drinks.

"You didn't sleep on the stone beds that night, did you?" Gunny asked seriously.

The stone beds were the graves in the Island Cemetery on a hill overlooking New Harbor. The fact the cemetery was situated between two of the favorite bars on the island, bars that sat in two favorite marinas where racing sailboats were parked for the night, and the fact that racing sailboats are not the most comfortable for sleeping, all combined to make the stone beds a viable alternative for nightly accommodations.

Especially viable for sailors passing by after last call with a snoot full who would invariably pause and light up a joint with a buddy or two.

And it was especially attractive when you found a young lady racer chaser who had a grudge against her family and insisted on making love on each of the gravesites of her deceased relatives. A bucket list of another kind! Really. It happened!

"Gunny, I'm the MFO. I don't sleep in the cemetery. I paid for my bed. In fact, I paid for your bed as well. I paid for everyone's bed. I hope you used it!"

Gunny sipped from his glass. There was quiet as they both dwelled on the fond memories of boys gone crazy in their chase for sailboat greatness, but not far away was the reality of what Z was facing.

"Where are you going to sleep tonight?" Gunny asked seriously.

"Sleep? Not sure when I will sleep again, Billy. Not sure." Z reached into his coat pocket and pulled out a plain white envelope and slid it along the bar. It was stuffed with $100 bills, a stack about an inch high showing plainly.

Billy stashed the bills in his shirt.

"That's for the rest of the season. You've still got a few regattas to do, Off Soundings, the Benefit Cup, Island Cup. Just keep winning." Z raised his glass and then finished off the contents with a quick gulp. "Gotta go."

He got up and Billy shook his hand, holding it while looking Z in the eye.

"Trophy at the 'Horse tomorrow. I guarantee it. I understand you gotta run, but if you can, be there, at least for one sip. The guys would like it."

Dr. Z smiled. "I want to be there, but…." He held Billy's gaze and then with one last squeeze of his hand, he turned for the door, left and didn't look back.

Billy sat down truly wondering if he would ever see Dr. Z again.

"I think you need this," Jerome said, as he slid another Mt. Gay ginger in front of Billy.

"Thanks," he mumbled and tried to picture where Z might go. Run or hide? What would Billy do, he asked himself. Where could he disappear to? A sudden thought struck him as paranoia seeped into the room one more time.

"Jerome!" he snapped, getting the bartender's attention.

"Yeah?"

"Not a word! Understand. Whatever you overheard, you heard nothing." Billy zippered his mouth in a friendly gesture to his friendly drink supplier.

Jerome held up both hands, palms out, all innocence.

"Hey, friend, I'm too busy to overhear anything."

Billy nodded his head in understanding, then downed his drink in one smash gulp and slid the empty glass toward Jerome.

Billy stood up, took a second to fish a one-hundred-dollar bill from the envelope in his pocket and dropped it on the bar top. "Thank you, my friend. I'll see you next time." Then he headed for the door and the crew van parked in the marina parking lot a few steps from the club.

He took a lungful of fresh air in the ghostly glow outside, and gazed up at the near full moon overhead. He laughed. He had forgotten to admonish Z on the simple screw up that had forced the crew to crash in the van. Seems the motel reservations at the Holiday Inn were made in Bridgeport rather than the Holiday Inn in Rye. A difference of 35 miles. The crew opted for the van rather than make the drive.

"Hey, we'll be drunk enough to not notice," boasted pitman Toby Patton when they realized the mistake. "At least, it will give us an excuse to get that drunk."

He looked at the van with the extended cargo compartment that normally hauled electrical equipment for Darts Gorman, their navigator. It still had a couple of extendable ladders on the roof rack. For the weekends it was their main form of transportation and had seen a few miles over the years getting them back and forth to regattas around Southern New England and beyond.

He thought he heard Darts snoring from inside the metal chamber, and while he was pleased to see the front passenger seat vacant, reserved for him, he imagined the scene inside with the rest of the crew spread out on sail bags and foul weather gear. No rush to sleep, he thought. He pulled his sunglass case from his pocket, found a half smoked joint inside and quickly lit it up.

The night was warm and peaceful. A few stars struggled for attention in the moon's cast and broke through the dim yellow glow over the parking area. It came from a single light post supporting what appeared to be a naked 100-watt bulb on the roof of the harbormaster's shack on the edge of the marina. He could hear the halyards clanking nearby on the docks where a dozen chariots of competition gently rocked on their lines, lifeless fiberglass machines awaiting the human touch of their respective crews and the push of Mother Nature's breath.

That would come later in the morning.

An image of a sports car racing down some deserted highway drifted into his brain, likely carried on the THC molecules circulating in his bloodstream. He saw himself sitting in the car, next to the driver. It was Z, hands casually on the wheel, his eyes focused on the road ahead, ignoring that black cloud of turbulent air following them. Why was Billy watching the cloud alone? He couldn't decide if he put himself in the seat to experience the rush of living large or just the breeze in his hair and the intimate connection with the wind.

Poor Z, thought Billy! Trying to make a buck satisfying a mixed herd craving for escape and now, he was on the run. He pulled the envelope Z had given him at the bar and idly fingered the stack of rumpled bills. Used hundreds that must have come from a hundred different wallets and pockets of the ganja lovers across the region. Money that was now Billy's to do as he pleased. Resources to run the Smoked program through the summer. The payment that put the power of cash at his disposal while it put up another picket fence around his existence. It's not mine, he thought. It's for me and the boys, for Z, for Smoked, for the trophy tomorrow and the other trophies out there, yet to be won.

He flashed back to a scene at the Watch Hill Yacht Club one early evening after a race. It was a rare occasion because Smoked had been beaten, settling for a second-place trophy in the form of an engraved metal plate. In a rare fit of pique, Z had flung the plate off the upper deck of the club and the crew watched in stunned silence, along with a couple dozen other sailors, as it sailed gracefully into the harbor.

Z's regret was immediate.

"Oh, shit!" he exclaimed. "That was just plain wrong!"

The plate skipped twice on top of the water, like a stone, hit a boat on its mooring, and clanged up in the air to fall into the cockpit of another boat right next to it. The "oohs" and "aahs" from the assembled sailing crowd turned into hysteria as Z dove off the deck into the harbor twenty feet below and swam to the boat where the trophy plate had landed. He climbed up on board, retrieved it, and proudly held it high over his head to wildly cheering sailors who had not seen an owner act like that before.

Billy remembered what Z told him later, trying to be serious while wringing out his shorts.

"Trophies are not pieces of pottery or cheap loving cups or peanut dishes! They are a symbol of accomplishment. Our accomplishment! You don't throw away a paycheck, do you? Even if it's a small one. Don't you ever let me forget that!"

"You got it, Z! It's good to be the Trophy King, isn't it?! You are the cuphead!"

Billy could feel the envelope of cash in his shirt and laughed. Cash was good, too, he thought. Especially when it's there to help win trophies.

He finished the joint and savored the quiet for another moment or two. Even the halyard clanging had ceased tickling his ear. The very air had stopped moving. As he settled his butt into the van's passenger seat, with Teddy Trumanlee next to him and Darts' gentle snoring in the back among other body forms strewn about, he let his mind drift toward the lovely figure of his girl, Goldee. He felt comfortable with the idea of her sharing space inside a picket fence, someday down the road, with sailboats parked in the backyard, and another big day of undiscovered possibilities ahead.

22 - NIGHT FRIENDS

The door opened silently and Jimbo slipped into the dark room. He stood for thirty seconds and let his eyes adjust. Familiar shapes began to appear, in their remembered positions. The faintest light to his left filled a window covered with curtains. He stepped around the kitchen table and turned down the hallway to the closed door at the end. It opened easily and he covered the three steps to the bed quickly. In one motion he lowered himself down next to the shape laying on its side under the covers, slide his right arm under her neck, and his left hand gently over her mouth.

"Did you get the warrants?" he whispered in the Assistant US Attorney's ear. Eyes wide open, Molly nodded her head. Jimbo eased the pressure on her mouth, tracing his fingers over her lips and then moved his hand under the covers, settling below her breasts.

"Good. The raid is planned for Sunday dawn," he whispered again. "FBI, DEA and IRS will join you. Two trucks. Eight agents. If he has anything, you'll find it."

"What about you?" she asked quietly.

"I have another plan," he said softly and moved his hand to her breast.

"Then, we only have a few hours," she murmured and

snuggled her butt against his body. Her work was done for the day and this man was ready to play. Even through the bedspread, their desire was strong and shared. They clearly saw what they wanted. No one turned on a light.

23 - Walk of Shame

There was another metallic sound rolling around in Billy Gunny Gunning's dozing brain, but unlike the one from the jail cell, this one was steady, rhythmic, and soothing. Dreamlike.

It also bordered on annoying.

The contradiction seemed natural to his resting mind, where anger and frustration sparred with friendship and acceptance every day. He had learned not to fight it, but to let it play out, each thought, each sound, each subconscious cloud of neural action taking its own path. He was the leader, the head of a network of chaos that sizzled like a sparking electrical wire with a cut end, the electrons seeking a new path through the gaggle of synapses leading to some connection to reality.

The answer came like a light switch. It was the two marbles he had placed inside the aluminum tubing that framed the inner core of the sailing vessel number 23, a 26-footer, another Edge speed machine he had built with his own hands from the Dave Vee design drawings. Echoes of laughter rolled through his sleep as the small balls rolled back and forth inside the tubing with each movement of the vessel on the water. It seemed like such a good idea at the time!

So many naughty, funny ideas that were always a part of his approach to life. Make it right, build it fast, sail it true, but maybe kick it, just a touch with an ounce of disruption. Was it a cry for attention? A whimsical payment to have the last say? A memorial to the moment when decorum was replaced by anarchy?

And then the image of a face he knew appeared in his still sleeping mind, a young woman from days gone by, a chance meeting on the docks where he tended boats tying up at the local club. They always had an easy way of communicating, simple words about what they were doing, what they were thinking, and where they were going. She was from a nice family with some money, he was the young bonehead who liked to race boats and chase girls, but they got along easily.

And who were those two kids playing on the beach? Wait. They were sailing, too, messing around in boats! A tall blonde girl, capable and fresh, her eyes focused on all the world could offer, and the boy, a burly lad, strong and ambitious, good with his hands, ready to jump in, with a youthfulness unspoiled by disappointment. The spitting image of him and that girl from the docks. What part of the future was he seeing? Or was it another past?

The damn marbles started to roll again, but this time the sound shifted mid-roll and turned into the scraping sound of the van's side door sliding open, waking Gunny from his slumber to find the vision of Tank McHale, the morning sun blasting any hope of a return to his dreams.

"Time to go racing, Sleepyheads!" Tank shouted out in greeting, full of piss and vinegar. "The wind will not wait for your dreams. We're gonna have to catch her as she is right now!"

"Fok you, Tank! You should come knocking before you start rattling!"

"Well, my dope eyed friend, this van certainly was not rocking, so I don't need to be knocking!"

"Yeah," Billy said with resignation. "Not this zoo hole!"

He looked around at the bodies of his crew strewn about the back of the van, wedged against sea bags, anchor rode and a big old toolbox. Mostly, laying on the hard floor with the worn rubber mat under them. The pile began to move as the crew regained consciousness.

In minutes, shoes were on, shirts changed, and teeth brushed, rinsed with leftover beer. Nothing better! Long before social distancing was a thing, race morning breath was an effective tool against sharing the same bad air.

As a unit, they meandered down the dock, the click-click-click of Brian's steel toed boat shoe setting the tone. Suddenly, he stopped and put up his hand. Smoked was tied up in front of them and the boat began to rock as a blond head appeared from the companionway. It was, to everyone's surprise, young Johnny Flash. He turned on the edge of the deck and reached back to take the hand of another person who appeared from below. She was tall and slender, with long black hair and a mid-thigh high, deep blue, dress hanging loosely from her tanned shoulders.

She stepped barefoot over the lifelines, Flash's grip firmly on her left hand, guiding her onto the dock. She clutched her blue dress shoes close to her chest, smiled slyly at him then turned to walk up the pier. The boys were standing there all agape, smiling and nodding and chuckling as she walked proudly past them, the carefree model for the Walk of Shame.

"Don't wait to be good, you guys!" she said with a sense of purpose, soaking in their stares with a knowing smile. She strode confidently, her bare feet slapping at the metal surface. The dress shoes slipped easily into her left hand, a light jacket in her right, she turned to head up the ramp to the seawall and suddenly flashed Flash a smile over her shoulder.

The crew, to a man, turned their heads with her and watched Flash respond with an embarrassed wave and his own ear to ear grin. Then she was gone up the steps into the yacht club.

"What the hell, studhead!" barked Gunny, shaking his head in amazement. "That's about the badass-est walk of shame I have ever seen!"

"Who the hell was that cutie pie?" exclaimed Tank McHale.

Flash just beamed away, his eyes following her until she was out of sight. "Her name is Miss Teekee and she seems real nice."

"Ya think?" came the sarcastic laugh from Brian as he jumped on board and playfully smacked Flash on the belly. "I didn't think you had it in you."

"Or in her!" laughed Toby as he stepped over the lifelines and headed below. The rest of the crew followed suit, finding their way on board to begin their prerace routine. They each gave Flash a nod or pat of congratulations and, to a man, believed his night was clearly the better alternative than being cooped up in a barren van with seven snoozeheads.

"Okay, you swinging dicksheads, let's go win this thing and go home," Billy announced and within minutes the lines were cast off and Smoked headed out of the marina toward the starting area on Long Island Sound for the final day of competition in the ESYRU Championship. Billy had a funny feeling it was to be a day like no other.

24 - Let's Go Racing!

Not many organized sports begin the day of their scheduled event by searching for a place to play. Usually, the games are played in a stadium, on a field or around a track that has long been designated as the home field. The lines are already drawn and require, maybe, a touch up of white chalk. The fences are in place, the baskets stand tall, and the ticket booths are staffed, filled with change, sharing space with souvenirs and finger foods to sell to the spectators who park their cars and wander onto the hallowed grounds where the players will rise or fall to the level of the competition, and the voices of the faithful.

Not so much for a sailboat regatta. There are very few spectators and the officials, the Race Committee, start their day on a handful of boats, and head out early into nearby waters to start from scratch. They literally build a racecourse on the fly. The Principal Race Officer, the PRO, guides his team to the general area designated for the event and begins the process of laying out the course. His tools may include a wind stick, a 'hockey puck', an anemometer, a chart or two, local knowledge gained from years of racing in the same area, and always an opinion or two from his fellow RC crew.

His wind stick first finds the direction from which the wind is blowing. A piece of tape or string tied to the tip, free to dance in the breeze. The hockey puck, a handheld compass nicknamed for its size and weight, puts a number on the wind direction. Add a touch of geometry, a few carefully placed bags of air, and let the games begin!

"I'm reading 190-195, looks like about 10 knots," muttered Martin Gamble to no one in particular, eyeballing the strip of audio tape from a Meatloaf cassette that fluttered horizontally off his 12-inch section of a hockey stick salvaged from a Hartford Whalers game. A PRO for 15 years, Gamble always felt good about the first declaration of the day's weather pattern with the wind direction. It set the tone by orienting the axis for the racecourse. And it confirmed once again that he could see the wind.

Since this was the ESYRU Championships, several support boats were lingering nearby, their two-man crews ready to head out and drop the buoys in their correct positions to mark the racecourse

"I like 195, agree on the 10 knots. 10 and a half to be exact," answered the assistant PRO, Lenny Kane. He held his own hockey puck compass plus a spinning device that looked like a small fan. Known as an anemometer, it didn't blow a breeze on his face, instead, put a number on the speed of the breeze blowing in his face.

"Let's give it 10 minutes and check again. I'm thinking a 6-mile triangle, then up down to the finish, a total of 10 miles. One race, get everyone on the road heading home before Sunday traffic." Gamble smiled at Kane, displaying a confidence they both knew was just a start to the game.

"Early party! I like it!" Kane laughed.

"All subject to change, of course," the veteran PRO added with a bigger smile.

"Of course," Kane answered. He jotted down the numbers in his ever present notebook and took another wind shot.

"195," he read off his hockey puck. "Steady." Then he added,

"For now."

While the Race Committee brain trust planned their next move, the boats from the ESYRU began to appear on the horizon, coming from all directions. The annual championship event attracted over 50 crews in several classes to compete for bragging rights, pickle dishes and justification for a good old celebration.

Winners drank louder than losers, but in the end, it was all good clean fun, right? And while Billy Gunny Gunning and his crew understood, as well as anyone, the ins and outs, nuances, and shades of partying after a regatta, they were as finely tuned to what it took to make it a louder party, as winners. Preparation, planning, a good pair of sails, a few good pairs of hands, and a dose of good luck. He liked the way Woody Hayes' defined good luck when the legendary old time football coach at Ohio State declared, "Luck was talent meeting opportunity."

Billy and his boys had the talent. Now they needed the opportunity.

"Morning, Billy!" came the friendly greeting from PRO Gamble aboard the signal boat as Smoked motored by for check-in. "It's going to blow or it's going to suck, right?"

"We hope it blows, Martin. We hope it blows," Billy answered with a wave. He was pleased to see PRO Gamble running the show. At least we'll get a square line and a decent beat, he thought.

"Shit!" came a cry from Brian Bellows, sitting on the edge of the starboard side cockpit just behind Billy, intently spinning the drum on the big Lewmar winch, a vital tool in the sailboat racing arsenal. The jib sheet wound around the metal drum and magnified the strength of the jib trimmer who controlled the shape of the sail on the front of the boat. A mere mortal could grab several yards of the sheet as the jib switched through a tack from one side to the other, but as the boat came to course on the wind, the pressure on the sail required mechanical help to turn mortal muscles into

Superman muscles.

The normal click, click, click of the gears inside the drum sounded erratic at best. Suddenly, just as Gunny focused on it, the winch jammed and locked up with a sickening metallic crunch.

"Pawls are shot!" cried Bellows. Immediately, Toby, his head halfway out of the companionway, ducked back into the bowels of the boat and immerged a moment later with a tool bag. Brian had already lifted the drum off the spindle to reveal a vertical stack of roller bearings wrapped around a shaft connected to thick gears. The culprit pawl was a small wedge of metal that had slipped its designated slot where it sat dutifully and dumbly, performing an essential task.

As nuanced as the wind could be, sometimes it was pure power and strength that made the sails work. The thick gears at the base of the main spindle meshed with the indentations on the inside of the drum. As the grinder reversed direction of the handle, the gears shifted to the next power setting, tightening the jib sheet and, eventually, the jib would be trimmed. Without the pawls, the gears couldn't shift and would keep spinning in the same direction. No shift, no power, bad trim.

"Brian, like that cutie pie said, don't wait to be great! We need that winch, man, or we are dead on the starting line!"

"I got it, Billy, no problem, piece of cake. Can fix this in my sleep…."

Brian's show of confidence disappeared in an instant as he lifted the drum. One of the collars filled with the needle bearings that kept the drum spinning stuck to the inside of the drum. It popped off the center shaft and fell to the deck. The narrow rollers, about two inches high, shaped like thick needles, numbering two dozen, held together by the narrowest of margins in a circular metal framework, spilled all over the deck.

Tank McHale watched Bellows pull off the shaft, anticipating disaster, and was ready for the spreading chaos. His right foot moved quickly to catch three of the needle bearings sliding across the deck, stopping them from slipping over the side into the water.

"Son of a bitch, mother ducking jump ship!" Bellows shouted as he and Toby flailed their arms and hands, also grabbing for the bearings as if trying to corral a flock of dancing bugs. The dreaded sound of metal plinking on fiberglass could have spelled disaster for the crew of Smoked, but they contained the spillage.

Gunny watched in horror, thinking their hopes for the day were about to be gobbled up by the ocean. A second later, he realized they had saved the day.

"Damn, you guys are good! And you guys suck!" He shook his head. "Don't do that again! Now get the damn thing fixed! We have a race to win."

"Now is the time to find that gearhead in you, Brian!" Trip offered calmly, watching the boys bent over the broken winch.

"Alive and well, Trip," Brian muttered. "Alive and well."

"Twenty minutes, Billy!" It was Flash at the helm warning of the time left before their start sequence. Billy nodded to confirm as he checked his watch.

"Copy that, twenty minutes!" He turned to Brian and Toby, bent over the various parts of the disassembled winch. "Twenty minutes, guys? You good?"

Brian nodded without looking up, clearly focused, not allowing a negative answer to enter his mind. They had to be ready.

Billy turned his attention to the flags flying from the Race Committee boat, a classic old wooden design from the 1920's, over 50 feet in length, owned by the young scion of a famous family who made their fortune in coal. Easterly was scripted across the broad stern, and its appearance set a serious tone, a Corinthian air, to the event, harkening back to the days when rich men went yachting for the sport of it all.

While he certainly appreciated the sentiment, Billy knew it meant little at this moment because this was now and that was then. He was more interested in which direction the flags were flying and what course had been posted. The letter T was showing on the white board on top of the RC boat, with 190 and 2.0 posted below.

"We're going up, around, then up and down, two-mile legs, twice around." It was Darts Goman speaking quietly in his ear. Billy nodded and glanced at his navigator. "Right. I don't think the wind is going to hold," Billy answered. He looked at the instrument on the bulkhead against the cabin. It read 12 knots of breeze. A quick look at the compass set the wind direction a little west of due south.

"Ebb 'til noon, right?" he asked Darts and he confirmed the tidal change anticipated an hour after the start with a nod and a suggestion.

"I think we play the right side early, but left side second time up wind."

Billy looked at the ripples on the water's surface and didn't say anything in response. He just looked at his navigator and shrugged his shoulders. Plenty of time for that decision, he thought.

"Let's start with the medium one, but keep the light one nearby," he called forward to no one in particular. Trip Standish and Teddy Trumanlee were pulling sails around on the foredeck and were already thinking ahead. Trip just acknowledged with a wave and a gesture to the greenish sail bag laid out along the rail with the big M1 stitched on the end.

Billy waved back and smiled. He liked it when his crew was on the same page as him. It was especially fun when he wasn't so sure what page they should be on, but they always seemed to be ready to the point where they could put him on their page with a nod that usually proved to be the right choice. The game was always changing, one decision built on another, and all of it waited for Mother Nature to throw some dice, change her mind or just seemingly disappear, and let things stay as they were. Those were the rare days, when the wind blew steady from the same direction with the same speed, and sailors could take the time to relish in their choices, rather than hover on edge anticipating the next change.

"Having a little trouble, Billy?" came a shout from off to the starboard side. Billy knew the voice before he turned and saw his rival gliding up on the right. It was Montgomery Fillmore Prescott III on board LykytySplyt. Standing next to him was the police chief who arrested the crew the night before. Both were grinning ear to ear as they watched the small crowd bent over the broken winch on Smoked.

Prescott III made a big deal looking at his watch and shaking his head. "Time may not be on your side today," he shouted.

"There's always time for fine tuning, Prescott!" Billy shouted back. "Need to be ready to take advantage when the advantage shows its face. Good luck to you and the boys!" He threw a friendly wave and then turned his attention back to his own boat.

"Foking assholes!" he muttered, drawing a smile from Flash at the tiller.

"Eight minutes, three to our Warning," was all Flash noted.

On the Race Committee boat the PRO Gamble was eyeballing the windward mark boat as he dropped the orange inflatable buoy in the water two miles away. He had settled on 190 as the course, and the triangle with a windward leeward finishing leg was posted, and they were ready to go. Fifty boats in all, starting in four different classes. He looked at his own crew of flaggers and spotters, saw they were ready and then met his deputy eye to eye.

"We go! Course Tango," he said.

Len Kane nodded and spoke into the radio. "Mark boat, pin boat, this is Signal. We are go. Stand by for first warning."

"Signal, this is Mark boat, copy."

"Pin boat, copy."

Kane and Gamble traded looks again and a brief high five. Len went forward to run the start sequence and Martin took his spot nearby, ready to call boats over early and to make sure the team worked the start smoothly.

The start of a sailboat race is unique. It's fluid. It's timed to the second and there are no lines to follow. There are rules, but they do not define politeness. It's been called the Dance of the Lead Bottomed Money Gobblers and defines controlled chaos.

Each boat has a plan to time their approach to the invisible starting line marked by a buoy on one end and the RC boat on the other. The drivers sit about 35 feet behind the bow, depending on the length of their vessels, so they have no way of knowing exactly where the front of their boat is located. So, they must rely on hand signals and shouts from their bowman, and their own off angled judgement, to tell them how close to the line they are.

Normally, the starting line is set perpendicular to the wind, a 'square line', but sailboats can't sail directly into the wind. They have to angle their movement about 40 to 45 degrees away from the wind to generate forward movement. Of course, directly upwind is where their destination is located, the windward mark, so the variations of sailing angle create interesting dynamics. Throw in a dozen rules about boats meeting other boats and you have the potential for great fun!

"I want the right side, Flash!" Billy ordered his driver. Flash responded by looking toward the west. He turned back toward Billy and gently rocked his head back and forth, as if thinking about that directive.

"I'll get you there, but I'm not sure it will stick all day."

"Neither am I, but let's begin the proceedings there."

A shotgun blast from the RC signal boat punctuated their brief conversation, signaling the start of the five-minute sequence.

Their class was "in the box" and could start the dance, the goal to be in front heading in the right direction at speed when the five minutes was up.

25 - The Start

The crew on Smoked settled into their pre-start focus. The broken winch spun easily, repaired with minutes to spare. The sails went up, Flash called out his needs, and the boys responded by trimming and tweaking. "Coming down a touch here," he would call out and Tank eased the jib a bit and Gunny unlocked the mainsheet that controlled the big sail overhead. Feel is so important to the helmsman as the pressure builds and eases on the sails, the hull heels over, and the water rushes underneath. Flash was as good as there was, a former collegiate champion, and a proven performer in this fleet. His focus and feel were downright scary.

As the timer ticked down, Flash drove Smoked to the pin end of the line, the left side, steering parallel to the start line on starboard. That gave him the right of way and he niftily weaved his way through several competitors coming in the opposite direction.

"Up here, then around," came the call and the sheets were trimmed in as the bow turned closer to the wind. They slid up to the bright yellow balloon buoy that marked the pin end of the line, deftly turned around it, spinning 180 degrees and headed back the way they came, this time with the wind coming over the left side on port.

"Thirty to P down," came from Darts as he crossed through the cockpit from one side of the boat to the other with the rest of the crew. Not only were the dozen boats in their class moving on their own courses, but the crews were moving from side to side on each boat, using their weight to keep the boat as level as possible through the maneuvers.

Gunny looked behind and found Prescott III a bit to leeward and behind, charging in the same direction. He looked at Flash steering from the opposite side of the cockpit, pointing with his eyes at their rival. Flash gave the slightest nod and without looking back he steered away from the wind ever so slightly, picking up speed and moving in front of LykytySplyt's path.

"He's coming up," Gunny said as he watched Prescott steer toward the wind.

Seconds later, as Smoked passed behind the RC boat, Flash suddenly turned hard to the left. The bow of Smoked turned into the wind pointing directly at the back of the RC. At that moment, a long horn signaled the drop of the P flag meaning one minute to the start. Within seconds, Smoked came to a near halt and hung in the breeze, her sails flapping, effectively blocking anyone who wished to pass close by the stern of the RC.

LykytySplyt had to correct their course to avoid Smoked and turned down, to the right, to pass behind. Twenty seconds later, Flash pulled hard on the tiller and swung his bow left, catching the breeze in a sudden puff that pushed the anemometer to 17 knots. Smoked began to accelerate in the shadow of the RC boat, heading for the start line on starboard. They had rights.

LykytySplyt spun into a gybe turning 270 degrees to the right and coming out a couple of boat lengths further away from the line still behind the RC boat and now heading back in the direction she had been chasing Smoked. Prescott III hardened up on the wind steering a parallel course with Smoked, but several boat lengths away, ahead and to leeward. With 30 seconds to go before the start, Prescott surprisingly tacked onto port and started to close back in on Smoked, still on starboard.

Gunny muttered to himself, "He wants to hit us!" as he watched LykytySplyt aim right at them. If nothing changed, they would collide about a boat length from the start line.

The B Boys, brothers from Groton, were in the battle as well on Tomohawk and found themselves running alongside Smoked but to leeward and behind. Both had set their sights on the start line and were approaching max speed, anticipating their timing would be right on. The brothers saw LykytySplyt at the same time and shouted in unison, "Starboard!" They suddenly found themselves between LykytySplyt and Smoked, all three on a collision course, but Tomohawk would be hit first if LykytySplyt kept coming. Prescott certainly wasn't going to be able to cross in front.

"Starboard!" came the shout again, this time from Flash, louder than anyone had heard him shout before. He realized what was about to happen if Prescott did not tack.

"You have no rights in here!" Flash shouted again. This time he stood up and pointed directly at Prescott. Some might call it a "menacing threat" if they didn't know the mild manner driver, and it worked as intended. LykytySplyt began to tack. However, they may have overplayed their hand, and just as they began to turn, the B Boys on Tomohawk were forced to turn right, coming up hard toward the wind with seconds to go before the starting gun. It's called a luff and the maneuver was necessary to avoid a collision. However, it put Tomohawk in the way of Smoked.

Flash admitted later that, seconds before Tomohawk began to turn, a sudden vision of a sexy, dark haired woman in a short dress and wide "come hither" eyes popped into his mind and might have slowed his reactions. He might have let Smoked get too close to Tomohawk as they approached the start line, and when the B Boys began to come up, he might have already been too close, which left him with only one option; bail out of his starboard approach to the line and go into a full tack onto port.

"Tacking!" was all he had said. "Too close!" was all he heard from bowman Bellows.

The flapping of sails as three boats began to turn, all trying to avoid a collision, was lost in the distinct sound of the starting gun, followed two seconds later by a distinct horn.

"2-9-8, over early. 2-9-8, over early!" Gunny recognized PRO Gamble's voice announcing over the VHF radio that 298 was over early. That was Smoked's sail number.

"Ah, crap!" he said looking back at Flash.

"We'll go around the boat!" Flash responded, focusing on steering Smoked across the front of the RC, completing the tack onto port, avoiding the anchor chain and then bearing off down the other side of the RC, coming out the stern, gybing and hardening back up onto starboard tack where they had been less than a minute before. Both Tomohawk and LykytySplyt were also on Starboard, but at least 100 yards ahead. The rest of the class spread out ahead of them for the two-mile beat to the windward mark.

Gunny could see a Bravo code flag flying from the backstay of Prescott's boat and what appeared to be a continuing conversation across the water between him and the B Boys with occasional hand gestures and loud retorts that carried across the water. Another Bravo flag appeared on the back of Tomohawk.

"Who the hell is Prescott protesting?" Gunny asked in disbelief. The red code flag is flown when a boat plans to file a protest because someone did not honor the Racing Rules of Sailing, like the most basic rule - starboard has rights over port.

"Wrong tack, wrong place, wrong human," was offered by Tank near the port side winch as he trimmed the jib. The rest of the crew sitting on the rail were buzzing as well with their take on the situation.

"Okay, settle down, meatheads! We are climbing out of this.

This is the land of opportunity. We've all been here before, so focus on ahead and fok what's behind."

"One steel toed boot up his ass, that's what's gonna be behind," shouted Bellows. And seconds later, he added, "Puff in ten." "Got it, thank you," answered Flash as he watched the water rippling ahead and to the right. The darker color meant stronger wind, and he was ready for the extra puff which would change the angle of the boat slightly. And so it begins, he thought. Gunny was pleased to hear his young bowman focusing on the job. The protest, whatever it was, would happen after the racing. What happens over the next hour was what really mattered.

26 – EARLY ARRIVAL

Jimbo felt lucky today. He knew Dr. Z and his crew were racing for the ESYRA Championship and they would probably win. And if they did…hell, even if they didn't… they would end up at the Seahorse for some sort of a celebration. And if they were heading to the Seahorse after the race, Dr. Z was sure to be there too.

The Seahorse was a shrine of sorts for hundreds of mariners of every size and shape who frequented this part of Connecticut for fun or business. It was a bar, for sure, unique in its precarious location on stilts clinging to a rock at the mouth of the Thames River on the Groton side. It clung to the precious hard surface like a child to his mother's breast. The river rumbled by inches away, but the warm and sturdy bar was a safe place to nestle. The wood plank building had been around as long as anyone could remember.

The owner, Big Charlie Mann, never told anyone the name of the original owner who built the first structure as a home. However, he was super proud of his grandfather, Little Bob Mann, who turned it into a bar just two years before prohibition laws shut down the serving of booze. His grandfather used it as a home, but with an unusual cast of family members, and their friends, who visited frequently and, well, let's face it, used it as a speakeasy.

It's location a hundred yards into the river, and Little Bob's close connections with the city council, made it a blind spot for the local cops who were charged with enforcing the laws of the 1920's. An "open tab forever" bribed the local powers that be and made it easier. In later years, with prohibition lifted, the open tab continued for the right people, making permits for water pipes and electric power easily attainable in a spot that today might be considered an environmental liability.

Since then, the Mann family had tended bar, patched planks, held on when the wind blew and worried when the water rose.

Sure enough, when Detective Hurley parked his motorcycle in the private lot in front of the stone monument that marked the entrance to the rickety wooden boardwalk that extended from land, over the river, to the Seahorse's front door on its little rock island, he saw Big Bob's son, Little Zak Mann busy nailing a new plank into the hand railing that lined the bridge.

"Bent any nails yet?" he playfully shouted with a raise of his hand in greeting.

"Bend this," Zak responded with a grin. "Never wasted a nail in my life!" He finished off the board with a definitive slam of his hammer, driving the last part of the nail to its head. "Not counting the few that might have ended up in the river!"

He laughed, smartly spun the hammer and slid it into the tool belt hanging loosely around his thin waist. He looked at the stranger with long hair, a headband, goatee and mustache. He glanced at the motorcycle and wondered what drew a biker to a sailor's bar.

"A little early to be partying," Zak murmured.

"Never too early, my friend," he said with a big grin. He took a step onto the walkway and felt the whole wooden structure move a fraction. He grabbed hold of the handrail and started walking confidently toward the building on the stilts sitting on rocks in the river. "Especially when I'm feeling lucky!" he said over his shoulder.

Zak nodded and went back to tending to the handrail sections that needed fixing. He had seen a lot while working his dad's place. He couldn't remember the last time a biker in leathers showed up.

Hurley walked carefully along the wooden boardwalk, getting comfortable with the slight movement under his weight. Something one had to get used to, but it only took two or three trips. The walk back to the parking lot was the tough one because, regardless of how much you might have had to drink while visiting the Seahorse, the walkway moved enough to make you think you had maybe one too many. Of course, those who actually had one too many did not notice as much.

He paused at the door where lobster buoys hung in clusters overhead and looked to the north up the Thames River to see the spires of New London on one side and the office towers of Encore Pharmaceuticals on the other. The Gold Star Bridge stood tall and proud spanning the river, gleaming in the midday sun. The Long Island ferry was slowly making its way past the local marinas, trying not to throw off a wake. He quickly counted a half dozen pleasure craft and a couple of fishing boats all intent on their day. He couldn't resist a smile.

Then he pulled out a knit hat, opened the top buttons on his shirt, put on a sneer generated by the angry bone stored in his bag of tricks that allowed him to become someone else. He then opened the door and stepped into the shrine.

27 - Big Mo and the Lobsters

I've stopped apologizing for sleeping on the porch of the Seahorse, the longtime home away from home of sailors from everywhere. Something special happens when the fog hangs low on a spring morning and a splash of red and white light tickles my closed eyelids. The multiple lights flash for three seconds duration and alternate color every six seconds from the beacon 90 feet atop the New London Harbor Light. It was built in 1801 on the other side of the river, long before the Seahorse appeared. However, it is a relative late bloomer compared to the lobsters that live just below the porch.

The porch was built a few years after they plopped the wooden structure down on the rock formation called Billy Island. The name came easy one spring morning after a storm swept down the river and a billy goat appeared on the rocks. No one could say whether he was thirsty or not, but soon enough, a legend grew. Nothing better than a cozy shelter surrounded by water, reachable by a long wooden walkway, open for business with six kinds of beer on tap and a fully stocked liquor cabinet. And a porch a few feet above the muddy river. My porch.

I've been around long enough and have slept there enough times to call it my porch without any hesitation. Friends who know about my habit, even strangers who first learn about it, don't seem to care much about it anymore, so, until someone says move on, I'll stay and keep on. Not bothering a soul. Picked out a corner spot a few years back and have been there ever since. When I'm not doing other stuff, of course.

Understand, it's not because I don't have a place to stay. My 30-foot fishing boat over at Shipyard East is a perfectly good place to crash or even entertain. However, sitting on my boat has never been the same as sitting on the porch, primarily because my mind doesn't quite reach the special level of understanding it reaches when I'm along the river by the bar listening to the lobsters from my wooden Adirondack chair. And while it might seem misnamed, the chair, sitting on a wooden porch over the gentle flowing waters of a coastal river in Connecticut, it is right. The broad slope of its shoulders, the deep seat for your butt cheeks and the solid under-the-knee support, coupled with wide arm rests, make it the ideal human holder when getting off your feet is a priority.

Of course, it has taken years of experimenting to come to this realization. There is a specific mix of alcohol, THC and hours awake that is required to reach that moment of deep consciousness where natural things seem to take on their own rhythm. Some might call it semi-consciousness, but certainly not unconsciousness. It's a world in between, where the present goes quiet, the past comes into perspective and the future appears as if it were the past. What's clear is the clarity I experience when I awake. An understanding fills me, and I can go forth into my day with the kind of confidence that fearlessly embraces all that happens. Even if my memory appears a bit fuzzy at times.

That is why this Sunday morning I awoke to find a man standing along the railing not far from where I rested and, unexpectedly, a hiccup disrupted the smooth karma of the day. He glanced at me, nodded a friendly acknowledgement, then returned to gazing upon the river. The ferry to Long Island was just passing by, pushing a wall of white water in front of it at ten knots, the rear deck showing several cars and trucks, indicating another full load from New London destined for Greenport, New York.

"Gonna be a great day!" I heard him say. He smiled and turned back inside through the door slider that led to the bar. I stood up easily and walked over to the opening, sticking my head just far enough inside the room to adjust my vision in the darkness and, of all things, I see him taking a seat at the bar. Another hiccup corroding my day! He had slipped onto the barstool positioned in the southeast corner of the bar. My barstool!

28 – THE TAIL

Bob Smoot, the guy with no nickname, sipped his coffee without moving from the binoculars propped up in the back of the nondescript van parked on LaSalle Street, near the corner of Claremont in the Bronx, New York City. He focused on the garage door behind the metal gate half a block away, excited still on his very first stake out as an FBI agent. His partner, Bob "Smitty" Smith, a ten-year veteran, was next to him, bored to distraction.

The tree lined street was shrouded in shadows cast by the six story apartment buildings on both sides that blocked the morning sun. It was a quiet neighborhood a couple blocks from Riverside Park, protecting the East River on Manhattan's Upper West Side. The 125th Street station for the New York City subway was two blocks to the north. A nail salon, a florist, a dry cleaner, and a dentist's office lined the street at sidewalk level. There was a bar, too, called Moody's Grille.

The opening between buildings was the focus of Smoot's binoculars. Right next to Moody's, it led down a slope that followed the natural curve of the terrain to a basement storage area. A small box truck could slip down the driveway with careful navigation over the curb, between a lamppost and a tree and through the wrought iron gate. It wasn't a real driveway per say, but on occasion, it was used as one.

It was ideal for deliveries of booze and ribs for the bar. It was also convenient for Luiz Salano who packaged Z-Weed for Dr. Z, cutting 15-to-20-pound bales down to 1 oz. baggies. He handled about 10 or 20 of them a month from a quiet space in the basement of the Kafé de Kuomo in the building across the driveway from Moody's Grille. The aroma of freshly brewed coffee was the most intoxicating smell on the street in the mornings. Smoky barbeque ribs with Moody's tangy sauce competed for the attention of the passersby in the afternoon and evening. Every few weeks, the smell of pot would slip into the wind, but most folks didn't care, and no one went looking for the source because, well, they already knew.

Luiz and Dr. Z enjoyed each other's company and often partied in the third-floor apartment where Salano ran his marijuana distribution network. He was a key cog in Dr. Z's enterprise, the connection to the street and the customers who paid the freight. On this Sunday morning, Z woke up on the couch to the smell of coffee and Luiz standing over him with a morning offering.

"Black, as usual," Luiz said shoving the cup in front of his face. "Drink it and then I need your help. You owe me!"

Z moved slowly, feeling the effects of the good buzz he put on the night before when he surprised Luiz by showing up at his door late and then dropping the bombshell that deliveries might be curtailed in the immediate future. Both understood the nature of the game they were playing, but Luiz didn't seem too pleased. After a few drinks and a joint, he changed his tune. He had done well the last couple of years as the "Z connect" as he liked to call himself. The dawn of a new morning came with a different attitude.

"Maybe it's time for a small break," he suggested hopefully, coming to grips with Z's explanation that law enforcement might be closing in. However, he wasn't quite ready to give up the cash flow.

"This morning, we move the rest of what I have," Luiz commanded. "You drive, then we take a break!"

Thirty minutes later, agent Smoot spotted Luiz at the gate. The target swung the gate open and stepped back to let a red sporty hatchback up the driveway. Luiz closed the gate behind, jumped into the passenger seat and they slipped over the curb and onto the street.

"That's him. That's Luiz!" he nudged his partner Smith, almost spilling his coffee cup with the sudden movement. "We have to get moving. They are heading down LaSalle, the other way!"

Smith slipped quickly into the driver's seat, thankful for some action, started up the van and spun a U-turn to get behind their target.

"Who's driving that Z?" he asked. Then he jammed on the brakes because the sports car stopped half a block down the street, double parked in front of the florist shop with the sign, "Pott's and Posey's", hung over the entrance where pots of plants and colorful bouquets were displayed on the sidewalk, inviting customers into the store.

The two agents watched Luiz jump out of the car and run into the store carrying a box in his arms. The sudden Bat-turn left Smith feeling totally exposed and he decided to keep driving beyond the sports car. Smoot kept his eyes ahead, but Smith got a good look at the driver as they rolled by. He didn't recognize him. Their assignment had been to keep an eye on Luiz Salano, but this was somebody new. He drove on, turned at the next corner, and pulled to the curb. Smoot jumped back to his spot at the rear window and kept an eye on the target.

In a moment, Luiz returned to the car and had apparently exchanged the box for a paper bag. The sports car pulled off, continued straight down LaSalle, zipped under the overpass that carried the #1 Broadway local, and headed to the middle of

Morningside Heights. Smith pulled another Bat-turn and took up the tail, holding back at least half a block. He had ID'd the car as a Datsun 280Z and silently thanked his lucky stars. The red Z stuck out in this city of five million cars, compared to a black Chevy or blue Ford.

For the next few hours, Smoot and Smith tailed the red Z to a couple of dozen stops, and observed Luiz get out of the car each time with a package only to return moments later with a stuffed paper bag. The bags contained cash, surmised Smith. Luiz could be seen counting the contents when he returned to the car and stuffing the bills back into the bag, tossing it into the rear seat, and then making a notation in a notebook. It looked like a regular UPS delivery operation. At each stop, Smoot pulled out his Nikon with the 500mm lens and snapped a photo of the red Z in front of the location.

Three times Luiz met different men in front of buildings, another next to a bus stop, and what appeared to be a college student in front of a deli near Columbia University. Smoot documented it all as evidence for AUSA Molly Fitzgerald and her NEOCDETF. He remembered feeling very important sitting in his first task force meeting just two days ago.

"We have a tip from local police this guy is dealing in quantity," Molly had explained in Bridgeport. "I want to know where he lives, what he eats and who he sees," she demanded, looking right at him. Smoot was the new guy among a dozen agents from DEA, FBI and both New York and Connecticut State Police. Scraps of information were pinned to a couple of bulletin boards showing the early stages of the Z-Weed network.

At about the same time that Smoot and Smith followed the red Z out of the driveway under the Kafé de Kuomo on LaSalle, 120 miles away a whole basket of dots fell into place. Molly and a half dozen agents served a search warrant on Dr. Z's house in

Glastonbury, a nicely appointed suburban community just outside Hartford.

The agents found only a couple of ounces of marijuana, but they found a plastic tub with a blue cover in the garage under a stack of paint cans. The container held $278,450 in bundles of cash. Further inspection of the backyard revealed buried coffee cans of cash worth an estimated $100,000, mostly in $20s and $50s. Unfortunately, that cache had suffered water damage due to leaky tops and many of the bills were rotted and useless.

Molly sorted through a desk while her agents were digging up the yard and discovered tax returns for the prior three years. They indicated Dr. Z and his wife, Camille, had earned an average of about $36,000 a year. Molly made a call to the local IRS office, and they sent over an agent to secure the paperwork.

Handwritten lists were also found with apparent nicknames and dollar amounts that Molly believed was a record of workers who were being paid by Dr. Z. The ton of marijuana that had been confiscated from the sailboat the day before had opened the flood gates of evidence. The cash found at the house, the bits of apparent payday notes, and the out-of-whack tax returns were enough for her to feel confident she had a case against Dr. Z to prove he was involved in an ongoing criminal enterprise to smuggle marijuana.

She couldn't help but smile.

As the agents began packing the evidence into a police van, Molly made a call to her boss, US District Attorney Frank Murphy, District of Connecticut.

"I'm glad you called, Molly. I think we've tracked down your guy," Murphy said when he came on the line. "We've traced a license plate to this guy "Dr. Z" and he's in New York City with that distributor you like, Luiz Salano. Smith and Smoot have been following them."

Molly was standing at the desk in the home in Glastonbury

and was looking directly at a photo that was apparently Dr. Z and his wife, Camille. They were standing in front of a red Datsun 280Z sportscar.

"A red Z?" she asked.

"A red Z," Murphy responded. She could imagine the smile on his face.

"Well, god damn hurrah!" she responded, her smile equal to her boss's. "So, forget Luiz for the moment, we know where he lives. Tell Smith and Smoot to stay with the Z! And issue a BOLO as well, will you?"

"Will do!" Murphy responded and signed off.

"And Frank, let's just stay close to him. No need to pick him up just yet. He may lead us to a few other connections."

"You got it!" Murphy said and rang off.

Molly hung up feeling buoyant, but cautious. She walked into the living room where Dr. Z's wife was sitting quietly and alone on the couch.

"Camille, when is the last time you spoke with your husband?" Molly asked.

"Yesterday afternoon," Camille answered truthfully.

"Where was he, do you know? Where is he now?" Molly probed.

"I don't know"

The two exchanged glances. Molly could see Camille had been crying, but seemed composed now.

"You are in trouble, Camille. And so is your husband."

Camille nodded in understanding.

"I am not going to arrest you right now, but I suggest you contact a lawyer. If you do hear from your husband, you must call me." Molly paused and handed her a business card. Camille took it and nodded again.

An agent came up to Molly and handed her a clipboard with

a handwritten list attached. Molly glanced at it quickly and nodded, then handed it to Camille.

"This is the list of items that have been seized under the search warrant. Please sign here."

Camille signed.

"And Camille, there is no place to run, so stay close. We will be meeting again," Molly advised her in as friendly a manner as you could expect from the person who had the power to make your life miserable.

Camille nodded grimly, resigned to the fact that even if she had not returned to the house earlier that morning after moving some things to her friend Brooks' house, there was no where she could run or even wanted to run. "The Ugly" was here and so be it.

Another American Dream turned into a nightmare.

A few moments later, as the agents were ready to leave, Molly stood looking at the plastic tub filled with cash.

"This was a good catch, Molly," said one of the agents. He was Sam from DEA. She nodded and looked at him. She realized this was the first job they had been on together and in fact, she had only spoken to him once before in their very first meeting when he arrived, freshly assigned to the task force, only two weeks ago. She made a conscious effort to hide the fact she had not seen that much money in one place before, this close, right there within arm's length.

"We still have to catch the big fish, Sam." She laughed. He nodded.

"We'll get him, Molly. Hooks are in, just need to let him play out the line." Sam's confidence came from years of chasing bad guys. When they made a sighting, it was hard to escape the net of the Feds.

"Hey, anyone heard from Jimbo? Detective Hurley?" she asked the two other men on her team. Both were from the FBI.

"Not a peep. He said he was on a mission!" came the reply.

"I heard." She turned and climbed into the car. "Okay, guys, let's get this stuff cataloged. We can't let this one get away."

29 - THE WIND SHIFT

Victory did not come easy. It did come smart. In fact, it took three legs of smart sailing to get back in touch with the leaders. Prescott was out front with the B Boys sniffing a couple of boat lengths back. Smoked another five. Coming into the final downwind mark, Smoked was nose to tail on Tomohawk and faster. However, the B Boys got to the zone around the mark first. Smoked was required by the rules to give room by allowing Tomohawk to sail where they wanted.

They went right for the mark, of course, but in a rare snafu, Tomohawk's spinnaker halyard hung up on the chute douse and they were forced to steer a wide angle around the mark. That left an opening for Smoked and Flash took advantage, sneaking inside the B Boys while they struggled to pull their wind filled sail into the boat.

Flash and B One, close friends and frequent competitors, shared an icy stare. B One snapped a one fingered salute as Smoked spun around the mark in the exact spot where Tomohawk had aimed. He clearly was pissed that the snafu had cost him a position. Flash offered a small grin in return and then turned his eyes hard left to insure Smoked missed the inflated buoy as they pirouetted around it. He saw he had two feet to spare. They came out on starboard tack and headed for the left side of the course. Just sixty feet ahead was the transom of LickytySplit and the rotund figure of Montgomery Prescott III at the helm.

"We have to get right!" came the call from tactician Teddy Trumanlee. He was the wind guy and he pointed to the righthand horizon. Billy turned his head and looked.

"Good call, Teddy!" he nodded then turned to Flash. "We have to tack now."

Flash took a quick glance right to check on Tomohawk, now behind and to windward. He guesstimated there was just enough room to squeeze in front on port before they got back up to speed.

"Ready about," Flash responded to Billy's call, turned the tiller and sparked the crew back into action. The symphony of movement took all of ten seconds as the jib and main were eased, shifted, and retrimmed on port tack, sending Smoked heading to the right at speed.

B Two on Tomohawk saw Smoked tack, cross a half boat length ahead, and wondered why. The breeze was decent right here and the entire fleet was heading off to the left on starboard! Then he saw what he didn't see. Ripples!

Up ahead, B Two watched the dark patch of water suddenly change to a lighter blue patch, and the ripples that reflect the light ceased to exist, leaving only a stillness on the surface, a "flat spot". A mirror like patch of water with no wind. The boats heading left were on the righthand edge of the dark water. All of them were moving on starboard tack, so the crews on the rail were looking right into the wind. The flat spot was visible, but it did not appear to be moving nor was it very large. It may have been a mirage because they were moving away from the flat spot. For that moment. To the average eye it appeared the breeze was holding.

Suddenly, the flat spot grew and crept closer because the unseen cloud of wind got smaller. The trailing edge of breeze just blew on by and suddenly all the boats who went left were coasting to a near stop in a now, very big, flat spot. Ugly, even!

If Mother Nature is anything, she is relentlessly fickle.

To the right, on the western edge of the racecourse, a zephyr was gently blowing from an island left over from the glaciers that carved Long Island Sound eons ago. Upon the island sat a famous stone lighthouse called Execution Rocks. The century old structure, complete with tower and light, warns sailors of the shallow dangers lurking right in the middle of the Sound. It comes with several ghostly and grisly stories. It also, by its mere shape, has an effect on how the wind and tide flow around it.

Some say it was once used by the British to punish revolutionists whose transgressions against the King earned them a stake on a rock that was only accessible at low tide. Out rowed the jailors with their prisoners, in came the tide to drown them. The bodies often left to remind others of who was in charge.

The other legend spoke of a serial killer who finished his victims on the rocks. Yet another story is told of boats filled with immigrants crashing into the shallows on their way to the harbor in New York City, literally drowning their hopes and American Dreams.

Billy preferred the legend that the west to east ebbing tide swirled around the island and spun a current of half a knot from the north to the south. He knew this current and rode the zephyr toward it. He glanced to his left and nodded at the drifting fleet that was once ahead but not now. Smoked was making trees! Trees moving in the background as if coming from the front of the masts. They were moving ahead ever so slowly.

There was flat water everywhere and Smoked ghosted along drawing the pressure from 30 feet up. There was a new wind coming and the first puffs were theirs, and theirs alone. The legendary current proved to be a reality and Darts stuck his head up from the nav station below to confirm it.

"We are getting the kick from Execution!" Darts declared with a touch of, 'I told you so' in his tone. Billy watched the speedo jump half a knot. Unnoticed on a highway, but a rocket booster for a sailboat racer getting through a flat spot.

Billy Gunning had sailed long enough to not be surprised by Mother Nature's actions. However, he still got a big charge when what he thought would happen actually did! Much of the space he sailed in was invisible to the naked eye. All you could do was read signs, feel the tickle in your ear, on your cheek, a ribbon dancing on a stick, a memory of how the water flowed, even a sense of hydrodynamics that might allow you to predict where water gets pushed to, and what the physics teacher was talking about back in 12th grade.

Popcorn clouds in the sky over land meant sea breeze on the water!

The invisible wind could no longer hide as it touched down on the water's surface and pushed gently at Smoked's sails. Cat's paws tickled the glassy mirror next to them. The gentlest of ripples indicating a big righty. A 40-degree shift. A header. Just what they wanted!

"Tack back!" called Billy and the ballet commenced again. As the crew completed their dance and settled back on the rail on the starboard side, the speedo number climbed, and the boat came alive. They were fetching the finish line a mile ahead, on their nose in a freshening breeze, and no one else had it yet!

"Who's gonna deal with the laundry?" came the question from driver Johnny Flash. He and Billy could see the red code flags hanging from the backstays of LykytySplyt and Tomohawk. Red was Bravo and Bravo meant protest.

"Not going to worry about what happened at the start," Billy answered. "Not 'til we get to the finish. Focus!" He pointed ahead at the finish line marked by an orange buoy and the big white RC boat holding anchor. Flash didn't answer, allowing his eyes instead to lock on the tell-tails, those strands of yarn flying along the front edge of the jib indicating the flow of air across the material. Back and slightly up was good and his hands adjusted the tiller as needed to keep them flying.

They were the only two facing into the boat which allowed them to see to leeward where the rest of the fleet was struggling with the fact they were suddenly behind. The whole racecourse had shifted, like a tablecloth spun under a spread of cards, shaking up the hands already dealt. Everyone looked different, and Billy's boys looked good.

In some races, when there is a dramatic wind shift, the Race Committee either kills the race or shifts one of the marks to keep the course square to the wind direction. The attitudes change based on the level of the event and the competitors involved.

A 40-degree wind shift is big, but on the last leg, you let them go, especially when the fleet is already on that leg. Whomever is in the right spot when Mother Nature burps deserves what they find. That was the attitude of RC PRO Martin Gamble as he sighted the finish line under the orange flag amidships the committee boat. He looked around at his crew of five; spotters, signalers, recorders, timers. They were prepared to call the finish of the race.

"Here is 298, standby. Three. Two. One. Gun!" he sounded to the old man holding the shotgun next to him.

The veteran sailor squeezed the trigger and "Boom!" went the gun. Like a switch, the gunshot sparked a simultaneous jolt of joy and happiness from the voices of the crew sitting on the rail of Smoked. The sound of Victory.

"15:29:33!" announced the timer sitting on the cabin roof next to the scorer with eyes on the passing boat and ears tuned to the PRO. She jotted the time next to the sail number on the score sheet.

"Looks like Tomohawk 311 will be next. This is a horn,"

continued Gamble. And the RC staff kept track of the finishers one by one. Montgomery Fillmore Prescott III in LykytySplyt finished third. There were no shouts of joy when they crossed the finish line. The crew sat on the rail and stared straight off the boat, as if each crewmember was contemplating where he screwed up.

The cockpit brain trust stood quiet in the back of the boat. Prescott at the wheel was the only one who moved, pointing behind him to the red code flag Bravo flying on the backstay over his head as they crossed the finish line.

"We are protesting Tomohawk and Smoked!" he shouted to PRO Gamble, who responded with a wave of acknowledgement.

"You got that, Stacey?" he asked over his shoulder to the scorer. She nodded and smiled. "Prescott just loves to keep us after school, doesn't he? What a blowhard!" She shook her head in disgust, realizing her job wouldn't be done until after the protest hearing, and that would cut deeply into her party time.

"Among the best," Gamble muttered under breath, then turned back to continue the litany of finishers.

Onboard Smoked, the boys were in full beer-party-victory mode, tasting and toasting, sharing handshakes and pats on the back for a job well done.

"We are the best! Super excellent cool!" shouted Gunny, holding his beer high. "'Til next time! Then we have to do it again!"

"Good call on the righty, Teddy!" Gunny nodded toward his tactician who returned a nod.

"I calls 'em when I sees 'em!" he laughed.

"And here's to Dr. Z! I'm sure he was the missing link working the 'Zephyr by the Rocks'. Super-secret MFO Z, if he really exists!" It was bowman Brian, gently tapping his steel shoe against the repaired winch that had performed flawlessly during the race.

"Where the hell is he, anyway?" asked pitman Toby Patton.

"He is here, Brian!" Billy explained. He pounded his foot on the deck and gestured around the boat. "He's right here, all this shit, that is where he is. It's his. He's the MFO, And you are still a POTRAF! Enjoy it while you can!"

The crew looked around at each other and Tank lifted his beer can in a toast. The others followed. "Slam it boys, for Dr. Z!" he cheered. And they all drained their beers and tossed the cans into the cockpit with that distinctive sound of hollow aluminum bouncing on fiberglass. It was another sound of Victory.

30 - Story Time

Sailors who spend any time on the water understand the need to learn navigation. The job of navigator has taken on a romantic air through the centuries, slotted just one step below a skipper, because as daring do as you might be at the controls of your vessel, be it a supersonic jet or a lumbering sailboat, you aren't going to be doing much heroic stuff if you don't know where you are going!

There are no dotted lines to follow on the water, only compass directions. Grabbing bits of information, to determine where you are, where you are going, and what will be in your way on the way, is the first step. Interpreting what that information means, and how to use that information efficiently comes next. It's a process.

One of the many keys to navigation is understanding the difference between true north and magnetic north. It is such a basic premise that it is often hidden under the layers of instrumentation and calculation that provide the answers when you plug in a waypoint on your Global Positioning Satellite device.

Volumes have been written by scientists who have studied the phenomena. It begins in the liquid core 1800 miles below the surface of the earth where a magnetic field is created that extends into space, wrapping completely around the planet. We base creatures on the surface see its effect when the little magnetized needle on our compass wiggles and points north. Magnetic north.

If you know one point on a compass, you can figure out the rest and adjust your course appropriately, assuming you have a destination in mind and a map that shows you where it is located. Do you see where I'm going here? It's all about a point of reference.

Oh, one more problem. The magnetic point of reference changes every few years! While GPS devices are programmed to figure that change out, in Southeastern Connecticut, where the Seahorse Tavern provides a popular point of reference for sailors, the variation between true and magnetic north has shifted about 18 degrees over the years, and there are reports that the annual deviation is increasing.

Big Charlie Mann and his son Zak, the owners of the Seahorse, understood. They knew where the sailors were headed. For years, they've bellied up to the bar and enjoyed the revelry and fellowship that is an essential part of drinking. To help them, embedded in the bar top is a special wooden compass that shows North. It's a nice piece of work created by a talented artist who wishes to remain anonymous. I don't even know his name!

The carved dial is ornate and sits under a piece of glass with a special wedge of wood shaped like an arrow that points to magnetic north. Ironically, the overused saying around town is "Let's get lost at the Seahorse!" even though the tools are right there to keep you on course.

Most sailors understood immediately the artistic wheel pointing the way to where you wish to go. It's actually, pretty cool! It shows off the north, south, east and west points on the compass, their attendant degrees and one very cool element. An arrow-like sliver, painted red, that points to that point where the north end of the magnetic field begins. It's a sliver of wood carved into the compass face, not free moving, which would be nice, but it's there. Did I mention it was very cool?

There is a minor problem, however. Every few years the artist is forced to appear at night and rebuild the wooden compass to shift the red sliver to its new direction. Change is constant, or so they say. Meanwhile, the one thing that hasn't shifted in some time is my barstool which sits right in front of the bar compass.

Today, the man from the porch was sitting on it, right there, checking out the compass and sipping his drink. I paused in shock for only a second and slid up next to him on another stool.

"Don't think I've seen you sitting on that stool before!" I offered cheerily and waved to young Zak behind the bar for my usual Mt. Gay rocks.

"First time in a long time," he responded in a friendly voice and waved his drink at me before taking a sip.

The stranger was a scruffy guy, probably in his 30's, dark hair, full around the ears but a little short on top revealing a high forehead. A few days growth of whiskers around his scraggly mustache, plus the unlit cigar in his mouth gave him the aura of someone living under the Gold Star Bridge.

His open work shirt was covered by a leather vest with the New London Motorcycle Club logo stitched over the right breast.

"You guys don't act like the part you look!" I said with a big smile.

"What part?" he snapped with a hard look at me.

I sipped my drink and laughed.

"Motorcycle gang! The leathers! Right out of a Southern California biker flick! From what I've heard, you guys are really just a bunch of nice guys!"

He held my smile with a cold look, but only for a few seconds before he smiled broadly himself and turned back to his drink.

"You writing a book? Maybe trying to become a Prospect?"

"No, no! I don't ride. Just saying! Your club is a bunch of good guys from what I've heard. Raise money for charity and all with your rallies."

"It's the leathers, right? You see leathers, you think Hell's Angels. The Pagans? Am I right?"

"You got me. I'm stereotyping."

"Do you see an axe handle?" He smiled again, looking around in mock surprise. "How would you feel if I called you a sailhead just because you had a fleece vest on?"

I laughed again and nodded.

"Well, you would be right. I am a sailhead, but we don't all wear vests. At least not all the time, all together."

"Well, here's to bikers and sailheads!" he said with a raised glass.

"And vests!" I added and we clinked.

We sat there for a few moments quietly contemplating the refreshing taste of our drinks and the oddity of the empty bar, except for Zak and us two vest-wearing strangers snug against the bar compass.

"So, first time in a long time for you. Can I ask why you chose to sit in my seat?"

"Your seat? I did not know." He looked around, apparently for a name plate, making a big deal of not finding one. However, he did stand up and step back with his drink in hand. Then he gestured with a nod for me to reclaim it. I did.

"Mind if I sit here?" he asked as he slipped onto the stool I just vacated. His exaggerated politeness only heightened my sense of embarrassment, but really, sometimes, you have to claim what's yours. No one else is going to do it for you!

"Sure, no problem. In fact, let me buy you another. Zak, one more for my new friend here."

I stuck out my hand.

"I'm Mo. They call me Big Mo here. It's like a second home actually. Sorry about being so prickly."

"Jimbo," he said shaking my hand. "Jimbo Hurley."

"Pleased to meet you, Jimbo," I said.

"So, this must be the sailing king's seat?" he asked pointing to the bar stool upon which I sat, in front of the compass art, the view I was used to for as long as I can remember.

"I'm not the king, that's for sure. Well, maybe for one year they let me be in charge, but it's like herding cats! As soon as you think you're in charge, they bite you in the ass and drag you down the road they want to travel."

"Cheers for the chain of command!" he toasted again, finished his drink, and slid the empty glass along the bar as Zak dropped a full one in front of him.

"I tell everyone who complains about a problem that they're the chairman of the committee to fix the problem!"

"Problems? You have problems? I thought you guys were so carefree and talented, didn't give a shit about problems."

"You're right! It is just a sailboat race, isn't it? Lots of sailboat races," I admitted. "It's the challenge against Mother Nature and the camaraderie that comes with a joint purpose." I hoped I didn't sound too righteous.

"Joint?" he asked with a sly smile.

I nodded, knowingly. "Yeah, there's that. And the drinking. There is some of that, too, my friend!"

We toasted again and shared a good laugh. I was liking this guy.

"I'll bet there are wacky stories to tell over the years," he said.

"A few. Can't help when a bunch of yakheads get together and imbibe."

"Sure, every gang is like that," Jimbo laughed.

"The Waitress Float Test comes to mind," I continued. A rack of stories popped into my mind. "The BlowHard. Bloody Race to No Where. Ray Greene. The Walk of Shame. SBORC."

"SBORC?"

"Shit Box Ocean Racing Circuit. That's our Wednesday Night Race Series. Run what you brung!"

"Sounds like it's all fun and games with you guys," Jimbo laughed.

I looked at this motorcycle clad stranger with the scruffy face and got serious for a moment. It was clearly the rum and my fuzzy brain that was behind the talking.

"You have to realize, sailboat racing is one of the absolute hardest sports in which to do well. Unless you're lucky!" I took another sip.

"Sometimes you have to create your own opportunity," I advised, holding my glass up. "Nothing happens unless you have a boat." I felt a rant coming on and was full on ready to take advantage of my, best I could tell, newbee.

"First you need a smooth bottom, slippery even, so your boat glides through the water with minimum of friction. Then you need a fine-tuned rig that holds the sails, and they have to be shaped properly, selected for use based on the wind strength and direction." I could see his eyes starting to roll back in his head.

"If they are too old and stretched, the shape will not work with the wind. Slow. If they are too small, you're underpowered. Too large, overpowered. Slow, and slow again." My hand demonstrated the angle of attack of a hull sitting flat in the water and then heeled over enough to power through the water.

"Then let's put humans on board, make them pull the strings at the correct moment, adjust the strings for the few degrees of nuance that translate to a difference between 4 knots and 4.3 knots. Then, adjust the weight distribution on the boat by moving people around so the keel gets to working, and the power goes forward toward the mark instead of sideslip away from the best angle. The angle of attack is the key, but it changes based on the wind strength,

the waves, the course you want to sail to get to the next mark.
And just when you settle into a groove, the wind shifts, or changes
strength, or another boat comes screaming in from the side and
demands you get out of the way because they have rights over you,
so you have to readjust the strings, the angle of attack, the angle
of heel…and don't forget there's six or eight people on board, each
with a job or two or three to do, and to do it at the precise time that
job has to be done to accomplish one or two of the adjustments.
So, you need a good crew boss, like an orchestra leader. And by
the way, who the hell is steering this bucket through the water
where the waves are working with or against the wind. And did I
mention the tidal current which is shifting the entire playing field
one way or the other, usually so imperceptibly that you don't notice
it right away until you wonder why you overstood the lay line
to the rounding mark. The marks are anchored, you see, so they
don't move. Everything else does! And missing the lay line, that's
usually the fault of the tactician who doesn't touch any strings, but
determines the fastest path to the mark, reading the wind on the
water, sniffing out the next shift, and making sure everyone is ready
to make the next maneuver."

I paused to catch my breath and realized my new friend was
now sitting with his mouth agape, apparently amazed by my rant.

"Then dealing with the mistakes, when someone doesn't do
their job, or living off the good feeling of success knowing full well
it won't last!"

Jimbo kept looking at me. Then he shrugged his shoulders.

"Why the hell do you put yourself through that?"

"Because," I said, turning to him with a big grin. "When you
get it right, there is nothing better!"

He nodded and raised his glass in salute.

"And the parties are usually kick ass!"

"I'll bet. Is there one tonight?" Jimbo asked.

"Probably. They are finishing up the ESYRU Intergalatic Regatta over in Westmont. I'm thinking they are going to win it again, and we'll likely all be here in a couple hours to celebrate! Be a good time for you to meet some of the guys, maybe think about joining up! Ah, wait a minute. Rules prohibit signing up a new member in a bar."

"Rules. You got rules? Why is that?"

"Well, your $25 entry fee will never get to the treasurer!" I laughed and pointed to our drinks. "It usually ends up right here."

"Doesn't matter. I'm not so sure I'm ready to join your gang just yet!" he laughed, "but I am interested in meeting Dr. Z."

"You know Dr. Z?" I asked, surprised.

"I don't know him. I know of him. There was an article in the paper last winter about a race in Key West. Local boys make good, kind of thing."

"Yea, I saw that article. They got close." I finished off my rum drink and asked young Zak to bring us another round. I looked at my new drinking buddy with a new sense of curiosity.

"You will…if he shows up," was all I said.

Suddenly, I felt like the drug smuggler's wingman again! I was acutely aware of the cash still in my pocket as if it started to buzz. I couldn't help wonder if I was about to become a part of setting up a drug deal.

31 - Steal a Boat

Karl stood outside QuiKee Gs and pondered the Albanian flag decal that he had plastered over the double door entrance the day after they took over the franchise. The bright red background caught the eye immediately and focused one's vision on the doppelganger eagle in black that dominated the image. It was a weird eagle to say the least and he always thought it more a dragon from ancient times. It appeared as a mirror image of a half bird crying out in anger. Or distress.

A reflection of the conflicted lives led by Albanians? He wondered. Their history littered with shared battles against invaders from every surrounding country at one time or another; from Western Europe to China, from the Ottoman Turks to the Serbians, the Germans, the Communists, even the Italians at one time or another tried to shackle Albanian independence.

Karl firmly believed it was a conflict between right and wrong, but one could never tell which side was which. So, you did what you had to do to get along. He and Mike came to America to chase a dream of prosperity without conflict. Mike convinced him selling gas was better than smuggling guns. It appeared that was the case. He pondered the American flag hanging alongside. Was that the flag of success and no conflict? He wasn't so sure.

They had a hint of success for a few days recently and both

were pleased to learn that their missing deposit from several days ago had been made good by the Shoreline Trust Bank. However, things had changed since the bridge was fixed. They needed to do more, or their dream was over. After several nights of intense conversation, Karl explained his plan to Mike and how it could change things. It was a simple albeit dramatic plan, and clearly toyed with the mirror image of good and bad, right and wrong. In the end, Mike agreed it was something they had to do. To succeed.

"Are you ready for this?" Mike asked him from the driver's seat of their small box truck as he pulled to a stop by the pumps right in front of where Karl stood. His expression was clearly one of resignation.

Karl gave him a small smile and a nod, then turned to the pump and inserted the nozzle into the truck's gas tank. Karl looked at the two cars filling up nearby but focused on the four empty pumps with no cars. He was more determined than ever to go through with the plan. The nozzle shut off as the truck's tank filled, and he carefully screwed on the gas cap. He then jumped in on the passenger side.

"Let us go make it rain, my friend!" and they drove off the lot, turned south onto Route 12 and headed toward the marinas in Mystic. He couldn't help but remember the start of another adventure back home, many months ago, where the mountains, danger and a big payday awaited. He was confident this time would be different.

32 - The Trip Home

About the same time, 100 miles to the southeast, Billy Gunny Gunning looked for a plan to get his boys on the road, to head home to celebrate at the Seahorse. Montgomery Fillmore Prescott III stood in the way, again, attempting to implement his own plan to steal the regatta. He had filed protests against Tomohawk and Smoked, and like all protests, it just prolonged the weekend.

While Billy really liked the Westmont Harbor Yacht and Tennis Club near Rye, New York, he had his fill of the weekend and Prescott's B.S. While he appreciated and respected the rules of racing, and fully understood the right of protest protected all racers who felt they had been unfairly limited in their ability to compete, Prescott's claim was crap!

"We were on port tack and they were on starboard," admitted Prescott in front of the panel of the same three judges who had rejected his case the day before. The six of them sat in a wood paneled room. The judges, the protestors, and the protestee. "We made a big effort to avoid them by tacking, but they didn't give us enough room!"

Sailboat racing's primary rule to avoid collisions starts with "starboard has the right of way over port." You learn that on day one. However, a nuance of the rule prohibits the boat that has the right of way from "hunting" for the boat that does not. Essentially, you can't make it harder for the give way boat to avoid you. You must give them the opportunity to keep clear of you and your right of way express. It's a nuance, for sure.

If the port tack boat doesn't avoid the starboard tack boat, then it falls back on the right of way boat to take evasive maneuvers so there is no collision. Avoiding a collision was of primary importance in the minds of the rule makers.

"We headed up to avoid LykytySplyt," testified B One of the B Boys from Tomohawk. "They had no regard for port-starboard and tacked way late! We were forced to change course."

"You didn't protest them, did you?" asked one of the judges.

"Why bother?" shrugged B One. "We beat them straight out, fair and square to the finish. We didn't have to protest to beat them."

"They hunted us!" Prescott complained. "We were trying to get out of the way, but they came after us! They turned right down at us!"

Another of the judges asked Prescott if he saw the other boat, Smoked, to windward of Tomohawk.

"Yeah. Yes, they were in the way, too!" Prescott answered. His eyes lit up as if he had found a new idea to run up the flagpole. His voice went up an octave as he lashed out at Billy, pointing to him. "Clearly they were forcing Tomohawk into us. It's their fault for all of this. He should be thrown out!"

"You do realize they were forced over the start line early because they turned away from you and Tomohawk?" the judge asked seriously and pushed the model boats on the table between them to demonstrate how Smoked was early for the start because they turned away from the potential collision.

"Well, I don't know about that…" Prescott stopped in mid-sentence. He looked at the model boats and pushed them around as if looking for a pattern that would fit his narrative but could not find one.

"I have a question, Prescott. May I?" Billy interjected, looking at the judges. They nodded together.

"Were you on port as you approached these two boats?" he asked simply, pointing to the Tomohawk and Smoked models on the table.

Prescott looked at him as if it were a trick question.

"Port or starboard, man? C'mon!" Billy pushed.

"Port," Prescott said quietly. "Obviously. I said as much."

"Were you able to cross us? Pass in front of either boat?" Billy continued.

Prescott stared at the table. He said nothing for a full ten seconds then shook his head. "No."

"Thank you!" Billy said with relief as if pulling the obvious answer from a child. He looked at the judges and shrugged his shoulders. "I think that is all we need to know."

The head judge looked around the table at the assembled group and put out his hands. "Anyone have anything else to offer?" All shook their heads, although Prescott looked as if he was about to say something and then thought better of it.

"Gentlemen, if you would leave the room and wait outside. We will come up with our final decision. Thank you," the head judge announced.

Outside the three sailors could hear the noise from the party in full swing coming from the Westmount Club bar down the hall. Billy had a mind to head that way when he saw Tank and B Two coming down the hall in the opposite direction with drinks in their hands.

"They deep in the rule book?" Tank asked, cracking a smile as he handed Gunny a rum and ginger. "Deliberating or debilitating?"

"If it's deep, it's dumb," Billy laughed. "I suspect the wheels of justice will move swiftly here. Basic Rule 10."

Prescott stood off to the side a few feet and watched the four friends sipping their drinks. He seethed quietly, fearful he had lost another championship. He looked up to see Tank walking toward him.

"Hey, Monty, word of advice," Tank started. Prescott involuntarily took a step back.

"Fok you, McHale!" he said, defensively.

"Hey, asshead, just a note. You should work that outhaul and the Cunningham a bit more going upwind. Maybe you'll find those few tenths you need to keep up. With us." Tank offered him a big, friendly smile as he grandly gestured to include the Tomohawk boys.

"Yeah, well, trim this!" was the response from Prescott, grabbing his crotch.

Tank took another step forward, but he stopped short as the twin doors to the protest room opened.

"Gentlemen! We've reached our decision, please rejoin us," announced the head judge.

Just as Billy had predicted the protest was disallowed citing Rule 10. The panel of judges sat stoically as they handed each racer a single sheet of paper with the decision. No one said anything, which was just fine for Billy's way of thinking. He traded smiles with B One from Tomohawk. Prescott crumpled up the page he was given and tossed it back at the judges and stormed out.

"Asshole," muttered the head judge, shook his head, scooped up the page into his briefcase and headed out himself. "Gentlemen, 'til next time and, if we are racing here with that guy involved, I'm sure there will be a next time." Everyone chuckled and followed him out the door.

The party with the full fleet was in full swing as they entered the club bar. Jerome the bartender saw Billy walk through the door and held up a drink for him with a big hello. Billy took it with a nod and joined the rest of his crew hanging by the dinghy centerpiece that stuck out from the old wooden bar. Not five minutes later, Commodore Montgomery Fillmore Prescott III, wearing a silly fez with tassels, a relic of some tradition his club persisted in upholding, grabbed the microphone by the upright piano in the corner that had been turned into a trophy platform, and started the prize giving ceremony.

Cheers went up for each boat as they were announced, even those who finished at the back of the pack. The biggest cheers were reserved for the crew on Smoked.

"For the third year in a row, in a different boat this time, Smoked with Dr. Z and Billy Gunning. ESYRU Champions!" Prescott sounded enthusiastic even though many believed it pained him greatly to be saying Billy's name.

Billy went up and grabbed the trophy, holding it up for all to see. It was a wonderful piece of metal, shaped like a punch bowl with handles on top of a tall wooden tower about 18 inches high, brightly varnished and covered with shiny brass plaques noting the year and boat name of previous winners. It was called a Perpetual and the boys from Mystic would keep it for a year before returning it in time for next year's championship regatta.

Brian had acquired several small party poppers and he and Toby ran around the room shooting confetti all over the assembled mob of racers who reveled in the moment. The only complaint was the confetti mixed with the cheese dip and, in some cases, racers' rum drinks.

In the end, everyone had a good time and soon began stumbling out to their cars and the prospect of going to work the next morning, carrying good memories, and a hangover or two.

"We ready to go?" Billy asked Toby. "Where's Tank and Brian?"

"They went outside already. Tank said he had something to do and took off with Brian," Toby answered between the last sips of his drink. "Probably taking a piss!"

"Teddy! Darts! Trip! Let's go, Seahorse bus leaving on track three right now!" Billy slammed his glass down on the bar, tipped his hat to Jerome, turned, and wandered down the hallowed hallways of the club with glass trophy cases filled with pewter, silver and glass bowls, plaques, and pendants. An old club with lots of history, he thought. The pomp and circumstance really didn't reach him.

And you had to split your allegiance with the golf and tennis crowd as well! Not for me, he thought as he stepped onto the porch with the spectacular views of the harbor and the sound. Well, maybe there was a hint of envy…Nah!

Out front, Billy saw the van backed up by the youth sailing building. Darts was already sitting in the driver's seat. He waved frantically as if suddenly he was in a hurry. Most of the racers had found their way to their cars and left. Others were hanging nearby, getting in their last goodbyes.

"Gunny, you forget something?" came a yell from behind. Billy turned to see Trip coming down the steps of the club with the trophy in his arms.

"Oh shit, that monstrosity!" Billy laughed. He had left it next to the bar. He loved winning it, but after two years of it sitting in his den, next to dozens of others, its cache' had worn a bit thin. He stopped for a moment and admired it one more time.

"It is a pretty serious thing, isn't it? I feel like we are stealing a piece of ancient history from this venerable club!" Billy observed seriously.

"Well, if they learned how to sail better, maybe they could keep it locked up here," Trip suggested dryly and carried it off toward the van. The side door slid open, and everyone climbed in.

Billy jumped in the passenger's seat, glad he didn't have to ride in the back. He turned to count heads and stopped short.

"Whiskey Tango Foxtrot?" he blurted out.

He expected to see bodies everywhere, but three of his crew were sitting sideways on two coolers behind the driver's seat. Trip, Tank and Ted looked at him with shit eating grins on their faces. Trip had the trophy tucked next to him between two sail bags. Billy turned further and saw Brian, Toby, Flash and the woman who had greeted them that morning, Miss Teekee, sitting next to Flash. Those four were ensconced comfortably on a large paisley couch that took up one side of the van.

The door was pulled shut by Ted and Darts slammed the van into gear, spun the tires on the loose gravel, and headed out of the yacht club parking lot.

"Is that the couch from…?" Billy started, looking at Darts.

Darts looked at him and nodded with a big grin.

"Yes, it is! Youth sailing be dammed, we have liberated it!"

"Whohoo!" came a rebel yell from Brian.

"We deserve it, Gunny, my man! Three days of kick ass sailboat racing and 90 miles of comfort on I-95. Only way to travel!"

"But the youth sailors…that's their couch!" Gunny responded.

"No sailor ever learned how to sail on a frigging couch, my man. Couch is for traveling in style!"

Tank ranted on and traded high-fives with everyone. He was in hand grenade mode having pulled off the theft of the day.

"Did you not like Monty calling you an asshole?" Billy chided him.

"I offered him some friendly advice. He acted just like an asshole, so, I followed his lead!" He let out a cackle that was typical when he was in his 'piss on you' mood. "And, as I said, we have to make our guest comfortable!" He nodded toward Miss Teekee, hanging next to Johnny Flash who sat there quietly with his arm around his new-found girlfriend and a big smile on his face.

Trip handed Billy a joint and he took a hit. He handed it back and reached over to tap the trophy wedged in between Trip and the back of Darts' seat. "Well, good foking job, you cupheads! Let's go baptize this baby one more time at the Seahorse!" And they headed for I-95 as the sun headed for the horizon in the western sky behind them.

Back at the club, Commodore Prescott noticed something was wrong as soon as he walked by the Youth Sailing office and saw the empty front porch. The couch was missing! He immediately assumed Billy and his unruly gang had stolen it, and he wasted no time heading for his sporty Alfa Romeo. He jumped in, ignored the faint lingering odor of piss, slipped it into gear and sped off to give chase. He knew where they were headed, and truly believed he was the one to teach them that "no one foks with the Commodore!"

33 - ROLLING ROLLING ROLLING

Back in the city, Dr. Z shook Luiz's hand and apologized one more time.

"We knew this was possible and now we know...this is possible," he offered. "Stay low. When things clear up, I'll be in touch."

"My friend, you stay low. It's been a good run and it's not over yet!" He stood by the iron gate at the top of the driveway next to the Kafé de Kuomo and waved him on, closing it behind as the red Datsun 280Z turned onto LaSalle and headed for the highway.

For just a split second, Luiz caught the eye of the dark-haired driver of the van that pulled out from the curb across the street and headed in the same direction as the Z. He suddenly realized he had seen that same van a couple of times already today. Once in the morning, parked on the same corner, once during their delivery tour when he was sure it had been behind them. Or was it the blue van he remembered passing on Amsterdam Avenue going in the opposite direction? That one had two men in it, just like this one.

Luiz' hands locked the gate with practiced movements as the van disappeared around the corner and his mind rifled through the images of the day. "Damn, Dr. Z!" he said out loud to himself. "I don't think you are alone!" He walked down the driveway toward his workshop and decided he would best be served if he went to visit his sister in Arizona. Like today!

On the street, Dr. Z zipped through an intersection, under

the elevated tracks and turned left on Broadway then left again onto 125th Street, under Riverside Drive and under the elevated train tracks for Metro North until he reached the entrance to the Henry Hudson Parkway for the run up the west side of Manhattan. The late afternoon Sunday traffic was moving, but he was lucky to get over 30 miles an hour. The further north he went, the more traffic he hit. It was bumper to bumper by the time he approached the Cross Bronx Expressway. Folks heading west for the George Washington Bridge and New Jersey fighting with folks heading east toward Long Island and Connecticut.

He remembered the Yankees were playing the Red Sox that night and the Stadium, just over the Harlem River to his right, was attracting more than the usual flow for a Sunday in New York City. As much as he thought about being chased by the authorities, and as often as he looked in his mirrors, memorizing what he saw around him of the cars behind, beside, and ahead, the more he felt trapped by the sheer inability of the city's roadways to handle the number of cars and people who used them. He felt utterly powerless, his surroundings frozen on the west side of New York.

Thankfully relief appeared after the Cross Bronx where the east west travelers and the baseball fans left his world to continue on their own quest. His speedometer ticked upward as he headed north. Soon he was ripping along at 45 miles an hour! Cars began to pass him, and he felt a sense of freedom. Even the air flowed more freely!

He looked to move into the passing lane when he noticed the blue van about ten car lengths behind, holding steady in his lane. He spotted it only because it had been there, sticking its high windshield above the others behind him, a seemingly permanent blue bump among the many nondescript vehicles that had appeared in his mirror back on the Henry Hudson Parkway. Moving slowly had kept his worry about being chased simmering on low, but now.…

He slipped into the passing lane and accelerated, resorting to a weave from lane to lane, pushing 60 miles an hour where he could, intent on putting in some separation. After five minutes, he settled back into the righthand lane and sure enough, now about twenty lengths back was the blue van with the two guys. He ruefully laughed about choosing the color red when he picked out his 280Z a few months back. He suddenly wished he had chosen a grey Chevy sedan.

34 - A Bridge Not Too Far

Back east, Mike was very conscious of the speed limit as he and Karl worked their way down into Groton and then to the shoreline in Mystic. Their plan weighed heavily on him, and although he had accepted the right and the wrong of it, he was sure the local authorities would see it only as wrong. So, he wanted to remove any excuse they might have for interaction.

No one paid them any mind.

They eventually pulled into the small marina called Mystic Shipyard East just on the other side of the Mystic train station and parked against the tree line at the far side of the lot. Karl pulled out a drawing that he had hastily created on the ride from QuiKee Gs and pointed to some key elements in the structure drawn on the paper. Mike studied it for a moment and nodded. Karl folded it up and returned it to his jacket pocket. Then they jumped out and unloaded the back of the truck, carefully placing two coolers and a long, bulky object wrapped in a tarp into a two-wheeled dock cart.

Karl counted three people in his line of sight, boaters wandering the docks, intent on their business of finishing up their day on the water. He was pleased there were only three. He thought that if he owned a boat, he'd be spending as much of the daylight as he could on board, on the water, enjoying the boating dream. Then he refocused and got down to the business at hand.

Down Dock B they went, pushing the cart with their load.

Halfway down Karl stopped behind a lobster boat tied between four pilings. The first thing he noticed was a billboard like structure on the roof which made it look like it was more than a lobster boat. Karl shrugged, but then spotted the name RUMRUN painted in blue across the stern.

"This is it!" Karl exclaimed. He was pleased. It was about 30 feet long, had a high roofed cabin, open on the side where the steering wheel was located. The engine compartment was right in the middle of the boat under a sliding gray box with a flat surface. Right next to the wheel was a circular winch that led to a block and tackle hanging outboard from the cabin roof. It was the standard gear used to haul lobster traps from the depths. Behind him, the open deck was roomy, ideal for a crew to haul and drop lobster traps or to run sailboat races. Apparently, that's what RUMRUN was used for according to what Big Mo had told him a couple of weeks back on their drive to drop off the load of weed. Lobstering by day, sailboat Race Committee on Wednesday nights.

"How do we get in? You got a key?" Mike asked as he surveyed the boat.

"Big Mo gave me the 'combo,'" Karl explained as he grabbed the pad lock hooked through the latch on the cabin doorway that led below. "Christmas summer inside out!"

He rolled the four columns of numbers on the lock to 6-0-5-2. As predicted, the proper combo was marked in red, so anyone could match up the numbers with ease. He popped the lock and folded back the door, revealing a small cabin below. A bunk on the right with a blanket covering it, big enough for one and a half people, maybe just Big Mo thought Karl. On the left side, a second bunk turned into a storage shelf with three small milk crates filled with stuff. In the bow, a square hole that led to the anchor chain storage. A small portable toilet seat shared space with a line of code flags hung between two bulkheads. Karl was impressed.

"Comfy, utilitarian, small but useful," he nodded his head as he looked around. "Don't think I'd live here, but we could if we had to!" He looked at Mike who was hanging above the stairs looking in from above.

"No place to sit," Mike observed.

"No time to sit for us," Karl returned and looked under the stairs to find the battery switch. He flipped it to the upright position then looked further along the bulkhead before he found a key on a floating fob. He tossed it to Mike.

"Let's go boating!" he said with a cheery smile.

In minutes they had transferred the load from the pushcart on the dock to the deck of the boat.

"Better than a donkey!" laughed Karl.

Mike stepped in behind the wheel and started the engine while Karl loosened the dock lines. In a minute, they were off, navigating between the pilings to clear the marina. Karl had to push off on one turn and was saved from a dunking by a conveniently located handle on the cabin. They headed out onto the Mystic River and turned south.

"About 30 minutes to the Thames River and New London," Karl announced. He bent over a chart of Fishers Island Sound recovered from down below. "We should be getting there about sunset and that will be just right! Keep driving and don't hit anything!"

"Since when do you know anything about marine navigating?" Mike asked with a smile, keeping his eyes on the channel ahead.

"Look, it's simple. You got red buoys and you got green buoys. Stay between the red and the green. It's like a mountain path."

"With a better donkey!" repeated Mike.

The sun was painting the western sky orange as they motored along, peaceful as two fishermen out for an evening's sojourn.

Karl lifted the bulky package off the deck, arranged it on top of the engine box and slowly unrolled the tarp. He felt a tingle in his gut, not so much a foreboding as much as a premonition that tonight would be one of their best adventures.

35 – Toll Booth Tragedy

The music blasted through the van from the radio and the sailors were blasted on a combination of weed, beer, rum, and victory. Flash and Miss Teekee were having a wonderful time nuzzling on the corner of the comfortable couch, and everyone else was singing to the sounds of the Police.

"Every step you take, every move you make, every breath you take, I'll be watching you!"

This van was definitely rockin', and no one was gonna be knockin'! Darts had the speedo pegged at 75, top end for his overloaded workhorse, but he didn't care. He didn't do drugs, but he enjoyed every party, and let the flow of energy coming from the back of the van extend pressure to his right leg, keeping the pedal to the metal.

Speaking of metal, Brian was tapping on the side of the van with his steel toed boat shoe in time to the music. Toby surprised everyone with his voice, hitting the high notes, and the low, strumming an air guitar as if it was glued to his fingers.

"Who knew he actually knew all the words!" Tank commented.

"Total airhead!" Trip added as he mimicked the air guitar action. "Get it?"

"You're the airhead!" shouted Brian.

"Total deadhead," was Teddy's response. He knew Toby's real

musical preference.

As high as everyone was, it wasn't important that the cacophony be in tune. It was loud, proud, and you could feel it in your bones!

Gunny was loving it too, feeling the buzz, letting his mind wonder to where he wanted to be next. Visions of his girl Goldee filled his heart and soul, and he expected to see her at the Seahorse soon. He was keeping time to Brian's beat with his own hands on the dashboard, like he was a born drummer in need of some Caribbean skins to help fill the noisy space.

Duran Duran filled the moving party of sound next, and the bodies continued to rock and sway. Tank pulled a hat from a backpack and slammed it on Gunny's head. The black bowler with a brim immediately transformed Gunny into the personae of the lead singer of ZZ Top. He loved that band! All he needed was another year's growth on his beard. As if a planned mix tape, the next song up was none other than "Tube Snake Boogie"!

"I've got a girl lives up on the hill, she won't do it, but her sister will. It's the tube steak boogie! It's the tube steak boogie!"

The boys were raucous, and the decibels increased even as Darts hit the brakes and the highway flow of traffic began to slow. The traveling party had reached Madison, and it was time for another toll booth.

Back in the day when the boys were living it up, the state of Connecticut collected about $60 million a year from toll booths set up along the Connecticut Turnpike from New York to Rhode Island and north to Massachusetts. Over 30 million cars and trucks made the trek each year in both directions.

If the partiers in the van were carrying a crystal ball, they would have seen a horrifying accident a few years down the road that eventually led to the closing of all the toll booths in Connecticut. Fortunately, none of them were involved when a tractor trailer plowed into a line of cars waiting to pay their $.35, killing seven. Amazingly, that crystal ball also would have shown part of a bridge collapsing over the Mianus River along the turnpike. To fix that problem, federal funds were used, which led to the real reason to close the tolls, because using federal funds prohibited states from collecting tolls. A weird web, yet to be weaved!

The amazing thread tying that future story to the present - minutes before the bridge collapsed, Gunny and Tank, on a delivery, drove over it, dragging a boat on a trailer. One of those moments to come that neither could guess, nor could they even now, in a wild party van, anticipate how lucky they were about to be.

But back to our current story. The van stopped on this evening two cars behind a road yacht. One of those big ass station wagons with four doors, wide fenders, fake wood paneling on the sides, chrome everywhere there was an edge, topped off with a full metal roof rack. Evolved from "depot hacks", the station wagon was the workhorse of the American family, deep into the American Dream, well before the minivan was invented.

Inside this Buick beauty was a college aged couple dressed in black. Tucker and Tiffany were out prowling after another gas and go robbery. The busy service plaza just east of New Haven was their most recent target, and they had brazenly walked out with a bag of cash and coins they gleefully threw in the back seat, along with their distinctive head masks with college logos on them. Today's logos were UCONN and PC. Unfortunately, Tiffany's sexy caresses of Tucker's crotch during their getaway distracted him so much he forgot to get off at the exit before the toll, and here they were, trapped in the exact change lane.

Tucker, as cute as a summer breeze, sat frustrated because his efforts to toss quarters into the automatic coin collector basket had failed repeatedly. A red and white wooden gate blocked their way, waiting for Tucker to pop the coins. Six lanes of traffic spread out to the right, all with toll takers taking change and making change. Tucker and Tiffany sat in their lane, the wooden arm not responding. And the world backed up behind them.

Tiffany had a mouth on her that could run like an angry rooster, and she was letting poor young Tucker have it with a steady stream of criticism. She had removed her caressing hand and Tucker, normally quiet and reserved, suffered the ultimate indignity of having quarterback good looks without the innate ability to hit the side of a barn with a quarter. Several of them were scattered on the ground from his previous failed attempts. However, he realized that even when he scored, the gate was not moving.

"What the fok is the problem here?" Gunny said as he watched the show from the van two cars behind. He stopped his drumming and watched for another ten seconds.

"Jeeezzzus, Mother Aunt!" he finally shouted, opened the door, and got out.

"Where you going?" asked Darts.

"To fix this, man! We have to get home!"

Billy crossed over to the driver's side of the big wagon and laughed at the similarity of this big Buick Electra to Teddy's Roadmaster that prowled Block Island in the summer. As he approached the window, he could hear the woman yelling at the driver.

"You stink, Tucker! What the hell! You can't even throw like a girl! I don't understand you! Why are you so uncoordinated?"

Tiffany grabbed a quarter from the bag in the backseat, then flipped a hook shot out her open passenger window, over the roof of the car in a rainbow effort toward the catch basin, only to bang off the edge and up into the air where Billy reached out and snatched it, much to the surprise of all three of them.

Billy dropped it in the basket, looked around, saw a dime among the change on the ground, picked it up, and tossed it after the quarter. "Was that so hard?" he admonished the pair in the car, while at the same time felt some sympathy because the woman next to him continued to squawk.

"You see, even ZZ Top can do it! You suck, Tuck! It's so damn easy. Next time I drive!"

Tucker gave Billy a soulful look, as if to say, man, save me, please! Billy started to nod his head, but his eyes were drawn to the red and white wooden gate because it had not moved. The money had gone in. He heard it register in the catch basin. Billy saw it get swallowed up in the cash hole, but the gate had not moved! Another five seconds passed and still nothing.

"See, it wasn't me," pleaded Tucker. "The frigging gate is broken! Look, Tiff, it's not moving! It's not me, the state is the one to blame. It's broken!" The sound of his whine mixed with vindication was too much for Billy to listen further. He walked up to the gate and gingerly touched it. It didn't budge. He walked around in front of the gate, put both hands on it, and it wavered, but still didn't open to allow the cars through.

He looked around for help, but all he saw was the back of a toll booth collector to his left, working the next lane, his gloved hand taking cash and dumping it in a cash register, handing out change and a receipt, if requested.

"Fok it!" Billy blurted and pulled hard on the gate and it came off in his hands, intact. Now, he stood there, a line of cars in front of him, which had built to half a dozen, and it appeared down the road an endless supply was on its way. He tossed the gate off to the side where it bounced off the ground, one end hitting the toll booth next to him and then rebounding to crash against the big Buick. It scared the bejesus out of Tiffany, sitting on the passenger side ready to provide advice. Billy quickly jumped to the gate, pulled it off the car, and made sure it landed off to the side.

"Okay, come on! Get going! Move! Move! Move!" Billy yelled, gesturing frantically. Tucker pulled away just as Billy looked back to see Tank and Teddy standing next to the van. He thought he saw Tank taking a piss against the side of the van. With the land yacht rolling, the line of cars started moving, one honk quickly followed by another, and Billy, feeling the cloud of impatience building, ran back to the van and jumped in.

Darts hit the gas and the van moved as Billy closed his door, but the back door was still open with Teddy outside. He jumped in. Tank was right behind, and with a hop, skip, and a jump, threw himself halfway into the back, grasping for a handhold. Teddy grabbed one hand and Tank grabbed the trophy with his other. The van picked up speed. A few feet before the toll booth, Tank pulled himself in, but the trophy silently slipped out the door a micro-second before Brian, sitting on the forward edge of the couch, slammed the sliding rear door shut. Darts accelerated through the toll booth, crunching over the downed wooden gate, and the line of cars behind did the same, all following closely the car ahead, taking advantage of the opening and getting on their way. And if they saved 35-cents today, so what! No remorse to feel because it was now a state problem.

In the confusion and adrenalin rush, no one noticed that the trophy had fallen out of the van! Billy was focused on the broken barrier that he had ripped off from its mooring. All he could think of was 'destruction of state property'.

"Ah, Darts, keep the pedal down, man. I don't need anyone blaming me for that mess!" Billy muttered while watching the toll plaza recede in the side view mirror.

Tank was thankful he was in the van and not under the wheels. He zipped up his fly, popped another beer and caught his breath.

"Good thing you're a track star!" Teddy offered, clinking his beer can with Tank's.

"Back in the day, maybe, but that was scary!" Tank shook his head in relief. "Say, did I ever tell you about the year I beat Yogi Berra's son in the 100-yard dash!"

"Yes, we've heard it! A dozen times!" protested Toby. Everyone laughed.

Back at the toll booth plaza, Mel Wisnieski, working the booth next to the exact change lane, turned his head and noticed a big Buick station wagon accelerating away and an empty bracket where the red and white barrier arm was supposed to be.

"Well, god damn!" he said indigently. "Son of a bitch busted through the gate!" He eyed the license plate then reached for his phone, dialed a seven with one hand, simultaneously grabbing a dollar from a car in front of him and returning exact change with the other.

"Brad, we have a blow through on lane 7. Busted up the barrier! License Echo-Lima-Xray – 3-5-7. The gates down, everyone's ripping through!"

"Okay," returned the bored voice on the other end. "I'll contact the Staties. Echo-Lima-Xray-3-5-7."

Trooper First Class Rudy Godman was on his lunch break sitting at the other end of the toll plaza facing southbound. He was jotting down info on a robbery at the service plaza back up the road when he heard the call on the radio from dispatch asking for an immediate response. A quick U-turn put him on the northbound side, and he started looking for a Buick station wagon with fake wooden panel sides and a young couple inside. He flipped on his emergency lights as he entered the stream of traffic coming out of the toll plaza and took up the pursuit.

A couple of miles down the road, paranoia set in for the first time with Billy Gunny Gunning. The brief flurry of action at the toll left him wondering about the cops. He flashed on Dr. Z's brief encounter with him the night before and had to laugh. Did I put myself on the same fateful course? Chased by the cops? He looked behind at his guys still enjoying themselves, abuzz again after the pause in the party, and happy Tank didn't get scrapped off at the plaza.

"The couch!" Billy blurted out. He realized that his boys had stolen the couch from a very prestigious club. Someone surely had seen them. Was that going to create an issue if they should get caught? Or even just stopped?

"What about the couch?" asked Tank.

"What if they come looking for it?"

"They'll never find it!" Tank protested.

"Bullshit, they probably watched you steal it! And certainly, who do you think they will suspect?" Billy laughed at Tank always going to the obvious, but most unlikely solution as long as it fit his narrative.

They looked at each other for a moment, each trying to find an answer to the paisley elephant in the van.

"Oh, shit!" interrupted Darts from the driver's seat. Billy looked over and saw what Darts had seen in the rearview mirror. The blue lights of a state trooper coming up behind them. Darts pulled into the righthand lane.

The sound of the siren reached them and everyone suddenly shared Billy's paranoia. They all looked at each other, then the couch, and back at each other as it became clear there wasn't anything they could do sitting there, trapped!

"They must have seen us at the toll booth and want to scold us for busting through the barrier," Teddy offered, the wise old man pretending to possess the understanding of an adult.

"You think they might scold us for stealing the couch, too?" Brian asked.

"Hey, remember when we stole that picnic table from Pequot House dock on Fishers?" Toby offered with a wistful smile. The famed bar on the more famous island a few miles from Mystic, across the sound, had more than a few famous stories. Toby was ready to tell one of them because the back doors of the van provided a crazy solution that was suddenly on his radar scan.

"Yeah, that table fit so perfectly across the back of your Whaler, so we grabbed it and took off!" It was Flash, who pulled himself away from kissing the cute, dark haired Miss Teekee long enough to offer his two cents. He had been there when they stole the table.

"It was your idea, wasn't it, tablehead?" Toby laughed, pointing at him.

"It would have fit so perfectly alongside my dock!" Flash was suddenly energized remembering the story.

"What happened?" asked Brian, the youngest among this crowd.

"Hell, a Coast Guard patrol saw us and when they lit us up, we flipped the table!" Flash gushed. He gestured how the table had flipped off the back of the boat, over the engine, and into the water. "The Coasties were so close they ran right over the table as it floated just under the surface of the water. With a sickening crunch of wood on fiberglass and metal, the collision ripped up their hull and engine prop, bringing the chase to an end in the middle of Fishers Island Sound!" Flash laughed hard at the memory. Everyone else tried to remember the last time he has spoken so many words in the same moment. No one could.

"What?" Flash protested.

"We're not flipping the couch out of the van!" Billy shouted as everyone started laughing at the image of the USCG floundering, and Flash and Toby motoring away.

"We had to stay low for a couple of weeks, but I don't think they knew who we were, still," Flash bragged.

"They are not coming for the couch!" Teddy shouted, frustrated no one seemed to be listening to him.

And just like that, the flashing blue lights and the blaring siren came up to the van in the passing lane, and kept on going. Everyone held their breath and then cheered as they watched the patrol car pass.

Billy sat back and let out a deep breath. When the threat of enforcement disappears, so does any sense of guilt. Can't convict a man you can't catch! He laughed and reached for another beer. Tank was passing them out to everyone. Suddenly, a tiny voice joined the verbal fray from way back in the van.

"Anyone want mushrooms?"

It was Miss Teekee. She had pulled out a handkerchief, set it on her lap, and opened the folds to reveal a pile of mushroom stems and caps.

"And what pile of cow dung do these come from?" asked Tank.

"I grow them at home. It's dung from Stonington if you must know. Jester Miller's Farm." She smiled so sweetly that all the boys were gazing at her in awe.

"Good dung if it's Jester's dung, I always say!" Tank joked. He reached for a cap and popped it into his mouth.

"I'll try one of those. Cubes, right?" Trip Standish asked as he reached into her lap and picked a stem from the pile. "Psilocybin Cubensis. The Magic Mushroom." He let it melt in his mouth and sat back on the couch, as if settling in for a long ride.

Blondie came on the radio singing, *Colour me your colour, baby, colour me your car. I know who you are. Call me!* Everyone seemed to be listening as if the mushrooms required a certain amount of concentration that beer or weed did not. It didn't last long.

"Well, looky here, boys and girls. The coppers got their man. And their girl!" Billy pointed to the shoulder where the flashing lights of the state trooper's vehicle lit up the Buick Electra wagon in a blue glow. The driver, Tucker, was out of the car and talking to officer. The woman, Tiffany, was leaning out the driver's window directing her thoughts to the police officer. Billy could swear he heard her yelling "…and don't you hurt him, Officer, he doesn't deserve it! He doesn't know what he…." and the rest was lost as the van drove on down the road. The last thing Billy saw was the Trooper looking in the rear window. He remembered the plea for help from the fellow's face back at the toll booth and sent him a good thought.

"I hope the sex is good," he muttered. Darts looked over.

"What? Sex is good? You bet it is!"

Billy just laughed and shook his head at his navigator. Goldee's face popped into his vision, and he settled back for the rest of the ride. He really hoped she was going to be at the Seahorse. He wanted to be the rock 'n roll tonight. He looked at his watch. Just another half hour or so. Then he let his mind dwell on her face and her body.

"Yes, the sex is good!" he said aloud even as her body began to melt in his brain, as if the mushrooms were turning her into a colorful cartoon character, but the lines blurred, separated, and the color began leaking out! The music of Foreigner filled his ears from the radio and the lights on the highway, in the 'solset' glow of dusk, seemed to move with the music.

"I've been waiting for a girl like you to come into my life. Been waiting for a girl like you, your loving will survive!"

36 - DR. Z CATCHES UP

⬛⬜⬛⬜ ⬛⬜⬛⬜⬛⬜⬛

Dr. Z tried not to worry about his wife, Camille. She had not answered when he called home. He pulled into the East Haven rest stop out of pure paranoia because that blue van was still behind him. The two guys in it were either tuned in to the same world he was by pure happenstance or were in full surveillance mode. He assumed the latter. He watched them park between two trucks while he stood by the line of pay phones. No answer at home.

She must be at Brooks', he thought, and that was good. It was also bad because it meant that the law was on his case from the found load of weed on Ishkoodah. Maybe Camille did call Nick, the lawyer. He felt like he was one of those high flying, girder walking, steelworkers, out on a beam, miles above ground, exposed to the world, but ironically no one was coming near him. Fear? Caution? Patience? Let him dig his own hole, or burrow deeper into the warren and ferret out others, so they can hang back and catch everyone.

What if he just ignored them?

He hung up the phone and walked slowly to his car. He momentarily let out a curse as a big ass station wagon passed him on the shoulder of the entrance ramp on the edge of control. Somebody's in a hurry, he thought.

He re-entered the highway slowly and sure enough, he watched the blue van moving behind him. He pulled into the passing lane and let the power of his 280Z take him away. The straight six opened up its 190 horses and pushed him back in his seat. He loved the speed. He remembered skateboarding down Fort Hill in Groton during high school. No one could touch his fearless denial of gravity's wicked punishment should he clip a sidewalk crack and go ass over teakettle.

For several minutes he lost sight of the van and kept going fast.

Then the toll plaza outside Madison. He pulled a quarter and a dime from his dash tray and glanced in the rearview mirror. For just a split second, he saw no blue van. He wasn't convinced. They had been hiding there since he left New York. Visible, once in a while, then gone. It was making him a bit crazy. He slowed and he saw something shiny ahead.

It made no sense. Right in front of him, on the pavement, 100 yards out, wobbling on its wooden pedestal, in the glare of the toll booth lights, was the same damn trophy he had seen the night before while sharing drinks with Gunny in the bar at the Westmont Harbor Yacht and Tennis Club. It had been sitting on the corner piano with the other trophies up for grabs in the regatta.

Even as he watched, a slow-moving car clipped it with its rear bumper, and it spun off to the right and fell on its side.

"Whiskey Tango Foxtrot!" Z shouted to himself, hit the gas and his sports car jumped forward. A leap like a panther. Just before he reached the trophy, he spun the wheel expertly to the right and jammed on the brakes, ending up parked perpendicular to the flow of traffic, right in front of the toll booths. For a split second there were honks as the two lines of traffic moving toward him were forced to stop.

He opened his door and there was the trophy within arm's reach. He grabbed for the one remaining handle on the metal loving cup on top of the wooden pedestal and lifted it into the car.

He could see a couple of the brass plaques had been knocked loose and were lying on the pavement, but he ignored them. Instead, he punched the gas again and spun in a tight righthand circle, just missing the cars coming at him in full honk. He completed his 360 degree turn, ending up back in the far left hand exact change lane. There was more honking and fist shaking as he squeezed in between two cars in the moving line.

He realized the cars were not stopping at the toll because the normal barrier was nowhere to be seen. As each car realized they didn't have to wait for the gate, they accelerated away from the plaza. He did the same, but when he looked up at the traffic behind him, the blue van was now only five car lengths behind.

"Fok!" he cried, feeling the bat-turn induced adrenalin pumping in his blood stream. And now the two guys were back in his brain, and his line of sight. He made another quick decision and cut sharply to the left behind the brick building that housed the toll booth offices between the north and south bound lanes. He found himself in a parking lot where the toll takers kept their personal vehicles. He weaved between two lines, over a median strip of grass, narrowly missing a toll worker heading into the office from the south bound side with what appeared to be a pouch of money. Suddenly, he was in the fast lane heading south, and he accelerated with the flow of cars leaving the plaza on the other side.

Less than a quarter of a mile further, he saw a narrow opening between the wooden guardrail that separated the two flows of traffic. Normally, a police car would be sitting there waiting for some call to action. It was empty so he slipped in and rejoined the north bound flow of traffic.

"I'm not trapped if I keep moving," he thought to himself. In a moment he rejoined the Exact Change lane and slipped back through the toll booth where he had just picked up the trophy. There were workers moving toward the lane, but he motored away, then checked his rear-view mirror again. This time nothing. Were they ahead of him? Did they follow his second bat-turn through the parking lot?

He saw nothing ahead and felt safe, for the moment. He matched the 65 mile per hour speed limit and moved to the righthand lane so he wouldn't arouse suspicion. He smiled and shook his head, as if a red 280Z could hide anywhere! Then he looked at the trophy in the seat next to him.

"Good on you, boys!" he gushed, genuinely proud of his team. Surely, they were the winners. No one else would be coming this way at this time of the evening. He was familiar with the prize since they had won it the previous year, and he had personally handed it to Gunny to keep on display. It was clearly tattered from its dalliance on the toll plaza. One of the handles on the loving cup had broken off. He had no idea how it ended up abandoned there, but he knew where everyone was heading next.

He looked in the rearview mirror again and saw nothing that would click on his paranoia. Had he lost them? Were they ever really there? If they were following him, why hadn't they picked him up? He thought about his wife, hopefully safe at Brooks. He thought it better that he stay away from her for the time being. He thought about Billy and the boys getting ready to celebrate. He looked at the trophy and realized it needed to be a part of the celebration. And so did he!

Seconds later a pair of headlights in his side mirror caught Z's eye. A fast mover in the passing lane. In a few heartbeats it was there and by; a red convertible, top down, had to be doing 90. He recognized the Alpha Romeo immediately and the shock of white hair on the driver. "Monty?" he asked in surprise.

Z backed off on the gas, settled down to 60 miles an hour, and reached for his patience zone. No sense in trying to keep up. That was a "pay attention to me" zone he wasn't interested in joining. He assumed the only reason Monty would be in this neck of the woods was to join in the party at the Seahorse. As odd as he thought that to be, it was the only rational explanation why he would be speeding this far east on the turnpike.

Sure, there was his sister, Goldee, and Billy. Z wondered if that was such an issue the Commodore would be ripping up speed limits to do something about it. And what could he do anyway?

"Well, looks like we gonna have a hell of a party at the Seahorse!" And he drove on into the darkening evening after one more look in his rearview mirror. It looked clear for the moment.

A few miles ahead the van cruised comfortably at the speed limit in the middle lane of the three-lane highway. Bob Seger's rock ballad "Against the Wind" took center stage on the radio. Any song with reference to wind was enough to become an anthem for this load of sailors, at one level or another. They were all singing in the back, rocking on coolers, and nestled in the comfort of the paisley couch.

"I was livin' to run and runnin' to live. Never worried about payin' or even how much I owe. Against the wind. Running against the wind. We were young and we were strong, running against the wind."

The music was a mellow magic carpet ride for their z-weed filled brains mixed with beer, rum, and shrooms. High on winning, drifting without responsibility. Darts alone had to worry since he was behind the wheel as they rolled over the Connecticut River, the next party stop at the Seahorse just 15 minutes ahead.

"Oh, crap. Here comes another one!" Darts cut through the mood. Billy looked over and saw what sparked the driver's concern. More flashing blue lights.

"He's chasing somebody!" called Toby looking out the rear windows of the van. Everyone in the back craned for a look and sure enough, they could see the blue lights and a pair of headlights in front of it.

"He's probably chasing us!" Brian offered. He was having trouble picking out what headlights had the blue flashers above them.

Within seconds, the first pair of headlights appeared next to the van, passed on by and then suddenly, adjusted speed to slow down, falling into pace with the van, running right next to the driver's window.

"Holy Fillmore, Friends. Guess who's back in town?" It was Billy who had immediately recognized the red Alpha Romeo convertible. "It's the Commodore. Hizz horror, hizzself!"

"I could smell him!" blurted Brian. "A bucket of piss, man Winner piss!"

"What the hell is he doing up here?" Tank asked, sitting behind the driver's seat. He pulled himself up to peer over Darts' shoulder so he could get a better look at the car next to them. It was definitely Monty behind the wheel, and he was apparently angry, judging from the yelling and gesturing in the general direction of the van. He seemed to grow angrier after a few seconds because whatever he was yelling wasn't being heard, what with the rush of air at highway speeds, and the fact the window was closed on the van.

"He is not happy, boys!" laughed Tank. "Drop the window, Darts. What's he want?"

The peel of the police car apparently chasing Monty now reached everyone's ears as the window came down. They could also hear a human voice yelling from the red car, but the words were indistinct, although Brian thought he heard the world "bastard" in the tirade. Suddenly the Alpha Romeo accelerated sharply, cut in front of the van, then continued into the righthand lane and adjusted speed again until it slid back to a parallel track with the van on the other side. Monty edged closer until he was just two feet from Billy in the passenger seat.

Billy was impressed with the highway gymnastics and rolled down his window to wave at Monty.

"Are you crazy, man! Whiskey Tango Foxtrot!" Billy yelled.

"You bastards! You stole my couch! Pull over!" cried Monty. He was hopping mad.

"You're crazy, man!" Billy responded. "We don't have your stupid couch!" He then turned to Darts. "Keep driving, do not stop!"

Another bleep came from the police car, this time it was right behind the Alpha Romeo. Then many more bleeps as the cop closed right up on Monty's bumper. The commodore looked in his rearview mirror, realized his chase was over and began to slow.

"Keep going, Darts!" Billy ordered and offered a wave back to Monty as the van separated from the sports car and the chasing cop. Billy watched the two cars fall behind and pull over to the side of the highway.

"Picnic table maneuver?" questioned Toby again, sitting in the back by the door. "We can just slide it out! Maybe pull off at the next exit. Dump it in the woods." He had already figured out what he thought was the best plan of action.

Billy put his head back in the seat. He was still impressed with Monty's reckless maneuver to switch sides around the van while careening down the highway with a cop on his ass. He was also pissed that the daydreams of him and Goldee, making wildly hallucinogenic love in the Seahorse, had evaporated.

"Toby's right," offered Teddy. "Monty is going to turn us in to that cop and then he'll be coming after us for the couch! After Monty gets a ticket, of course!" He laughed at the image of Monty's life going to hell in a handbasket because of his obsession with putting the crew that vanquished him on the racecourse in their proper place. Wherever that was.

"We have to dump it, Gunny! Out of sight. We never happened." It was Tank offering his solution. "It's not going in my living room, that's for sure!"

"It's just a couch, right? What's the big deal?" It was Miss Teekee, sitting close to Flash in the back corner.

"It's Westmount Harbor's couch, Missy," corrected Teddy Trumanlee. "It's a symbol of their power. Their supremacy in the pantheon of yacht clubs across the Sound!" he said dramatically.

"They'll track us down!" offered Brian.

"Shut up, you Dumpheads? Is that what you want to be?" Billy yelled. His head was spinning.

Billy turned to look at his crew in the back, three on one side hunched on the ice coolers and sail bags, four sitting comfortably on the couch on the other. Then he noticed something wasn't right. He looked around again.

"Where the fok is the trophy?"

"Trophy?" asked Tank. He turned to where it had been stashed among the bags behind the driver's seat. Then he remembered his dash into the van at the toll plaza. "Oh, shit! I think it took a trip on its own. At the toll plaza."

Tank remembered grabbing for a hand hold as he jumped back into the moving van as it pulled away from the busted barrier, and the impending sword of punishment for anti-social behavior, not to mention destruction of government property.

"I must have knocked it out back at the toll plaza. Sorry." He shrugged his shoulders.

"Jessszzuss!" Billy shouted and shook his head. Then it hit him. The plan came into focus in an instant.

"The bridge." It was Flash speaking as if he read Billy's mind.

Billy looked up at his blonde helmsman sitting stoically against the back door, nestled close to the visiting dark-haired lady of the morning. They both smiled and nodded.

"Yes, Flash. The bridge. We dump it off the Gold Star Bridge."

37 – Rocket's Red Glare

Karl and Mike had never been on the Thames River before. As they made the turn up Pine Island Channel past the legendary New London Ledge Light, they were greeted by flashing lights of a Coast Guard patrol boat. In fact, the small boat turned right toward them and pulled up alongside. Karl and Mike looked at each other in panic and both moved to the starboard side to greet the patrol.

The young sailor with the red life vest waved, gestured up river and pointed to the east side. "Captain, just to let you know, we have the USS Philadelphia heading out to sea. Will be along here in a minute or three. Please keep to the east side of the channel."

Naval Submarine Base New London is America's primary east coast home for the US Navy Sub Force. Subs travel the Thames River frequently heading for offshore duty around the world or returning from same. It was not unusual to see a sub in the river, with two or three patrol boats as escorts. However, neither Karl nor Mike had ever seen a submarine, much less been in a boat on the same river.

Karl was a ball of tension even as he returned a friendly wave. He took a deep breath as a reflex action and tried to make himself six feet wide to block the guardsman's view of the tarp partially opened on the engine cover just behind him in the middle of the boat.

The patrol boat swung back toward the middle of the river. No one looked back.

"That was close!" Mike suggested. Karl flipped the open tarp back over the two rocket launchers laying in the open. The pair of PXF 44's had been removed from their crates stored at the QuiKee Gs and wrapped in the tarps. To the untrained eye, they looked like bulky fishing equipment wrapped in a tarp. No one was supposed to see them.

"We have to deal with a submarine now?" Karl asked, slightly pissed. He imagined many patrol boats all looking for the slightest disruption of normalcy. He looked upriver and saw at least two more points of flashing lights indicating a patrol of some sort.

"Maybe tonight is not a good night," Mike said from behind the wheel. He was enjoying himself playing captain. He kept the throttle forward as the speedo tickled eight knots. He was enjoying the scenery as well, marveling at the beautiful homes scattered along the point with their sweeping porches overlooking the harbor. They motored passed a wooden structure on stilts clinging to a clump of rocks. A porch surrounded three sides of the building and looked as rickety as the long, narrow walkway, also on stilts, that connected the rock pile to the shore. The wooden sign on the sloping roof caught the last rays of the sunset which reflected off the greenish white lettering that spelled out "Seahorse Tavern".

"Now there's the American Dream!" he proclaimed to Karl.

"It's just a bar, best I can tell," Karl answered. "How about those houses right there? Those are not little boxes! That's a dream!" He pointed to the high peaked roofs and spacious yards hugging the rocky edge of the river. Mike steered closer, both to comply with the Coast Guard request, and to get a better look.

"I could live there," Mike admitted. Then they both noticed a change. As if a line had been drawn at the property edge of the last home, a stand of high trees appeared, then a fence and suddenly, the view shifted from high end residential to full on industrial. Four smokestacks jutted up from brick buildings, and pipes ten feet off the ground crisscrossed an area leading to huge fuel storage tanks painted with the logo for "New England Oil", a regional gas distributor.

Next a massive office building appeared up on the hillside, then another. A sign on the building read "Encore Pharma LTD".

"Drugs and fuel. That's not a 'dream', that's reality," scoffed Karl. He was referring to the big pharmaceutical conglomerate that owned Groton and provided a dream path for thousands of workers. The names of equally large oil companies were plastered on the storage tanks. A large tanker tied up at the fuel dock under the tanks appeared to be unloading its cargo as they passed by. Karl could not help but imagine the thousands of cars that were part of the thousands of dreams that were destined to run on its liquid load. He felt connected to them, hoping they would all end up at QuiKee Gs.

The lesson continued as the huge complex of the Globolus Marine Boatyard came into view. One of the main cogs in the military industrial complex, it produced submarines every year for the US Navy, and had been producing navy ships of one kind or another since the turn of the century. Liberty ships, PT boats, sub tenders, and parts for all, including the first nuclear powered sub, the Nautilus, had provided work for thousands, and remained the region's largest employer.

"That's how you protect the American Dream," Karl offered to his companion, pointing at the nose of a submarine sticking out of a massive green shed, tended to by a pair of yellow cranes. "Another being built!"

"And another, like this one coming!" Mike added looking ahead. On cue, the USS Philadelphia appeared ahead, following a single patrol craft with a flashing red light. Its partially submerged black shape pushed a white foamy bow wake as it glided effortlessly through the water. Mike pulled back the throttle to cut their speed in half and they both watched in awe as the cigar shaped weapon, as long as a soccer field, slid by. Three men could be seen on the conning tower on the submerged hull, their heads and shoulders sticking out from the winged sail. Behind them three camouflaged antennas rose up over their heads. The number 690 was painted in white on the side

The sheer size was impressive, especially the long flat surface of the tail end of the ship where the missiles bays hinted of the world changing destructive power at rest. It was especially impactful for two Albanians who had seen war on a much smaller scale in their native country. They drove donkeys over mountain trails filled with machine guns. This hulk sliding through the water with a low rumble was filled with nuclear bombs. Or so they thought.

"That is a big gun," Karl said, almost under his breath.

They watched transfixed for several moments as the small entourage went by. Both continued to track the two patrol boats long after the tail fin of the sub had disappeared beyond the New London channel markers. Karl was pleased to see them turn back toward the harbor, their blinking lights turned off and the patrols tied up at a pier across the river. Karl turned his attention toward the railroad bridge now about a half mile ahead of RUMRUN. The sun was down, the sky was holding some orange tinted light, but he was looking for the increased darkness and not another charming sunset.

"No one has to die tonight, my friend. We are only helping ourselves, our dream." Karl had moved right next to Mike at the wheel. His tone was almost philosophical. Ahead of them loomed the structural jigsaw of steel that is the truss bascule bridge carrying trains over the Thames River. A large steel cradle on the western side held counterweights to their left. When the bridge opened to allow boats through, the entire span pivoted on that end, opening a 100-foot channel between the pilings.

Behind the train bridge towered the dual span of the Gold Star Bridge, twice as high off the water, carrying north-south traffic on I-95. It was also a steel truss structure arching high over the river in a lattice work of steel beams creating an open box. The beams angled diagonally with triangles of support between the upper and lower sections. The roadways, 80 feet wide, sat on top. More than 400 steel bolts held each of the dozens of metal plates to the beams. There were tens of dozens of beams, forming an immovable steel framework and everything multiplied by two. The northbound lane had been only added a few years previous, mirroring the southbound bridge.

The entire erector set construction was balanced on a series of concrete arches several hundred feet apart secured to the river bottom. For anyone who spent time looking at the underside of the bridge, the massive structure was impressive. A million tons of steel went into supporting the 50,000 cars a day that rolled back and forth. It was all very symmetrical except for the trusses directly over the center of the river. They were arched to allow passage of high masted ships underneath. For the most part, only the Coast Guard training vessel Eagle, at 147 feet, was tall enough to reach that height with its towering masts.

Surprisingly, with all its bulk, only four points of the strong center span were attached to the concrete arches. The seemingly out of proportion base supports, looking very much like tiny steel pyramids, carried the load. Not unlike skinny ankles on a gorilla, thought Karl, when he had inspected the bridge earlier in the morning from the public boat ramp underneath. He pulled out the pencil sketch he had made and laid it in front of Mike again. Two roadways, four arches, eight points of contact were all that held up the center sections.

"All we have to do is hit these two points, cause some damage and the safety fears will cause panic and close the roadway," Karl said emphatically. He circled the targets, one on the front edge of the north bound side and one on the southbound side. "It won't come down, but it will wake everyone up."

Mike nodded his head.

"And it will close everything down! Just like a couple of weeks ago!" Karl practically shouted. He looked around as if his shout might have awoken anyone on a nearby boat. He saw nothing.

"Shkodran, I'm committed to this plan. I understand what we must do. I want to do what we have to do." Mike spoke slowly, looking directly into Karl's eyes. He used Karl's family given name to emphasize his willingness to go on. And how serious he was. He had not been that supportive when Karl first presented the plan the night before.

Mike literally was preoccupied searching for a distributor of Ding Dongs to satisfy the one lady who asked for them when Karl broached the plan. Mike was a guy who liked to deal with the money. He didn't like gun play, even though he had been through enough of it. Enough to convince him they had to change their lives and now here they are, chasing the dream, and rockets were back in play! He came to realize it could work. That bank lady had pissed him off enough that maybe he could consider it partially revenge. That was an emotion he knew, and he decided he could live with.

"I have no doubts, Mirilind," Karl answered with his friend's real name, just as he had done. "I think we go up just past the railroad bridge and we will set up there." He glanced over his shoulder again toward the Coast Guard pier south of the cluster of steeples that provided a good landmark for downtown New London. There was no movement that he could see.

They motored under the closed train bridge and then Mike

eased the throttle to idle, allowing RUMRUN to drift. Karl pulled back the tarp and revealed the two rocket launchers from Delroy in Jamaica. Known simply as "Panzerfaust", they were German made, shoulder mounted and fired one rocket each, designed to kill a tank.

Mike went to the cooler at the stern, removed the two rockets, and watched Karl insert them in the front of the barrels. A probe extended from the nose of each projectile designed to ignite the explosion upon contact.

"You take the southbound side, I'll take the north, okay?" Karl said. Mike nodded and picked up his weapon. For a moment he was confused. "I'm actually aiming at the north side, where the southbound traffic is, correct."

Karl smiled, looked at the two bridge abutements as if trying to sort it out himself., then finally pointed up river. "The far side. Aim at the far side."

Mike nodded, nestled his right eye against the sight and tried to control his breathing. He could hear his heart pounding.

On the roadway above, Billy was pleased to see there were no cops standing by on the median where they normally parked to await their next highway law breaker.

"We are doing this. Are you ready?" he said to his boys in the van.

The van slowed in the righthand lane at the top of the bridge then pulled over into the breakdown lane and stopped near a light pole in the middle. The traffic was light, the sky was near dark, the lights of the bridge dropped pools of brightness on both sides of the road. The fence was a line of one-inch square metal bars standing vertically about eight feet high along the roadway.

Billy opened his door, jumped out and ran to the back of the van, pulled the handle, and opened the double doors. Flash tumbled out followed by Miss Teekee. She stepped aside and held the left door open, while Toby and Teddy jumped out. Flash grabbed an end of the couch and it began to slide from the van with Trip and Brian pushing it from inside. In short order, Tank popped out of the side door and the couch was carried by the others right up to the fence.

"Tank, get by the fence," yelled Billy. He looked out through the fencing and saw a flash of light from the New London Ledge Light three miles downriver where the Thames joined Fishers Island Sound.

An answering wink appeared to the right from the New London Harbor Light, the third oldest lighthouse in America. It had protected British sailors from the rocks during the War of 1812, submarines since the 1900's, fishermen and ferries every day, all of them navigating the mile-wide channel beside sailboat racers and cruisers, living the dream of a new world, a daily life, a moment to remember. A moment to regret. The flashes of light a background to those moments, the punctuation that never played a role in real history except to tickle a memory or place a corner on a life.

Five of them walked the couch to the edge of the bridge and lifted it up. Tank bent down and became the leverage underneath, pushing the couch as it was lifted over his head. It still didn't reach to the top of the fence. It was a beast with five guys manhandling it on the edge of their strength. Tank grabbed the bars from under the couch, lifted his leg and inserted his foot between the narrow opening, then pulled himself up to get a hold with his other foot. Billy stepped forward and pushed Tank on his butt raising him up so his back could take the weight of the couch. Together, with a multi-guttural grunt, they pushed the paisley sofa from the Westmount Harbor Yacht and Tennis Club junior sailing office up to the peak of the protective fencing and, after a moment of inertial resistance, reached the tipping point. With a final shove from Tank on the fence, it went over the top and fell, destined for the water

145 feet below."

"Let's get the fok out of here!" yelled Billy. His boys had pushed against the fence to look down, but there was nothing to see over the edge in the darkness.

"To the Seahorse!" Billy waved, pushing Brian and Trip ahead of him and they all jumped back into the van like a bunch of frat boys running from the dean. Their laughter sounded more like cackles as they reveled in the ghoulish behavior that had overwhelmed them in seconds and, suddenly, like the couch, was gone.

Down below, Karl had lined up the small pyramid support on the southernmost arch in the reticle of his rocket launcher's sighting scope attached to the side of the 3-foot tube. He took a quick glance to his left to see Mike in a similar position, aiming slightly more to the north and not as high.

"Ok, friend, let's do this. Aim and Squeeze!" Karl cheered.

Mike said nothing, holding his launcher gingerly, careful to avoid the flat panel of wood that was mounted on the top of RUMRUN. As he found out later, the panel was the board used to signal the configuration of the courses for Wednesday night racing. It was on the roof for visibility. Right now, it was blocking his view, so, he took a couple of steps back and leaned the back of his legs against the stern rail.

"Ok, I'm ready!" he announced to Karl as the tiny pyramid at the end of the concrete arch came into focus in his sight. His finger moved to the trigger gently. As he applied pressure, a light sound reached his ears as if someone was waving a flag. Even as the sound grew louder, he heard Karl shout.

"Now!"

They both pulled the trigger a second after the paisley couch, thrown from the top of the bridge over their heads by unseen perpetrators, crashed onto the cabin roof of the RUMRUN, crushing the course board with a muffled crunching sound. Then it bounced, flipped off the cabin roof, and crashed into Mike and Karl standing just below.

Mike's launcher made a big "Whoosh" as the propellant ignited sending the rocket from the launch tube. Unfortunately, the crash of the couch startled Mike to the point where he jerked the barrel down and pointed it directly into the open cabin. The rocket launched perfectly, flying through the cabin doorway, past the bunks below, and directly into the 2 x 2 foot anchor locker opening where the contact probe hit the inside of the very pointy end of the bow of the RUMRUN, and, as designed, ignited the explosive charge inside the projectile.

Instantly, the explosion blew out the hull, lifted the front of the boat up out of the water for a second, then it came crashing back down. Water started to gush in through the blast opening. The force of the explosion sent the 200 feet of anchor chain coiled up in the bow spilling through the hole, into the water and toward the bottom.

Karl's aim was also disrupted by the crashing couch and his rocket launched low above the water in the general direction of where he had pointed it. Like a stone, it skipped twice before it crashed into the base of the concrete support arch instead of at the top, where the small pyramid like footing was located. The fiery ball that ignited upon contact was quickly gobbled up by the river water, with seemingly no effect on the concrete.

Karl and his launcher, however, were knocked overboard when the bow of the boat exploded. Mike was thrown backwards onto the deck by the blast concussion and then something big and soft smashed against him. Deafened and dazed, he lay still for a moment. He slowly realized he was under a couch which had appeared out of nowhere. Then he heard a faint call. It was Karl, his voice trying to break through the incessant ringing in Mike's ears.

"Mirilind, Mirilind! Help me!"

Mike looked around and saw Karl had fallen overboard. He

struggled to move the couch off him, picked himself up, grabbed a life jacket stuffed under the stern deck, and staggered to the starboard side of the boat. He saw Karl treading water a few feet away and threw him the life jacket. His throw was accurate; it hit Karl right in the head, but he was too busy to grab it, trying to stay above water. In a second, he found it easier to simply swim to the boat.

Mike grabbed Karl's hand as he came alongside and pulled him onto the back of the boat. They both realized the boat was getting closer to the water, even as Karl was climbing on it. They were sinking! The bow was down, forcing the stern up, but the entire boat was heading only one way – down!

Then Karl saw the couch floating on the stern deck.

"Where the fok did that come from?" he asked incredulously.

"I think I heard it," Mike answered, then laughed because hearing was a problem, as if he was wearing earmuffs. He pointed up at the bridge. They both looked up, then at each other. Karl just opened his arms completely baffled by what had happened.

"Our shots missed and now we are sinking," he lamented. "Fok this country!"

"Get a life jacket on," Mike offered, grabbing a pair from the stern locker. "We'll have to swim for it."

The boat continued to sink and soon they realized they needed to jump off so they wouldn't get sucked down in the vortex. They floated nearby and watched the RUMRUN slowly disappear. Just the name was showing, then nothing but bubbles and then quiet. Seconds later the couch, floating invitingly for a moment, also disappeared. The rumble of the cars and trucks overhead took over the darkness.

"So much for the dream, my friend! I am sorry." Karl apologized, sputtering for air while blaming himself for the events of the evening.

"We try again tomorrow. Ding Dongs and potato chips," Mike laughed, but he was scared. He didn't like swimming. They both turned to look at the shore, then the other way trying to determine which was closer.

Then what they later referenced as a "miracle" occurred behind them. They heard a rush of water as if something was bubbling up from below the surface. Karl admitted he feared for a moment it might be a submarine, like the one they saw earlier in the night.

He was wrong.

It was the couch. It bobbed to the surface, rising out of the water. And it continued to rise, as if defying gravity. A second later, it stopped and floated, sitting askew on a self-inflating life raft that was part of the RUMRUN safety equipment. Apparently, the raft responded just as designed. Sitting in a cradle on the deck by the cabin windshield, it sank with the boat, but floated free when submerged, activating the HRU.

The hydrostatic release unit cuts the line that secures the raft to the boat when the pressure builds up under water. The freed raft floats upward and tension on a line attached to the raft, the painter, pulls open the valve that inflates the raft, forcing it out of its case and to the surface.

The couch's own descent into the river depths matched perfectly with the raft's ascent. Floating 15 feet in front of Karl and Mike was the assembled result of their good fortune. The couch on top of the raft.

Mike thought it looked like a throne fit for a pair of princes.

Karl thought seriously about giving God a second chance.

They swam over and carefully climbed on board. It was floating, but it was not stable. Karl managed to get on one end and helped Mike up. They sat for several minutes, catching their breath, each secure on an end as if they were ready to watch a TV program.

Soon, Karl realized the lights on land were moving upriver. Then he understood. It was, in fact, they and the couch, moving down river.

"I think the tide has us," he said. "We have to paddle to shore, or we'll end up with that submarine!"

And paddle they did. Carefully flapping their arms, for their floating raft was tippy at best.

38 - THE CELEBRATION

Little Zak had seen it before. A slow Sunday mid-evening, the crowd with a small "c", hovered over their drinks as if they didn't want to let the night end, but they didn't want to spend another dime for another round. He remembered when he would fret, thinking about the half empty cash drawer and worrying that this was not the best business choice to build a future.

I was well into my cups with my new best buddy, Jimbo, who was keeping right up. Rum and tonics go down like water and ice with repeated effort, providing you are not on your first campaign of slacking your thirst at the Seahorse.

"So, it didn't burn down, right?" laughed Jimbo.

"Hell, you can't light asbestos shingles with a Zippo," I laughed in return. We took another sip and a toast in our continuing game of 'can you top this?' We had been going for a couple of hours now and the latest story, "The Ram Island Arson Atrocity Legend" didn't quite live up to the legend itself, but most did not.

This legend dealt with a trophy that wasn't. The crew of racers on board ZoomNation had the best time in the fleet in the annual Around Fishers Island Invitational. The jagged extension of the north fork of Long Island, that arched off to the northeast, was the home of exclusive mansions, a marvelous golf course, and a convenient chunk of rock for sail boaters to circumnavigate. The Mystic Island Yacht Club used it for their annual event and offered a classic silver cup for the winner. However, you had to be a member of the club to take it home.

That apparently upset one crew member of ZoomNation, who slowly dismantled a wooden fence, stuffed the pieces under the club porch, and put his Zippo to it. He was stopped by his fellow crew and a few of the upper echelon of the club's Board of Directors. The end result: ZoomNation was not invited back for a year or so.

In many POTRAF minds, dimmed possibly by recreational additives, the suspension highlighted the attitude, back in the day, when yacht clubs would not invite crews, or boats with known unruly crews, to race, because they didn't live up to the Corinthian standards set by a bunch a white, rich guys in Breton red pants and blue blazers. These guys, all MFOs, had already won the race to the American Dream, enjoyed their fancy yachts, and had no interest in letting those POTRAFs, still struggling, into their parlor.

The economic snootiness was a good cover for the competitive fear that without the POTRAFs racing, the MFOs had a better chance of winning. Of course, that reasoning goes away when the MFOs remember who actually works the boat. And so it goes, on the water, where dollars face off against devotees every time the gun goes off to start a race.

On this night, there was no gun to signal the start of anything, but when Tank and Toby came prancing into the Seahorse, it signaled the start of the next phase of the celebration. And the end of my story swapping with Jimbo.

"Set them up, Zaky Mon, the boys are back in town!" chanted Toby, clearly feeling the effects of a 90-minute ride with beer, bong, banter, and cops, cooped up in an eight-foot van with nine knuckleheads.

Brian Bellows, Trip Standish and Miss Teekee popped through the front doors next, followed a few seconds later by Johnny Flash. They grabbed a table near the fireplace and settled into chairs. Another table was pushed from against the wall and soon there was a cluster for a dozen people right in the middle of the dining room floor adjacent to the horseshoe bar.

Carla appeared from the kitchen doorway and paused to take in the spectacle. She grabbed her pad from the nearby waitress station and drifted into the middle of the chaos.

"Carla! You are looking good tonight!" came the greeting from Trip.

"Somebody had a good day!" she answered, all smiles. A long-time server at the Seahorse, she had a special friendship with anyone who spent any time there. It was a unique connection built on a penchant to show extreme patience when delivering food and beverage to partiers of all types. She seemed to always be having fun!

"The best! Won it all, took it all, and threw it all away!" Brian chimed in. Ted immediately slapped him on the arm when he heard the 'threw it all away'.

"We not talking about that, Brian!" Ted admonished. He turned to Carla. "Throwing nothing away tonight, my dear! Just some menus and Mt. Gay tonics for everyone!"

"Coming right up!" Carla answered cheerfully and headed behind the bar to where young Zak was already pulling glasses and rum.

I had seen this all before, usually on Wednesday nights, when the racing crowd started to arrive after the weekly race series. Just like a men's bowling league, but different. Forty boats would hit the starting line after the workday, the first warning at five fifty-five pm, splash around for 4 or 6 miles and finish around sunset. Then on to the bar and the party. Midweek chillin' with a healthy dose of competition!

They called it 'beer can' racing. However, the chase was serious, the action could be dicey, and no one wanted to lose! It made me angry when folks would pass off the mid-week action as meaning nothing. I had been on lots of boats and every time the gun sounded, and the flag dropped, we were off and running! You're damned straight we took it seriously! When I did my share of Race Committee work and we made a mistake, no one walked away silently, sipping their carefree beer. They were all over our case with their own version of 'shudda, cudda, wudda'.

Everyone wanted to win, to hear the gun for first to finish. Of course, most people didn't. If they heard it, it was usually for soneone else. The usual suspects tended to dominate their class on any given night. Beer can this, my friend! You can drink anytime, but racing…? It foking mattered!

Darts stumbled in a second later, hanging on the shoulder of Teddy. It surprised me to learn later that Darts had driven the van back from the regatta at Westmont Harbor because he sure had trouble walking. Apparently, the mushrooms had taken him to a special place.Billy was next and surprised the hell out of me when he pointed in my direction from across the horseshoe bar. I waved as he walked toward me, but it was soon clear he was focused behind me where Goldee Golightly Prescott had been sitting with a couple of her friends. He walked right by me to where she was standing quietly, not moving, letting him come to her, and when he got there, threw his arms around her. They went all public passion right there in the bar with a lip locked hug and body press that would have brought a blush to a street pimp. They were clearly happy to see each other.

"Was it good?" she asked when they came up for air.

"Great weekend, great trip back, we pulled another one out of the dung heap!" He laughed and pulled her tight again. "I missed you. Let's take tomorrow off, just you and me!"

"I'm all in for that!" she laughed back.

Billy turned toward the bar and waved toward Little Zak,

signaling for two drinks.

"Congrats, Billy. Another big win, right?" I asked him and stuck out my hand. He grabbed it warmly.

"Big Mo, we kicked some ass! Got a little help from the current gods, but you know, the nose can smell it and we smelled it, sailed it and nailed it!"

"Meet my new friend here, Jimbo Hurley." The two shook hands, then Billy grabbed his drinks from Little Zak. "He's hoping to meet Dr. Z."

Billy looked at him for a moment, as if wondering why. Then he shook his head.

"Well, I'm not so sure that is going to work out tonight. He never showed!" Billy decided to leave it at that.

"That's too bad," Jimbo said nonchalantly. He took a big sip on his drink.

"I've been feeding him stories," I laughed. "All afternoon." I rolled my eyes as if it had been a huge burden. Billy just smiled.

"It's all lies, Jimbo. Whatever he told you, it's all lies!"

"Well, there's some good material there, Billy," Jimbo laughed. "What do I know? Entertaining as a cage of monkeys! We've been sitting here for days, it seems. He's got a ton of them!"

"Well, I'm sure there will be a new one to tell before the night is over," Billy smiled, pointing toward the crew around the table on the other side of the bar. "Anything can happen when these guys get together. Especially after a big win! You know how legends start, don't you?"

"How?" Jimbo asked.

"They start with a little lie!"

"Did you guys win a trophy?" Jimbo asked innocently.

Billy's face scrunched up and he shook his head.

"Yeah, a nice one. Same one we've had before. No lie there. Unfortunately, I'm not sure where the hell it is right now…Holy

Whiskey Tango Foxtrot!" Billy's mouth dropped in surprise. His eyes darted toward the front door, his attention suddenly interrupted by movement there.

"I don't believe it!" he marveled. "The Doctor is in the House!" he shouted. He tapped Jimbo on the arm and pointed. "There's your guy now! Lucky you!"

A chorus of voices joined in from the crew table as everyone turned toward the door.

"Z! Dr. Z! Holy shit, man! Z! You got the trophy!"

Chaos took over the room.

"There's the foking trophy, boys!" Billy shouted.

Sure enough, standing at the entrance was Dr. Z holding a large, somewhat battered trophy tower with a long base and a bent silver bowl on top. One handle appeared to be missing.

Dr. Z stood there basking in the cheers. He held the trophy high over his head, high enough to scrap the fish scale ceiling of the bar.

"Smoked, you rule!" he shouted.

The crew got up to surround him and everyone else in the bar turned their attention on the celebration. The trophy became the star for the moment as hands reached out to touch it, to make sure it was real, to examine it carefully to make sure it was the one they actually won.

Tank and Teddy looked at each other and laughed.

"I guess we should keep this one!" Tank said.

"It wants us more than we wanted it!" Teddy returned.

"Trophyheads, that be us!" They both tossed down their drinks.

Carla pushed her way into the crowd with a bottle of Mt. Gay fresh from the bar and poured the entire contents into the loving cup on top of the trophy.

"On the house, Boys. Congrats! You are the best!" she cheered as she poured.

That riled everyone up even more and they started passing the trophy around, as unwieldy a chalice of celebration as you'll ever see. Over the next several minutes everyone had a taste of victory from the cup.

Billy walked up to Z amid the joy.

"You made it, man! You must be foking crazy! There's no hiding here!" he said to his face.

"Fok hiding for now! I wouldn't miss this for the world! I don't feel like cheering in some dark hole somewhere!" he responded. The joy on his face and in his voice was genuine. "I'm sure there will be plenty of time for that!"

Billy took a sip from the trophy and passed it to Z. He drank lustfully, wiped his mouth on his sleeve and passed it to boat designer Dave Vee who suddenly appeared in the crowd.

"Vee! Vee! Vee!" came the cheer as the boat designer tipped the trophy and drank, spilling the rum all over his chin and chest.

"Z! Z! Z!" came the new chant easily switched without losing a beat. In a rare moment of choral animation, the crew marched around the table and through the bar. You would have thought a wedding had broken out and everyone was celebrating a moment of unbridled joy, swept up in victory again.

"It never gets old!" I shouted from my barstool next to my new buddy, Jimbo. He seemed caught up in the emotion of the moment as he raised his glass toward the happy group a few feet across the way.

I looked down at the compass embedded in the bar top right in front of me and I couldn't help but notice how right things seemed. The needle was pointing right at the celebration.

"Hey, Big Mo, you got a phone in here?" It was Jimbo asking. He was done toasting and now he wanted to make a phone call. I pointed toward the far corner on the way to the rest room and off he went.

I felt a hand on my back and realized it was Goldee with a playful tap as she walked around me to Billy, grabbed his hand and pulled him out of the pack onto the porch into the full moonlight. A slight breeze blew the warm June air through her hair and he threw his arms around her again and pressed her against the railing. Their bodies fit together well and they both pushed their desire with an openness that I'm sure had Billy thinking about taking her home right then and shifting the celebration into a whole new realm.

The noise from inside the bar faded away as their passion enveloped them in a bubble of their own. It was Goldee who heard it first.

"What was that?" she asked, as she pulled away and cocked her head toward the river.

"What? I'm so hard right now, my hearing is blocked?" Billy smiled, pushing against her.

From the darkness on the river the sound of water gently flowing past the rocks on Billy Island filled the air. In the ambient sound, the background of quiet, an ever-present sound forced you to pause and search for it, to pull it from your brain receptors to be conscious that you were actually hearing something.

"Listen!" Goldee whispered.

Billy turned his ear to the river and did as she requested. He heard the water flowing passed the rocks that held the stilts of the bar. Then he heard a splash. Then another, separate from the ambience. He focused on the sound and then several splashes together filled his ears.

"Sounds like someone's in a kayak or something," he whispered in her ear. They separated and both leaned on the railing, straining to identify the noise.

"Help! Help us!" came a voice from the darkness.

"Anyone there? Help us!" came a second voice, this one deeper.

"Jeeez, someone's out there!" Goldee said.

"Help!"

Billy ducked his head inside the bar and yelled to Zak.

"Zak, you got a flashlight? I need a big light! I think we've got someone in the river!"

Zak looked at me sitting by my compass rose and I knew exactly what to do. Being a bar, on a rock, in a river, required a certain amount of anticipation that, shit happens, the least of which is someone falling off the porch and into the drink. Next to the waitress stand, by the doorway that led to the rest rooms, sat a small closet with a flashlight and a 50-foot length of rope. Even a life jacket, if I remembered correctly, and sure enough, there it was in its orange glory at the bottom of the shelf. I grabbed it all and headed for the porch door.

Brian heard Billy yell for Zak and had already headed outside. He was soon followed by Tank and Toby and then the rest of the crew, ready to pitch in a helping hand.

Outside, the lights of the city of New London shimmered a mile or so upriver and the Gold Star Bridge further on offered its own tiara of streetlamps that crossed the open air to Groton on the east side. However, right near the Seahorse, it was dark. Only the light of the full moon offered any hint of illumination. On land, the lone streetlamp in the parking lot offered little help for seeing what was on the water where the walkway extended. The momentary sweep of the New London Harbor Lighthouse making its alternating red and white flashes every six seconds, did little but solidify where that structure stood.

I tossed Billy the light and he scanned across the river to the west and raised his hand to quiet the growing crowd of wannabe helpers and curiosity seekers who were spilling out of the bar to see what was going on.

"I see something!" shouted Brian. He pointed northward just off the eastern shoreline where the big rock promontory marked the edge of land. Billy shifted the light and probed generally where Brian pointed.

"Help us!" came another shout from the darkness and this time it focused everyone's eyes.

"What the fok!" Brian muttered as he saw the image come under the light. It was two men sitting on a paisley couch atop a life raft floating on the river.

"Are you kidding me! Isn't that the…." Brian's words drifted off. He just stood there shaking his head as he watched the floating apparition drifting slowly with the outgoing tide right toward the rocks where the Seahorse sat proudly for so many years.

"Coming through, watch out. Step back, watch your head!"

A commotion rolled its way out of the door and Big Charlie appeared with an 8-foot ladder straddled over his shoulder. He worked his way through the crowd to the north end of the elevated porch patio and expertly slipped the ladder over the railing, so it provided access to the rocks below.

Brian, the youngest and most agile on the crew, did not hesitate. He grabbed the rope out of my hands and swung his legs over the rail and onto the ladder.

"Gonna need a couple of hands here, guys! Anyone?" he called out. Toby and Tank responded and followed him down the ladder to the rocks below. They had no sooner disappeared over the porch when another commotion spilled out of the bar door.

"Gunning! Gunning! There you are, you miserable son of a bitch! You stole my couch!"

It was the Commodore of the Westmount Harbor Yacht and Tennis Club, Montgomery Fillmore Prescott III, and he was clearly livid, harried and red in the face beside himself. Following him closely was a uniformed State Trooper with the name Chiarelli on his pocket badge.

Billy turned at the noise and just laughed at the sight of Prescott. He continued to shine the light on the approaching life raft and couch with two men on it, even as Monty grabbed him.

"You shit! You stole my couch!"

Billy pulled away and looked at his rival.

"Monty, great to have you join our party! Now shut the fok up while we save a couple of lives here!" Billy nodded out toward the water and Monty took it all in for the first time.

"THAT'S MY COUCH!" he shouted when he realized what he was looking at. He turned to the State Trooper next to him. "See! I told you, these guys stole my couch! It's right there!"

The trooper stood by the railing and looked into the darkness. He was officially off duty, his last act of the shift issuing a speeding ticket to the man who called himself the Commodore. However, he decided to check out the nonstop claim that a couch had been stolen and there was some great miscarriage of justice underway. The fact they might find it at the Seahorse was the clincher. His beat covered Southeastern Connecticut, focused between Norwich, New Haven and the Rhode Island border. At worst, he thought, I'll have a night cap!

However, it appeared he had shown up in the middle of a water rescue and he stood by, observing, ready to lend an official hand. That's what cops do.

Goldee, on the other hand, smacked her brother on the arm, much to his surprise. He had not noticed her standing next to Billy as he walked to the edge of the porch and scanned the events on the water. He was seething angry at her boyfriend.

"Would you just shut up for one minute, Monty!" she hissed at him.

Monty turned in surprise, realizing it was his sister

admonishing him this time.

"Sis, what the hell?!" he answered. He just looked at her confused, pointing as if he was innocent, and the events unfolding in front of them were out of his control. He always felt that way when it came to his rival and his sister paired up.

The couch rescue had reached a critical point on the river. Brian could see that the two men were desperate. As they drifted closer to the rocks, they paddled harder which required them to lean over, allowing water to enter the already deflating life raft. It appeared the upper ring of buoyancy was leaking badly. The more they leaned, the lower the raft tilted, the more water spilled in, and the closer the couch came to falling into the river.

"Grab hold of the rope!" Brian yelled as he tossed one end of the line toward them. The two men were now close and the darker haired one on the right grabbed the flying coil expertly thrown. He held on tight. On the rocks below the porch, Tank joined Brian and they started to pull the floaters through the water.

A cheer went up from the dozen or so drinkers who had turned into an audience for the river rescue. I stood there and cheered as well and then I recognized the two men on the couch as the two men from the QuiKee Gs gas station up on Route 2A.

"It's Karl and Mike," I remember muttering under my breath.

"How the hell…?" came a mutter next to me. It was Dr. Z. who had joined the crowd by the rail. He recognized them as well. "Those are the guys, the humpers?" he asked me, looking for confirmation. I just nodded.

Mike and Karl hung on, but the life raft didn't. Not twenty feet from the rock that held the north side of the Seahorse above the river, Mike leaned over to add an extra paddle motion to help steer and slid off the couch onto the edge of the raft. The movement tipped things badly and water spilled over the edge held down by Mike's weight.

Simultaneously, Karl felt himself being pulled off the couch by the rope tug from the rescuers on shore, so he hooked the line around the back of the couch to gain some leverage. He held the line tight in his hands. That kept him from being pulled off, but now the pressure was on the couch and it shifted badly.

Things with air in them tend to tip when they become unbalanced and the back end of the raft tipped upward, flipping the raft near vertical. Gravity found the tipping point for the couch and it tumbled off the raft, with Karl pulling on the rope, sending all parts their separate ways.

Tank cursed to himself and gave up any hope of staying dry. He splashed into the water and reached for Mike who was partially covered by the inverted couch. Karl still held onto the rope and Brian, now joined by Big Charlie, pulled him toward the rocks.

Darts had seen enough from on the porch and jumped for the ladder and climbed to the rocks below. The crowd of onlookers cheered again as both men finally were pulled up onto the rocks. Tank had to swim a few feet, but was able to grab Mike by the collar and drag him ashore.

Karl never let go of the rope until he felt solid river bottom under his feet and literally crawled up the rocks to dry land, on his back, pulled the final few feet by Brian and Big Charlie.

"The couch! Don't forget the couch!" came the yell again from Monty, pointing as the six-foot overstuffed, over soaked, prize possession of the Westmount Harbor Yacht and Tennis Club junior sailing program, teetered on the rocks, one side secure, the other half in the water. "It saved their lives!" he added to the chuckles of everyone.

Darts and Toby splashed into the water and grabbed the floating end of the couch and jockeyed it around until all six legs were sitting on rocks.

Karl and Mike, soaking wet, sat on the rocks under the porch catching their breath. They couldn't help but smile at their good fortune. At that moment, Carla appeared from above like an angel, backlit by the porch lights, looking over the railing. She had an armful of towels and a look of concern on her face. She dropped the towels to Tank who passed them out to the pair of strangers. He couldn't resist.

"Who the hell are you coach potatoes?" Tank laughed.

Mike and Karl looked at each other, trying to determine what part of their story they were ready to tell.

"We went fishing," Mike offered tentatively, fighting off the shivers, wiping his face. He still felt as if he was wearing earmuffs and the world sounded so distant.

"For trout!" added Karl, who couldn't hide his smile.

"Trout? Shit, man, you picked the wrong river on the right night!" Tank laughed. "Good thing we like to party!"

"Where's your boat?" Brian asked.

"It sank," Mike answered. He looked at Karl and read his stare that clearly said, 'say no more'!

Then another commotion above as the State Trooper named Chiarelli stuck his head over the side and yelled down. "You guys okay to move? Come on up and get inside."

"Good idea," Tank added. "Let's get you a drink or two? You guys drink, right?"

Both smiled and got up shakily.

"We will manage!" Karl said.

He started to climb the ladder, with Mike right behind.

The handful of onlookers moved back and let the trooper take charge. Some turned toward the doorway to return to their drinks inside the bar. Trooper Chiarelli steadied the ladder and, as Karl reached the top, he recognized him from their encounter just a few days ago after the attempted robbery at the QuiKee Gs.

"Mr. Belmont. You're the guy with the sawed off shotgun!"

Chiarelli announced in surprise. "What the hell are you doing here?"

Karl took a moment to recognize the trooper and when he realized who he was, he blurted out. "Oh, you are the man of big bluster and no action, you prick! You have my grandfather's gun! You threatened me! I remember you. I thought I was dealing with the Sigurimi!"

Chiarelli was briefly taken aback by Karl's outburst. While he had no idea who the Albanian Secret Police where, he admitted he played the tough guy when he arrested Karl Belmont last week, but that was his role as a trooper, to keep the bad guys in line. Something about Karl had raised his police hackles. Even though the interview had not turned up anything incriminating, except the shotgun violation, he wasn't ready to trust him. The unfortunate residue of cop training. Still, maybe he deserves a break, he thought. He just went boating on a couch!

"Look, tough guy! You broke the law last time we met. That's what I do - enforce the law. Now, I'm going to treat this evening as if you were a victim." Chiarelli smiled and put his hand on Karl's shoulder in a reassuring manner. Then he moved in close and spoke into his ear.

"So, I'll be nice, let that remark go, get you warmed up and make sure you're good. Safe. Then I'll ask a few questions to find out what the fok happened here!"

Karl just looked at him with challenge in his eye.

"Bring it on, Kapitan!"

Chiarelli stared him back for a brief moment and then gave him a gentle shove toward the door. Mike, Tank and Brian followed right behind Karl, leaving a trail of water as they walked.

I watched Dr. Z walk over to the porch rail as Karl came up.

"Man, what are you doing here? What happened? Are you alright?" He sounded genuinely concerned. It might have had more to do with the uniformed trooper.

Karl looked at him and realized who he was talking to.

"Mr. Z-man, hello! Crazy night, eh? It's okay now. We got a ride...on a couch! A couch that tried to kill us!" Karl sounded unsure of what had just gone on. He seemed obviously shocked, was soaking wet, and suddenly surrounded by people he knew. He looked at me with a shit eating grin.

"Mr. Mo. Quite the welcoming committee!"

"Glad you're okay, Karl," I said.

I caught Z looking at Karl for just a split second and then a quick glance at Trooper Chiarelli who was looking over the railing at the scene below the porch. Z made the same motion with his hand across his lips as Karl had made back when they had first met a week ago at QuiKee Gs.

"You know the procedure," whispered Z and Karl repeated the motion - a casual as can be, slicing his hand across the lips. Z nodded his head and Karl moved toward the doorway.

"I've got to come to more of these parties," laughed Dr. Z as he turned toward me. "Good crew saves the day again!"

"This one is for the books, that's for sure. Where the hell did they come from?" I asked, totally amazed by what we had just witnessed.

"I need a drink!" Tank chanted walking by. He was clearly pumped from the exercise of couch rescue. He also was still a bit stunned that the paisley beast was back in their circle again.

"Well, they saved the couch, but they couldn't save the life raft. There it goes!" I tapped Dr. Z on the shoulder so he could see what I saw. The life raft had hung up on one of the rock outcroppings as everyone's focus had gone to the couch. I pointed to the raft, now floating free and unattached, half inflated, still floating. It was headed south out toward Fishers Island Sound.

"I've got one just like that on RUMRUN," I mentioned to him.

"Next stop Plum Island, maybe Montauk!" Z laughed. He

turned to head back inside. "Mo, come on, I'll buy you a drink. I have time for one more."

"Where you going? It's early!"

"Away, my friend."

"Well good, I'll do a drink. Besides, there's a guy in there who wants to meet you. I'm guessing for some business."

I don't know if he heard me because he was gone through the doorway and I followed him into the bar. The bright lights of the porch blinded me for just a moment. I took one step into the darkness and smacked into Dr. Z's back.

"Sorry, Z!" I apologized but he pushed backwards, turned quickly, and pushed me out the door against the railing. He looked me in the eye and moved close to me, nearly nose to nose.

"Morris, listen to me. This is not what I hoped for, but there are some folks in there who may be looking for me."

"Who's looking for you? That state cop?"

"It doesn't matter, my friend. Listen to me, I put something in your truck before I came in tonight. I had a feeling. Had a bad feeling all day, in fact." His eyes went dull as if he was suddenly in a dark place.

"Get rid of it, however you can. You know the procedure!" He made the same gesture he made to Karl a moment ago.

He then patted my shoulder, real friendly like, as if to say he trusted me, and he turned back into the bar.

39 - Good Night

When I got back inside, the party had resumed. The soaked Karl and Mike were sitting by the fireplace next to party central. Zak turned on the propane fired flames and they gave off the heat we normally enjoyed in the dead of winter. The boys were lapping it up. Tank, of all people, delivered to the wet ones two tumblers of what surely were rum drinks.

The rest of the guys had rejoined their own drinks. Carla flitted about making sure everyone was topped off. Billy and Goldee had grabbed a corner table right next to everyone and that's where Z headed as soon as he walked in.

I looked toward my barstool and saw three new faces standing right next to my buddy Jimbo. Two guys dressed as though they had just come in from a golf outing and an attractive blonde woman in a button-down shirt and lapel jacket, obviously not back from a day of sailing. The four were talking earnestly. I headed that way to grab my drink when suddenly Jimbo got up, reached down to his ankle, and pulled out a black billfold that flipped open to reveal a gold badge on a chain that he dropped around his neck.

He walked right passed me with nary a nod, followed by the two other guys who pulled badges from their pockets and slipped them around their necks. Their badges were slightly different from Jimbo's. An eagle stood over the blindfolded Lady Justice, holding scales and a sword. Federal Bureau of Investigation and the

Department of Justice embossed in gold over gold, let you know the source of their authority.

My drinking buddy Jimbo's badge was also gold, but Drug Enforcement Agency, Special Agent, and a big old U.S. were stamped on a blue background. The eagle was just as official looking.

The woman didn't move, content to stand at the bar and watch the three men move toward the corner table where Dr. Z was standing.

As I learned later, Dr. Z had walked into the bar through the porch doors and recognized two of the three new faces. They were the two guys in the blue van that had been in and out of Z's rearview mirror since early in the morning on the streets of Morningside Heights. The names on their ID cards were Smith and Smoot.

I had been trading stories all day with a guy who seemed nice enough, thinking he planned to meet Dr. Z to make a drug buy. What did I know? He was a foking cop! There to make a drug bust! God dammit! I have got to be more selective about who I sit and swap stories with! And the blonde? I had no idea, but I knew she wasn't on our side.

Right before my eyes, my new-found drinking buddy walked up to Z and started holding court. Or maybe, better to say, started making an arrest. Court would come later.

"Mr. Donald Zippermann, you are under arrest for violation of Title 21 US Code 848. You have a right to an attorney, anything you say can be used against you. If you cannot afford an attorney, one will be appointed. Please turn around with your hands behind your back."

The DEA agent produced a set of handcuffs and proceeded to shackle Z's wrists together. The two FBI agents stood nearby, scanning the crowd that had suddenly turned toward the legal confrontation.

"Who the hell are you?" Dr. Z asked.

"I'm Detective James Hurley, DEA. You are named in a federal warrant and we're going to take a trip to Groton Police station for some questions. You are being charged with running a continuing criminal enterprise."

Dr. Z looked at Billy and they traded a knowing look.

"Call Camille," was all he said. "Tell her 'the ugly' has arrived."

"Wait a minute, you can't do this! That's Dr. Z!" came the shout near the fireplace. Brian jumped up from his chair and grabbed Agent Hurley by the arm. Immediately, the two FBI agents stepped in and Agent Smith pulled Brian away. He was slammed against the wall and held there. Agent Hurley pivoted Dr. Z with one arm on his shoulder, another on the bound wrists, and directed him toward the main entrance.

Brian wouldn't rest easy. He kept struggling despite the much larger agent holding him against the wall.

"Let me go, you fok! Dammit. Get off me!"

The other agent, whose ID card identified him as Agent Smoot, pulled out a pair of handcuffs and in a matter of seconds had locked Brian's wrists together. Agent Smith pulled him away from the wall and led him off the same way Dr. Z was being led.

"There's no need to do that!" yelled Trip. He was joined by a cacophony of voices who could do little, but offer verbal support for their bowman.

"He's not going to hurt anyone!"

"He's just emotional!"

"Don't hurt him!"

"Leave him here, he's not going to interfere!"

It was too late. The law had spoken. The powers that be set their fence on a boundary line, and Brian was led off, one more violator heading for detention until the civil servants could sort out his rights.

"Stupid, stupid, stupid!" came from Darts, sitting in front of his cup of coffee, shaking his head while observing the whole situation. He did not like confrontation.

Billy tried to follow the arresting entourage, but was physically stopped by State Trooper Chiarelli who put his finger up as if to scold a child. Suddenly, the blonde woman who had been standing at the bar, where I had been drinking with Jimbo, appeared next to Chiarelli.

"Not tonight, Friend. Let it go! They'll get their day in court," she said in a pleasant voice.

Billy stopped and stared. "Who the hell are you?" he asked.

"I'm Assistant District Attorney Molly Fitzgerald. You boys have got yourselves involved with a major smuggling ring." She looked around at the crew, taking the time to make eye contact with each of them as they stood at the party table. "I'll be talking to each of you, soon. I promise, so, no long trips." She delivered it with a smile, as if that line had been long planned for the right moment.

"Son of a bitch!" Billy muttered. He looked over at Trip, helpless, and held his hands apart asking for someone to do something, but there was no response.

"Chiarelli!" shouted Agent Hurley at the front door. "Can you help us with transportation? You've got a car, right? We can use it right now!"

Chiarelli acknowledged with his left hand. Then he backed up toward the door and left. ADA Fitzgerald walked up to Billy and handed him a business card.

"Your Billy Gunning, right. Gunny? The leader of this group. The crew?"

"You busted up a good party here, Miss Fitzgerald. Don't think I have much to say to you." He refused to take her card, instead left her holding it up in front of his chest.

"Enjoy your party tonight, Mr. Gunning. You and I will be talking real soon, when you sober up." She looked at him and offered a sweet smile that Billy had to work hard to dismiss with a stone face. God, the law shouldn't look that good! was all he could think.

She gently slipped the card in his shirt, turned, and walked away only to be stopped by a voice from the other side of the bar.

"Excuse me, Madame, Miss A.D.A., aren't you going to do anything about my couch?" It was Montgomery Prescott III who suddenly appeared in the porch doorway. I had last seen him heading down the ladder to the rocks as everyone else was heading into the bar. He must have been checking on his couch.

"Mr. Prescott, I don't do couches. Not tonight!" And she walked out.

"Son of a bitch!" Prescott answered, shaking his head. He walked over to the bar and asked for a shot of Jack Daniels. In his hand he held what I recognized as a copy of the Racing Rules of Sailing, what looked like a small bag of M&Ms and a T-shirt. He dropped the stuff on the bar and plopped down on a stool to await his drink.

"This is all I could salvage from under the cushions," Prescott lamented to young Zak as he took his drink. He spread the T-shirt out to read the inscription on the back.

"Old age and treachery wins out over youth and exuberance!"

The crew started chanting again as the law presence left the building. "Brian! Brian! Brian!" followed by "Z! Z! Z!" There was confusion and chatter among everyone. No one could believe what had just happened.

"Who the hell was that bitch!" asked Toby. He turned and half yelled at the empty doorway where Chiarelli and Fitzgerald had just exited. "It's only grass!"

"Billy, we gotta get Brian!" Trip shouted. "And what the hell is

Z into? What is section 848 Title 21? Jeez!"

"Zippermann?! Did you know his name was Zippermann?" It was Toby shaking his head in disbelief.

Everyone turned to Billy looking for answers. He thought about telling them everything that Z had told him the night before at the Westmount bar. That the MFO of their racing campaign was a drug smuggler. He figured they probably now knew what was suspected by some.

"Well, it's not video stores, is it?" said Darts.

Billy laughed and shook his head. "No, you are right, Darts. It is not video stores. It's a bit smokier than that."

"Dope! I knew it," slurred Trip Standish, well into his cups, but suddenly speaking up. "I could tell, I could tell. He always had the best stuff!" There was a rumble around the table as everyone started talking at the same time, bragging they knew all along for one reason or another, that the man who had financed their racing lifestyle was a major smuggler.

"Dave Vee, we got a boat built on weed!" Toby said to Smoked's designer. He just laughed.

"At least it's not built with weed! You guys never would have made it to the start line! Where do you think the name came from?"

"We'd 'a smoked that sucker in the first five minutes," offered Tank.

They all laughed, sipped their drinks, and searched for more levity. Then Ted brought them to quiet when he asked. "So when is our next starting time? When does the class flag go up?"

"More important…who is paying the freight the rest of the way?" interjected Tank.

"Yeah, you're right, Tank. Billy, are we foked?" asked Toby.

Billy smiled, pleased to offer some good news.

"No fears, guys. Z has bankrolled the rest of the season. He had a premonition that the feds were closing in, so we are good. Off Soundings next week, Island Cup in August, The Benefit Cup, maybe the Vineyard Race, okay…if you think you can handle it."

That raised their spirits and sparked a call out to Carla for one more round.

"What about bail money?" asked Tank.

Billy paused for a moment and shrugged his shoulders. "We'll make it work. Maybe we can sell some Z-Weed!" Everyone laughed.

"What about the couch?" came the cry from Prescott at the bar. "You guys owe me a couch!" Monty had been slamming back Jack Daniels one after another and it was starting to show. He tried to stand up on the rung of his bar stool to get the crew's attention, but he failed and sank back on his butt.

Billy turned to him and let him have it.

"Monty, shut the fok up about your foking couch! I don't know or care how the couch got here, but you know what? Since you are such an A-1 asshole, I'm going to make a deal with you… if it's alright with our new friends Karl and Mike over there…" He turned to the now dry pair, sitting and drinking rum by the fireplace.

They had been watching the festivities. This group of sailors had saved them, welcomed them, dried them off, and gave them refreshments. They felt like they belonged. When Billy deferred to them during his tirade, they looked at each other then back at Billy and shrugged their agreement.

"…alright, it's okay with them, because they are the ones who brought us the couch. And we are the ones who are going to claim it as our own! It will become a new trophy and your Westmount Harbor Yacht Club can kiss our muddy asses."

"Muddy asses is right!" Tank shouted. "And the foking couch belongs here from now on!" he continued, as he stood up and gestured for everyone to follow him. At first, no one moved, uncertain what Tank had in mind.

"Hey, assheads, give me a hand!" he yelled again, standing with his arms open.

"Airheads, maybe, but not assheads!" It was Darts complaining about the name. "Call it the airhead trophy."

"Fok that! Raceheads is better!" Trip chimed in. "Or maybe sailheads. Or shipheads!" He got a laugh from Ted with that one.

"Rockheads might say it better?" Darts offered.

"Say what better?" Tank said, the frustration showing. "I'm just trying to get you knuckleheads to help me grab the couch." He turned toward the porch with a wave of his arm, dragged Trip out of his chair with him and then everyone got it.

I realized what was happening and tossed the rope that was lying across the bar to Toby who was next out the door. Soon, everyone was back on the porch. Four guys went over the rail, down the ladder, and tied on the rope. The couch sat in the muck of the tidal line that buffered the river and rocky island upon which the Seahorse was built. You could hear the sucking sound as the four guys unstuck the paisley couch. The four below lifted it up the ladder, and those on top pulled the rope until it slid over the railing and landed on its six muddy legs, and was pushed into the northeast corner of the porch. The couch fit nicely under the windows facing west so the evening sunsets, the flash of the New London Harbor Light, plus the twinkle from the city beyond, would entice anyone who chose to sit there.

Of course, no one chose to sit there just yet; except for Darts. The squish of his butt settling into the wet cushions sent groans from the crowd. Trip had to give him a hand to pull him from the mucky fabric. Groans evolved into laughter when Big Charlie, the Seahorse owner, showed up with a Polaroid camera he kept behind the bar, and soon everyone was on the couch to pose for a classic photo that still hangs over the rum bottles.

"You gonna clean off those muddy feet?" Darts asked Tank, pointing to the dark ooze that had spread from the couch legs onto the deck.

"Shhheeett! I am not touching that! Do you know what gets pumped into this river?" Tank responded with disgust.

Darts nodded in agreement.

"That has to be some kind of special mud," he exclaimed.

"Can't wait to see who wins that trophy next time," mused Teddy.

"Mudheads."

Everyone turned to look at Goldee watching the shenanigans around the couch. "Call it the "Mudheads" trophy," she said with a simple shrug.

Darts and Tank looked at each other, then back at her. Toby joined as well, having overheard her comment. Then they broke out laughing.

"Of course, the Mudheads," Toby laughed.

"It could even be the name of a club!" Tank added.

"A club? Like you mean with dues, a burgee…? God forbid!" It was Teddy half believing it was an idea to pursue.

"Sure, we could charge dues, enter regattas, have a clubhouse," Darts suggested.

"Clubhouse? You need to change sails, my muddy friend!" said Teddy.

"Well, don't be collecting the dues in a bar!" added Billy.

"Why not?", Toby asked.

"The money would never get to the treasurer!" Billy responded.

They all laughed.

"Now we have a treasurer? Great news!" Tank shook his head. "Can I have an expense account?"

"Well, I'm not paying more than $25 to join this club, and no one should have to vouch for you. Everyone gets in!"

"Why is that?" Billy asked.

"Well, how else would we get in?" Toby answered.

They all laughed and started back inside, nodding their heads, looking very much like bobblehead dolls as they walked.

"Did I ever tell you the story about racing lasers in the Mystic River against Dennis Connor and we flipped over..." Tank began.

"Yes, Tank, we heard it. A dozen times!" Darts cut him off as the crowd returned to their drinks.

Twenty minutes later, the party broke up. Darts dropped everyone off at Mystic Shipyard where their weekend had begun. Tank and Ted headed for the Groton Police station to check on jailbirds Dr. Z and Brian. Last I saw Commodore Prescott, he had passed out on the couch on the porch. I left him there.

Billy stayed behind and tried to reach Camille, but only got the answering machine.

"Z says 'the ugly' has arrived. I'm guessing Nick needs to call Groton Police," he said. He hoped that would be enough information to get their lawyer involved.

Then he drove home with Goldee. The way they were holding on to each other made me think I wouldn't be seeing him for a couple of days.

That left me at the Seahorse bar for last call with Karl and Mike. I turned back to my barstool only to find Karl sitting on it with Mike next to him, right where turncoat Jimbo had been sitting, in front of the compass on the bar.

I let them sit, and I grabbed a spot next to them. They had been through a lot, I gathered, because they were using the rum drinks as come-down medicine. In fact, their ordeal in the water had turned into an ordeal on land thanks to alcohol. They were tipsy for sure, but I wasn't in a hurry to leave just yet. I sat with them and sipped my last one for the night.

"So, guys, I'll give you a ride to your truck. Where we gotta go?"

"To the marianna in Miiistaac," Karl slurred, poking his thumb easterly.

"Yeah, I figured. Which marina?"

"By the brioodge road," Mike offered, no less sober.

"Which bridge?" I wondered if they were pulling me into a game of twenty questions. Or maybe they were just drunk!

"The railyroad swinging thingy," Mike continued.

"By the river," offered Karl with a big smile.

"Okay, great. I keep my boat in the marina by the river by the bridge. Which marina did you use?"

Mike pointed at me and nodded with a wide smile. I was impressed by his white teeth.

"That one! Yu-oar boat!" he said.

"Your boat, the loobstery boat," Karl agreed with another big smile. They both looked at each other and then back at me.

"My boat? Ok, that's the Mystic Shipyard East." I nodded and watched them grinning at me. Then it hit me.

"My boat? My boat?! At the same place my boat is at...wait a minute! Are you telling me you used my boat?!" I suddenly flashed back to my dope ride in the box truck with Karl to Charlestown when we delivered Dr. Z's load. Karl and I had chatted away and I had mentioned my boat, RUMRUN, and I do believe, lost in the moment of meeting a new friend, flying in that cloud of semi-bragging, pulling from my apparently overly generous good nature, that I may have suggested that my boat was available, if they ever wanted to go fishing.

I remember thinking that offer implied I would be with them, but it dawned on me sitting there with these two near drowned, couch potatoes, that I may have been misinterpreted! I do remember telling them the combination lined up with the red markings on the lock.

"You foking guys took my boat on your fishing trip?!"

"Christmas summer inside out!" Karl quoted me giving him the combo.

"We weren't fishing really, we were…." Mike suggested with a shit eating grin and a wag of his head back and forth.

"…working," Karl finished the sentence.

The image of the life raft drifting by the rocks under the Seahorse returned. How stupid to think it looked like my raft! It was my foking raft!

I pushed my drink away and stood up at the bar to face these two couchheads.

"Okay, tell me exactly what happened! How did you sink my boat?"

"We aimed the rockets…" started Mike.

"Rockets?!" I shouted incredulously

"…the couch fell on us…" Karl continued.

"…and the boat exploded!" Mike said. "Boom!" he shouted with his hands flying apart to demonstrate.

"…and the couch appeared like magic!" Karl finished with another big smile. He hoisted his near empty glass and finished it off in a toast to their lucky lives up to that moment.

"And the rockets? What…?" I shook my head in disbelief. The sudden realization that they would actually use the rockets they got from Dr. Z put me in another world.

"To jam up the cars. Make the fish run up our creek." Karl explained it, as if it was totally logical.

My feeble brain, addled with the intoxicants of the last few hours, finally put it together. These two "gas and go" jockeys tried to blow up the Gold Star Bridge, only to be saved by a stolen couch dropped off the bridge by the Smokedheads and sank my boat in the process. Sank the boat that presides over the local races. My boat, that I so generously let them use!

"Whiskey! Tango! Foxtrot!" I muttered.

I wanted to scream, but that's not me. I stood there for a second looking at the two. Then I moved for the door. I was seeing red. Maybe crimson!

"Time to go! Let's get the hell out of here!"

Young Zak waved goodbye, but I ignored him in my rush. I'm sure he had never seen me move out of the bar so quickly. Nor so angry. The two Albanians followed me, fully aware I was their ride.

I stormed down the rickety walkway; my footsteps pounded the ancient planks. I easily negotiated the swaying. I had done it enough times to anticipate every movement, and my raging sense of loss overpowered any effort by the little bridge to upset my balance. I was on a rocket ride of utter disbelief. The only distraction was the giggling behind me, mixed with "ooohhz" and "aawwzz", as Karl and Mike had a particularly difficult time walking, since it was their first time on the walkway, and they were drunk.

Blue lights greeted me in the parking lot where a Groton Police tow truck was dragging Dr. Z's Datsun 280Z away, apparently heading to the impound lot. For a split second that struck a chord in me, but the thought went away as Karl and Mike stumbled up, laughing about their excursion from the bar to the land.

"Get in!" I said briskly, jerking my thumb to my pick-up truck.

They both squeezed in the front seat, Mike leading the way, stumbling over a box that sat on the floor in front of the seat.

"I'm going to have to stock Ding Dongs Monday," he muttered as if he was explaining to Karl what his schedule was like for the upcoming week.

"Fok your Ding Dongs!" Karl muttered in return. He grabbed

the box and pushed it up onto Mike's lap to make room for himself in the righthand seat. "Fok this box, too!"

I looked at the box and realized instantly I had seen a similar one before. It was one of those office boxes where you might stuff extra files for storage. My continuing rage over losing my boat lifted for a second. That box had to be from Dr. Z, moved from his car because he feared exactly what happened would happen.

"Wait a minute," I said and reached over for the box. I lifted the cover to reveal a plastic garbage bag. I tossed the cover on Karl's lap and peeled open the bag.

Inside I first saw a hint of green and then realized I was looking at rolls of cash, wrapped with rubber bands. There was more cash with real dollar wrappers on them. I ran my hands down the sides of the box, and into the middle, and there was only cash! It was filled with cash right to the bottom! Twenties, fifties and one-hundred-dollar bills wrapped in all sorts of configurations.

I broke out in laughter the deeper I probed into the box. I laughed harder as I understood the magnitude of my discovery.

"Get rid of it, however you can." Those were the last words spoken to me by Dr. Z.

Karl and Mike were in awe of the box full of cash sitting right in front of them. I was delirious!

"That will buy a lot of Ding Dongs!" Mike laughed.

"Ding Dong this, my friend. I'm going to buy a bigger boat!"

"Now that's an American Dream!" exclaimed Karl.

I started the truck, put it in gear and drove off into the full moon night!

The End

Character List

The Storyteller
Big Mo

The Sailors
Billy "Gunny" Gunning – crew boss, MMFIC
Tank McHale – Trimmer, Billy's best friend
Brian Bellows – Bowman, youngest of crew
Ted Trumanlee – Tactician, trimmer
Gary "Darts" Goman – Navigator, oldest in crew at 35
Trip Standish – Mastman, long time sailor, big beard
Johnny "the Kid" Flash- Helmsman. Quiet, blonde, sees all.
Toby Patton – Pitman, resourceful
Dave Vee – boat designer
Montgomery Fillmore Prescott III – Commodore of ESYRU
Goldee "Golightly" Prescott – Billy's friend, Monty's sister

Dr. Z's Partners
Dr. Z – smuggler, MFO of Smoked
Camille – Dr. Z's wife
Luiz Salana – Z-Weed distributor
Hank – humper, sailor
Delroy Lawrence – ganja mon in Jamaica
Redbone – Delroy's # 2
Captain Tom – skipper of Calyopy
Tony Fanglioni – skipper of Ishkoodah, Camille's brother
Nick Cardman – Dr. Z's lawyer

<u>THE LAW</u>
Chief John Pastor – Police Chief Westmount Harbor
Lt. Arlo Raines – Jamaican Defense Force

<u>QUIKEE GS</u>
Mike Kansas – Mirilind Pasha Bushati
Karl Belmont – Shkodran Encheleis
Jacqui & Betsy - clerks

<u>NEOCDETF</u>
Molly Fitzgerald – Asst. US Attorney
Jimbo Hurley –DEA
Sam – DEA
Smith & Smoot – FBI
Trooper Chiarelli – CT State cop
Trooper Bill Cantor – CT State cop pilot
Officer Kolinowski – Norwich City cop
Chief Colby - USCG

<u>THE OTHER PLAYERS</u>
Tiffany & Tucker – Preppy Perps
Gina Sands – Bank VP
Rex – Bank Manager
Big Charlie Mann – owner of Seahorse
Little Zak – Charlie's son
Jerome – bartender
Carla – waitress

ACKNOWLEDGEMENTS

I was very fortunate to lose my first sailboat race and I have the sport of soccer to thank. I had never raced before, had no idea what I was doing, but ended up in the finals anyway - a match race against the owner of Campbell Soup at the time. He had just bought the Tampa Bay Rowdies NASL soccer team and I was going to be his radio announcer for the games. Soccer I knew. Sailing, not so much. And there we were, battling it out before the media and the players who had gathered on a beach to kick off the new team, and the new season, with a fun race in tiny boats. I was beaten, but I was hooked.

Fast forward 45 years and I've just finished my third novel where sailboat racing plays a major role. Where many of the people I have met racing have been turned into the characters who populate my stories, released to the page after spending a year or so in my head. Even longer for some. And now, hopefully, into your head, where they will tickle your memories, excite your desires and, maybe, send you off on an adventure of your own. At least, provide a few hours of escape from whatever dream you are currently living.

I love writing as much as I love sailboat racing and I soon found out you can't do either alone. I am forever grateful to those who played along with me, listened to my bull, suggested a different tack, shut me up, and helped with the trim.

Special thanks to Ghost Lady Courtney Moore (she's everywhere!), the English Teacher Hatsie Mahoney (I still haven't graduated), and the   Editorial Zoomer Loretta Vasso (okay, that's a good idea!). My buddies Ken, Tony, and Hutch for always bringing game. And a nod to all the MFO's who let me be a POTRAF. Get a ride. Get some bling. Get asked back.

Finally, special thanks to Frank Murphy, an exceptional sailor, race manager and storyteller who carries his own hand grenades and isn't afraid to use them.

None of this would be possible without the unconditional support of my daughter, Kristin and my companion of three decades, Pat Fritz. She has seen the sparks turn into an inferno and still manages to keep the porch from burning down.

Enjoy the read and never fear a bit of mud
on your nice yellow shirt!

Greg Gilmartin, June 2021 • www.greggilmartin.com

Spy Island brings local color to the national landscape of spies, secrets, love anbd Block Island. Here us a poem that hints of what is to come, followed by an excerpt from a chapter.

Spy Island is available in your local bookstore or at GregGilmartin. com

Spy Island – It's a Hell of a Tale to Tell

Booze and Bets. Broken Hearts. Stolen Secrets.
Old School Spies. Government Lies.
Sailors at the Oar drinking Mudslides.
A Murder. A Manhunt. Submarine Sabotage.
The Feds. The Reds. Digital Espionage.

Petrika's in the Cellar, Luke's on the Lam.
The Southeast Lighthouse is part of the Scam!
From Coney Island to Block Island,
You can Run. Hide. Spy.
But, Make no Mistake. They're Coming for You!
And Someone has to Die!

HERE IS AN EXCERPT FROM SPY ISLAND

16

WORRIES, RANTS AND PLOTS

Monday AM

However, when Luke woke up on Monday morning, bruised and battered from the beating he took at the hands of Misha's thugs, he wasn't thinking about Dr. Andrew Standord so much. His first thought was a wave of anger and hatred toward his card playing buddy Bailey. Followed by a feeling of shame for playing the role of idiot so well. A classic stupid pawn in another man's game! He was set up and fell hook, line and sinker.

He was in debt for over $100,000, money he didn't have a prayer of delivering by Wednesday. That was his salary for an entire year! What salary? He was about to jump into a rabbit hole that would surely cost him his job. Job? Job? How about his freedom? He feared for his life and fully expected further physical harm if he didn't deliver.

By Wednesday? Impossible!

Rene' was history, too. He didn't want anything more to do with her and was sure she felt the same.

And he was now faced with betraying his security clearance and his country, by stealing the plans for the SLACLONET 1000. He knew full well that opened him up to charges of treason and imprisonment. Embarrassment! End of life as he knew it! He had read all the security notices, watched the videos and heard the warnings of the GMBB security chief about "getting caught in compromising situations".

He tried to come to grips with betrayal but, he could only

muster a halfhearted effort. He really never thought much about patriotism while going about his daily life. Who did? As much as the flag was pushed on society, how many folks actually felt the power of that symbol? He thought of it more of a marketing scheme, like selling cars or beer.

He blamed the lack of leadership in America. The politicians who ran the government had done very little to bolster a sense of respect for the country. The White House was the ultimate seat of power, but it seemed ultimate power always attracted ultimate crooks, liars and cheats. He truly believed demanding respect wasn't the same as letting it brew a natural way. They lied and pedaled their influence and platitudes for the sole purpose of lining their own pockets, boosting their own ratings, maintaining their own place at the government trough. They didn't give a crap about this country beyond their own popularity! Why should he?

Stealing secret files wasn't as big a deal as getting your head bashed in. Or your life ended. And we've been at peace so long… the warnings about the enemies of our country fell on so many deaf ears, especially when they came from the bloviating clowns in charge. Their brand of patriotism was as empty and worthless as the rest of their blather.

Sure, men and women have died in the fighting, but in whose wars? Soldiering was a noble profession until you have to kill someone. Then who do you answer to? Where is the real threat? It's not who do we have to die for, it's who gets paid? The military-industrial complex! The defense contractors! The damn politicians! The policy makers! The whole charade depressed him as much as his impending doom at the hands of the Russian mob!

He had to sit down on the edge of his bed to calm down.

"Your life is over, Luke ass!" he shouted.

After a few moments, he stood up and walked to the

window of his third story downtown New London apartment with a view of the Amtrak swing bridge that opened at the entrance to Shaw's Cove on the West side of the Thames River. Fort Trumbull sat to the south, another bastion of patriotism built to defend from threats long ago. On the other side of the half mile wide, deep water port, sat Globallus Marine Boat Builders with her wharves and cranes and a warren of green and white work barns where the subs were built to defend tomorrow.

Great decisions often required great rationalizations, built in the depths of misperceptions, the heights of hopes, or the foolishness of wishful thinking. Luke experienced a moment like that gazing out his window upon the future.

"Unless," he thought aloud. "I can get away with it."

****

THE AUTHOR

Greg Gilmartin is a writer, TV producer, director and videographer. Born in the shadow of the parachute jump on Coney Island in Brooklyn, NY, his careers included stints as a car wash specialist, radio jock, USAF Russian linguist, automotive journalist, award winning sports reporter, talk show host and PA announcer for the Hartford Whalers. He is an active member of the Mystic River Mudheads and a certified Regional Race Officer for US Sailing. He has also written the novels Crew and Spy Island, available at all on line retailers. Greg continues to write along the waterfront in Southeastern Connecticut. You can reach him at: azrokx@gmail.com and keep up to date with his latest works at www.GregGilmartin.com.

Can't Sail In Jail!

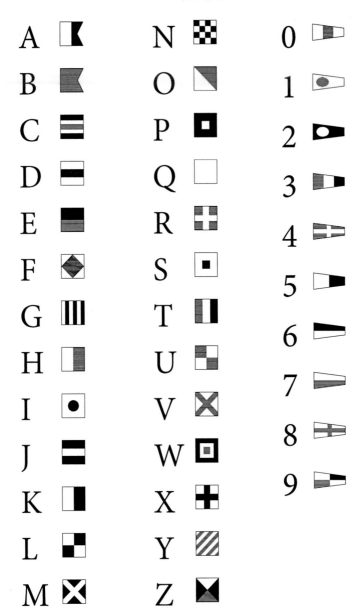

Can't Sail In Jail!